TURKISH COAST

Antalya to Demre
Second edition

Michael Bussmann and Gabriele Tröger
with walks by
Brian and Eileen Anderson
and Dean Livesley

SUNFLOWER BOOKS

Second edition © 2012
Sunflower Books™
PO Box 36160
London SW7 3WS, UK
www.sunflowerbooks.co.uk

ISBN 978-1-85691-426-0

Important note to the reader

Apart from the walks, this book is a translation from a series of *general*
guides originally published in Germany (see Publisher's note on page
8). We have tried to ensure that the descriptions and maps are error-free
at press date. The book will be updated, where necessary, whenever
future printings permit. It will be very helpful for us to receive your
comments (sent in care of the Sunflower Books, please) for the updating
of future printings.

   We also rely on those who use this book — especially walkers — to
take along a good supply of common sense when they explore.
Conditions change very rapidly in this part of Turkey, and *storm
damage or bulldozing may make a route unsafe at any time*. If the route
is not as we outline it here, and your way ahead is not secure, return to
the point of departure. *Never attempt to complete a trip by car or on
foot under hazardous conditions!*

Text (except the walks) translated and adapted from *Türkei — Lykische
   Küste;* text, town and site plans © 2005, 2006, 2008, 2011 Michael Müller
   Verlag, Erlangen, Germany; translation: Thomas Wilkes and Pat
   Underwood
Photograph credits
   © Michael Bussmann: pages 11, 27, 29 (top), 30, 31, 32, 34, 37, 45, 49, 60,
   65, 72, 74 (top), 78, 80 (middle and bottom), 98, 104, 110, 123, 141, 151,
   167, 170, 175, 177, 178, 181
   © Brian Anderson: pages 57, 94-5, 99, 100, 106, 112, 117 (top), 129, 133,
   135, 138-9, 154, 172
   © i-stockphoto: cover and pages 6, 17, 20, 24, 29 (bottom), 41, 43, 62, 71,
   80 (top), 81, 83, 87, 91, 92, 96, 117 (bottom), 122, 144, 164,
Walking maps: © Sunflower Books
Sunflower Books is a Registered Trademark.
A CIP catalogue record for this book is available from the British Library.
Printed and bound in China: WKT Company Ltd

Contents

● Preface _____

If the Bay of Antalya had its own flag, the colours would be aquamarine or emerald for the shimmering sea and, above, a fine gold line for the beautiful beaches, then various shades of green for the fresh-smelling forests and bright white for the summits of the Taurus Mountains, capped with snow for so much of the year. The star in the centre of the Turkish flag would be replaced by the constantly shining sun, and the crescent moon beside it by a column, symbolising the many ancient sites.

East of Antalya is the ancient landscape of Pamphylia — the 'land of all tribes', settled, according to legend, after the fall of Troy at the end of the 2nd century BC. Its coastline is supremely fertile: melons, bananas, figs, mulberries, oranges, lemons, and hotels all thrive here. Today this region is often called the 'Turkish Riviera' but, when you consider how many different nationalities visit today, the legendary description still holds true. While the Turkish Riviera is outside the scope of this guide, some excursions along the coast and in the hinterland east of Antalya are suggested.

The main part of this book concentrates on the area west of Antalya, known both in antiquity and today as Lycia. Historical descriptions of the wild, fissured Lycian coastal region abound with superlatives. Even Mustafa Kemal Atatürk, 'Father of the Turks', called it the most beautiful in Turkey. And the landscapes that sent so many writers into raptures have not changed for centuries.

Despite all the hymns of praise, Lycia's thinly populated coastal strip long remained untouched by tourism. It was so isolated that for a short time it even became a place of exile. Today, thanks to the building of Antalya's international airport, millions of visitors happily spend their holidays in the places where unwanted dissidents were once forcibly detained.

But the consequences of developing the coastal strip into one of the top locations for mass tourism cannot be concealed, even during the most beautiful times of the year. Many of the once-tranquil fishing villages have changed substantially in the last decade or so. Bay after bay is being opened up but, fortunately, the bulldozers still face several hundred kilometres of coast to plunder, so it will probably be at least another decade before the last idyllic places fall prey to big business.

The whole Lycian Peninsula takes in a very large area — running between Antalya and Lake Köyceğiz south to the sea. It is impossible to do justice to the entire spread *and* feature walks in one book, so this volume concentrates on the region between Antalya and Demre/Kekova, east of Kaş. A companion book, *Kaş to Dalyan*, takes in the rest of Lycia. When you've got all that under your belt, you

On a 'Blue cruise': a broad-beamed gulet *anchored in crystal-clear water*

might like to move further west with a third volume, *Bodrum to Marmaris*.

Antalya region highlights ...

... for lovers of beautiful beaches

If you love sun, sand and sea, the long stretch of coast between Antalya and Demre will enchant you, with scores of wonderful beaches and quiet bays. There are compelling attractions almost all the way along — with the **Olympos National Park** taking pride of place. The most beautiful beaches in the national park are at Adrasan, Olympos itself and Çıralı. Behind these beaches, hidden in the countryside, are scores of small *pansiyonlar* (guest houses) or 'tree houses'.

... for archaeology and culture freaks

A wealth of ruined cities — among them some of the most imposing in Asia Minor — testifies to the importance of this coastal region in ancient times. And you'll come across hundreds of elaborate rock tombs, a legacy of the puzzling Lycian civilisation. Among the plethora of sites, the following stand out.

Termessos — both a ruined city and a national park. In addition to the imposing tombs, Termessos is worth visiting just for the breathtaking views from its magnificently sited theatre. The entire site leaves one with a lasting impression of the transitory nature of power.

Aspendos — location of the best-preserved Roman theatre in Asia Minor, where regular performances still take place each summer. On the way to Aspendos from Antalya, you pass Perge, with Asia Minor's largest ancient stadium.

Phaselis — set in a pine wood within the Olympos National Park, near the sea, Phaselis is worth a visit for its wonderful location if nothing else. This ancient city once boasted three ports and one of the longest aqueducts in the Roman Empire.

Demre — where you'll find the Basilica of St. Nicholas (Father Christmas) and, on the northern outskirts of the town, the ruins of Myra, with an impressive necropolis and theatre.

... for nature and landscape enthusiasts

Off the beaten track, away from the tourist centres, there are still many unspoilt places left to discover. The harsh Lycian Taurus Mountains are characterised by summits rising over 3000m, barren plateaus, extensive pine forests, and impressive ravines — gouged out by roaring rivers over millenia. Below this backdrop lie hidden bays and sandy beaches from where you look out to a sparkling sea ranging from palest turquoise to deep blue. Below is just a selection of the most beautiful places to explore.

Olympos National Park — on the slopes surrounding the magnificent Tahtalı Dağı (2366m), the park is a story-book land of remote alpine pastures, chuckling streams and hushed forests. The park is famous among other things for the 'eternal flames' near Çıralı. These flaming fields, the mythical home of the Chimera, have attracted countless visitors since ancient times — and they are still quite an experience, especially at night.

Arykanda — cradled high in the mountains, with its backdrop a sheer rock face, this ancient site is even more appealing for its setting than the remains. Ancient doorways will frame your photographs of snow-capped peaks. The access road is spectacular.

Kekova Island — or, more particularly, the sea between Simena and the island of Kekova. In this lake-like area, with its many small islets, you can explore the famous 'Sunken City' on a boat trip.

Publisher's note

A couple of decades ago, we published Brian and Eileen Anderson's 'Landscapes' walking and touring guides to the Antalya and Bodrum/Marmaris areas. Their Antalya book was the first guide to several ancient trails which are today part of the Lycian Way. One of their specialities is 'scene-setting' in the introduction to each walk; another is botany. Brian and Eileen are still Sunflower authors, but these guides eventually went out of print. There was so much building work going on from the 1990s that the books really needed revision annually, but because of the long distances involved, coupled with rising car hire, petrol and accommodation costs in Turkey, this was no longer practical for UK-based authors.

We've been able to remedy the situation by finding two German authors who have been visiting and writing about Turkey for many years, and an Englishman who has his own guiding business on the coast. So this book has five authors, all with different interests. The walks were originally devised and written by Brian and Eileen; all were checked and rewritten where necessary by Dean just prior to publication, and everything else is down to Michael and Gabi, the main authors. Naturally this can lead to slightly different writing styles, but we hope it won't be a case of 'too many cooks'.

A few notes follow.

Keep in mind that if a hotel or restaurant entry says 'recommended by readers', this refers to recommendations by *German* users of the original guides (in print for decades and revised every two-three years). This does *not* mean, however, that the establishment is predominantly frequented by German clients; what Michael and Gabi always seek out is the place with a personal touch, whatever the price category or clientele. Just log on to some of the hundreds of web addresses they cite with their recommendations!

Dean was a find; he has lived in Turkey for over 25 years and helped research and implement the famous 'Lycian Way'. He has been involved in conservation for many years and now runs his own company organising activity, nature and cultural/historical tours from his base at Kayaköyü, near Fethiye. If you want to explore the area west of Antalya in depth — on foot or by boat, as a day trip or camping out under the stars — contact Dean at Seven Capes Sea Kayak Centre, www.sevencapes.com; (0252 6180390 or (0537 4033779.

One common thread binds all the authors: a shared love of Turkey's ancient history, landscapes and traditional hospitality. This shines through all the pages of the book — from the humorous boxed asides about mythological characters to their determination to retrace ancient walking routes despite the bulldozers and overgrown paths.

Key to the maps and plans

touring map	town plans	walking maps
motorway	P parking	dual carriageway/trunk road
trunk road	beach	secondary road/motorable track
secondary road	M museum	jeep track/path or old trail
minor road	mosque	main walk and direction
track	i tourist office	alternative route and direction
▲ mountain peak	post office	bus, *dolmuş* stop/petrol station
☀ viewpoint	BUS bus stop	*sarnıç*/tank, tap, water source
Δ campsite	TAXI taxi rank	mosque/ancient site
⁂ ancient site	car hire	windmill/viewpoint
9 location of walks	✚ hospital, clinic	building/castle, fort or tower

Country and people of the crescent moon — Turkey in facts and figures

Official name: Türkiye Cumhuriyeti (Republic of Turkey)

Geography: With a surface area of 779,452 square kilometres, Turkey is more than three times the area of the United Kingdom. Just three percent of the area is on the continent of Europe, with the remainder (generally called Anatolia) being in Asia. Turkey's highest mountain is Mount Ararat (5165m) in the easternmost part of the country. Turkey is one of the most seismically active continental regions of the world, with a long history of earthquakes due to tectonic activities in the fault line and the drifting together of the Eurasian and Arabian tectonic plates.

Political system: Turkey is a parliamentary democracy. The president holds office for a period of five years; the current incumbent (since 2007) is Abdullah Gül. From 2012 the president will be elected by popular vote; a one-term re-election is possible. The National Assembly (Parliament) is the law-making body and has 550 seats. For a seat in the National Assembly a party needs at least 10% of the national vote.

In June 2011 the reigning conservative AK party, headed by Prime Minister Recep Tayyip Erdoğan, won a third term, with just under 50% of the vote. Erdoğan is the only Turkish Prime Minister to have won three consecutive elections with an increasing majority each time. The AK party now has 327 seats. The second-largest party is the CHP (the Republican People's Party), with 26% of the vote.

The legislative session lasts four years. Laicism (separation of church and state) is guaranteed in the constitution.

Economy: After several boom years, with economic growth of 5-10%, Turkey has also been affected by the global economic crisis. As of press date, however, things were looking more positive for the future. According to the OECD, Turkey is one of the world's 20 largest economies. Its industrial sector, based mostly in western Turkey (textiles, chemicals, electronicals, motor vehicles and heavy machinery) accounts for 30% of GDP; agriculture (which employs a third of the total workforce) only 10% of GDP. The service sector contributes most — about 60% of GDP. The per capita GDP is just above Bulgaria's. But the overstretched budget is worrying, and the national debt could be more quickly reduced if more than only one out of ten people in employment paid tax.

Annual income (depending on the source consulted) ranges between £4000-£9000, but true figures are hard to come by on account of the black market economy. There are strong contrasts between western Turkey and the poor eastern provinces. At press date the minimum monthly wage was 760TL (about £320).

Population structure: In 2011 Turkey had approximately 74 million inhabitants (1960: 28 million); the average age is 28 (UK: 39.5). The population density is very varied. The administrative district of Istanbul with 1330 inhabitants per sq km is

clearly the most dense. The lowest population density is in the underdeveloped provinces in eastern Anatolia with only 16 inhabitants per sq km.

Sub-populations: 85.7% Turks, 10.6% Kurd, 1.6% Arab, and 2.1% mixed (Armenians, Greeks, Laz, Circassian, Georgians and Muslim Bulgarians).

Health/social: one doctor per 723 inhabitants. The average life expectancy for women is 73 years and for men about 68 years. Old-age pensions do not exist, nor are there any unemployment benefits.

Education: Eight years' schooling is compulsory. A third of all graduates go on to further studies at one of the 83 universities. The estimated illiteracy rate for women is approximately 18%, for men about 6%. However there is a strong contrast between east and west: in the western part, illiteracy is mostly confined to the older generation, whereas in the east (where child labour is still common) the figures include children as well.

Religion: 99% of the Turkish population are Muslims. The remainder are Jewish and either Syrian or Greek Orthodox Christians.

Military: The armed forces number 515,000 men and therefore are among the largest in the world (the second-largest in NATO). Military expenditure as a proportion of GDP is about 5% (about double that of the UK). This as come about because of ongoing conflicts with the Kurds in the east of the country and the power struggle with Greece. Soldiers are highly respected by the Turkish people.

Introduction

This book covers the coast and hinterland from the Köprülü Canyon National Park and Aspendos east of Antalya to Demre/Kekova east of Kaş. Most people staying here will be arriving at/departing from Antalya's airport. If you plan a longer stay and hope to explore more of Lycia, there is the option of moving west with *Turkish Coast: Kaş to Dalyan* and returning from Dalaman Airport; inexpensive one-way flights are easily bookable, and tour operators offer two-centre holidays.

When to go

Up until late autumn, the south coast of Lycia is shielded from the cool air mass coming off the Anatolian highlands by the 3000m-high peaks of the Taurus Mountains. Thus long hot summers alternate with short mild winters. There is very little rainfall during the hot season, while the winter months are wet. The **bathing** season around Antalya lasts from March until November, and many hotels are open all year round. But away from the main resorts, most guest houses are only open from Easter until the end of October. April, May and October, when the daily maximum temperatures rarely exceed 30°C, are the best months to visit (unless you will be spending *all* your time on the beach).

Getting to Antalya
By air

Most people reach the region on **charter flights** into Çalkaya Airport 15km east of Antalya. This airport is so popular that at time of writing there were (charter) flights from Birmingham, Bristol, East Midlands, Exeter, Glasgow, Humberside, London Gatwick, London Luton, London Stansted, Manchester and Newcastle.

Scheduled flights (with Turkish Airlines or BA) necessitate a changeover in Instanbul. From the United States it's rather a long haul, with flights by Turkish Airlines in cooperation with American Airlines and BA, stopping over in the UK.

Flight-only options are ideal for anyone who wants to make their own accommodation arrangements — or fly into Antalya and return from Dalaman (or even Bodrum). It's very easy to make your own arrangements on the internet, and perhaps book a **fly-drive** as well.

Prices are highest between April and October, when there are also more flights: expect to pay around £270 *including taxes*. But in 'off-season' there are some very economical deals — around £130 return or less *including taxes*. Obviously, booking well ahead (or at the last minute!) you may be able to better these prices.

The **travel documents** you'll need are listed on page 52 in the 'A-Z' section; for information about Çalkaya Airport, transfers, etc., see page 63.

Package tours to the Antalya area are offered by a huge number of companies and are perhaps the easiest option if you just want to stay in one place and haven't the time to make your own arrangements. All the major UK tour operators offer Antalya, but there are other specialists for Turkey. For a list of specialist Turkish tour operators, visit www.gototurkey.co.uk and click on 'Specialist Tour Operators' (in the USA/Canada see www.tourismturkey.org and click on 'Tour Operators'). The most popular resorts with the main tour operators, apart from Antalya itself, are Lara Beach, Belek, Manavgat, Side and Alanya (all to the southeast, the last four only briefly mentioned in this book), Beldibi, Kemer and Tekirova (all to the southwest). Naturally all tour operators will be only too happy to book you excursions to tourist sights outside the region, *gulet* trips along the coast, or even hiking tours. Often these excursions are offered at time of booking, or ask your tour rep about them.

The **baggage** allowance is usually limited to 20kg on flights, but if you are flying with a Business Class or other seat upgrade, or are staying longer than 28 days, you may be able to get this lifted to 30kg. Otherwise you are likely to have to pay about £3-7 per kilo for excess baggage (although if you're just a few kilos over they are likely to turn a blind eye). For **sports equipment** the rules vary between airlines: golf clubs and diving equipment are usually carried free, but sometimes they are classed as extra baggage for a flat rate of between £20-40. Bicycles, paragliders and surfboards can be charged at anything between £20-£100. Naturally you will want to check all this in advance — in any case you are legally bound to give the airlines advance notice of oversize baggage.

By *car*

Driving to Antalya is *possible* for those who have plenty of time (allow 4-5 days), especially if you want to tour and camp (campsite details are listed under 'Accommodation'). You will need an international driving licence, the vehicle's registration documents and valid Third Party insurance. On arrival, details of the vehicle will be logged in your passport, and you won't be able to leave the country without it. After crossing the Channel, you would make for the Italian port of *Ancona* for a ferry to Çeşme in western Turkey (Marmara Lines; www.marmaralines.com). Or take a ferry from *Brindisi* to Igoumenitsa in Greece (Anek Lines, www.anek.gr, or Minoan Lines, www.minoan.gr) — this is cheaper, but it's another 1000km to the Turkish south coast.

By *train*

This option is only for those really keen on rail travel; it is far more expensive than air. There are daily departures from London via Paris and Vienna to *Istanbul* (two different routes, each taking three nights). For details of this trip, see www.seat61.com. At the same website there are links for onward travel in Turkey itself but, since no trains serve the Lycian coast, at some point you have to change to a bus.

Getting around the Antalya region
By car or motorcycle

Having your own wheels makes travelling along the Lycian coast uncomplicated, but some caution is required. Once warrior-like Turks hunted on their steppe horses; today their great-great-great-grandchildren handle themselves with equal prowess in traffic — the combat cry has simply been replaced by the horn. For many drivers there is only one lane — the middle of the road. Overtaking on blind corners, driving the wrong way on a one-way traffic lane or street, not stopping for red lights: these things happen all too frequently. You will witness all this for yourself in time, but it pays to be aware of it from the start. If this is your first visit to Turkey or Antalya, a word of advice: don't pick up a car at the airport and drive into the confusion of narrow lanes in the old town looking for your overnight base. It's far better to take a taxi on arrival and pick up the car the next day.

You can **rent a car** in the tourist centres on nearly every corner whereas, in comparison, the number of places offering **mopeds, motorcycles** and **bicycles** is pretty modest. If you are interested in renting any sort of vehicle, you must of course

have your driving licence and passport or ID card. Some rental companies require that the driver is at least 21 or even 23 years old and has had their driving licence for at least one year. The cheapest (but at the same time the thirstiest) rental car is the Fiat 131, called *Sahin* in Turkey. The large international rental companies usually forbid you from leaving asphalt roads so that, strictly speaking, you would not be allowed to drive to any bays or ancient sites only accessible via tracks.

Prices are usually substantially lower from local hire companies than from the large international chains. Depending on the season, you'll pay between £13-26 per day with the smaller companies. They offer this price advantage by having an older and usually less well-maintained fleet of vehicles. The prices of the better-known hire firms differ little — again, depending on the season, they charge about £35-55 per day for the cheaper models. Which-ever you choose, the mileage is usually free. The best value is to book by the week before leaving home, and can be cheaper still if booked straight away as a **fly/drive**. Prices for motorcycles begin at approximately £20/day, scooters start at £15/day.

Do read the **small print**: make a note of the **insurance cover** specified in the contract, and particularly personal liability in the event of a claim. Note for instance that even with fully comprehensive insurance, under-body damage and flat tyres are not covered. Various rental companies accept credit card payment; gold cards usually offer an additional insurance protection/cover, which makes it unnecessary to take out passenger insurance or the like. If in doubt, ask your insurance broker.

Should you be unfortunate enough to be involved in an **accident**, you must *not* move the vehicle, but summon the police, no matter how remote your situation or seemingly minor the damage. A police report is mandatory for any insurance claim. *Do not sign any report which you cannot read* — or else make a note on the report that you could not read it. There are a few scare stories around about accidents involving personal injury to the effect that it's better to put your foot down and drive to the nearest police station as quickly as possible, lest you meet with summary justice at the scene. However well meant, this is totally irresponsible advice. You would be charged both for hit and run and for not giving aid, with far worse consequences than any possible reprisals at the scene of the accident.

Keep the following **traffic regulations** in mind: the **maximum speed** in built-up areas is 50km/h, outside 90km/h (with a caravan or motorcycle 70km/h, in a campervan 80km/h). On divided highways cars 110km/h, campervans 90km/h. On motorways cars 120km/h (with a caravan or motorcycle 80km/h, in a campervan 100km/h). The **blood alcohol limit** for drivers of *cars without trailers* is 0.5mg/l, for everyone else (including motorcyclists) there is *zero tolerance*, no alcohol permitted at all. **Mobile telephones** may only be used

Special advice for motorists

• Avoid driving at night if at all possible. Badly lit lorries and cars will be on the roads — to say nothing of people on completely unlit bicycles and farmers in dark clothing on their way back from work. The risks of an accident are also higher at night because you can't see the potholes and building works ahead, and they may only be marked off with some stones.

• If you are in the first row at a red light when it changes to green, look right and left before going ahead — not all your fellow road-users are interested in the colour play of traffic lights…

• In Turkey it is common practice to sound your horn before a blind bend. If the oncoming traffic does not hear anything, they assume the road is free. It is also common practice to sound your horn when overtaking!

• Exercise special caution on loose chippings, particularly on newly built stretches of road. Thousands of windscreens are broken every year. Keep well back from lorries!

• Take car after rain, especially if it hasn't rained for a long time; the roads may be like ice rinks.

• In order to curtail speeding, frequent radar controls are in place (minimum fine £35), and speed bumps have been added in recent years at the entrances to built-up and populated areas. For those who don't yet know their way around, these speed bumps can be treacherous, because there are usually no signs to make you aware of them, nor are they marked in colour (apart from large oil marks!).

Traffic signs — what's what?

Bozuk satıh — bad stretch of road

Dikkat — be careful; caution

Dur — stop

Düşük banket — unfinished road

Kaygan yol — slippery surface

Park (yeri) — car park

Park yapılmaz — no parking

Şehir merkezi — city centre

Tamirat — roadworks

Taşıt geçemez — road closed (driving through prohibited)

Yavaş — drive slowly

Yasak — forbidden/no entry

with a hands-free device while driving.

Petrol stations are frequent along the main roads and open seven days a week. Lead-free *(kurşunsuz)* petrol is readily available. Petrol prices in Turkey are slightly higher than those in Britain at time of writing, with a litre of normal unleaded costing about £1.35 (diesel £1.20). Don't worry if you have a **puncture**; the Turks are very helpful. Ask for the nearest *Oto Sanayi* — a group of workshops, usually on minor roads at the entrance to or exit from the larger communities.

By bus

The bus is the king of cross-country travel. The number of companies with networks serving the whole country is incredible, and the price differences are small.

The busiest companies use modern Mercedes or Mitsubishi buses, which are manufactured in Turkey under licence. Air-conditioning (take a jumper with you on the bus!) and video are standard; the majority of the buses also have toilets, tinted windows, special seat cushions, etc. Well-known companies are Metro, Ulusoy, Kamil Koç, Pamukkale and Varan. The better bus companies give you a token for your stowed luggage, so it's easily retrieved at the end of the trip. During the journey passengers are usually catered for by a young steward. Biscuits and drinks are distributed free of charge, as well as a Turkish eau de cologne *(kolonya)* for sticky and sweaty palms.

All the buses are non-smoking (but they stop for breaks approximately every two hours). The departure times listed in this book serve only as a rough indication and refer to data from the larger bus companies. Journeys with the smaller (predominantly local) bus companies invariably take longer, since they make so many stops along the route. Further information about bus travel can be found with introductory details about the towns and villages covered.

Bus fares vary little; on average one pays 3-4 pence/km, with the up-market companies charging somewhat more. So a trip from Antalya to Finike would cost about £3.50. Booking a ticket also includes a **seat reservation**, and you can choose your seat from a plan. Naturally the front seats are usually the best and most coveted, but wait: you may be exposed to the driver's cigarette smoke — unlike the passengers, the drivers *are* allowed to smoke on the bus!

Arrive well in advance of **departure time!** Buses leave

Buses are kings of cross-country travel.

punctually — and often up to five minutes early!

Turkish **bus stations** *(otogar, terminal* or *garaj)* are very like British and continental *railway* stations, with toilets, waiting rooms, kiosks, restaurants and shops. If there is no official 'left luggage', you can usually leave your things at the counter of your bus company. Bus stations are usually located several kilometres outside the city centres, so to get to them you often first have to take a service bus or *dolmuş*. But the well-known companies and local bus companies normally offer a feeder service with mini-buses from the centre of town. Smaller towns frequently only have a collection of simple bus company offices near the market, and the buses either leave from just outside the office or stop briefly on the town bypass.

At larger bus stations, **touts** working for different bus companies will try to persuade you to one ticket counter or other. Just ignore them, so that you can compare departure times and prices in peace.

By Fez Bus

The 'Fez Bus' (www.fezbus.co.uk) is a hop on-hop off service aimed at backpackers and independent travellers. From the end of April until the end of October a Fez Bus leaves Istanbul every two days and makes a circuit round half of Turkey before going back to the Bosphorus. With just one pass (which is valid for the whole season), you can get on and off as often as you want on whichever route you've booked, and you do not have to start at Istanbul. The basic route (Istanbul — Gallipoli — Selçuk — Köyceğiz — Fethiye/Ölüdeniz — Olympos — Antalya — Cappadocia — Ankara — Istanbul) is called the 'Turkish Delight Pass' and costs about £175, including an English-speaking tour guide. There are a great many add-ons, too — from detour routes on the mainland to *gulet* cruises and trips to Greece and its islands.

By *dolmuş* (shared taxi)

Shared taxis are one of the most popular ways to get around in Turkey. *Dolmuş* means 'full up'; in practice, this means that they do not operate to a strict time-table, but instead set off when the driver is happy that he has enough people on board. A *dolmuş* (usually a mini-bus seating from 14-20 people) can be recognised by a sign on the roof or hanging in the window indicating the destination. In cities there are special *dolmuş* stations for connections to outlying parts of the region, otherwise they leave from the town markets. In large connurbations some routes will have intermediate stops. Moreover, you can stop a *dolmuş* anywhere along its route by waving it down. The *dolmuş* is a boon for walkers!

Dolmus **prices** (specified by the city councils) are somewhat higher than bus prices in city traffic, but a bit less once outside the built-up areas. The fare is usually collected once you are underway. It's a good idea to take note of what your fellow (Turkish) travellers are paying, or you may end up paying an additional 'tourist fare'. The longer routes are broken down into sections, and you only pay for the stretch you travel.

By taxi

In the tourist centres you can find a taxi on every corner. The fares for longer journeys (for instance to some tourist attraction, site, etc.) are usually posted in the taxi in various currencies. For trips within the cities it's best to take a taxi with a meter or negotiate the price in advance. *Caution:* sometimes taxi drivers 'inadvertently' press their meter button, so as to make the fare higher. During the day *gündüz* must appear on the display (*gün* = day, *gündüz* = daytime; *gece* = night).

By train

Railways are not, so far, a significant element in Turkey's transportation network, and there are no trains operating along the Lycian coast.

By ferry

There are no ferries serving this area. The only regular connections are from Fethiye to Rhodes and Kaş to Kastellórizo (covered in the *Kaş to Dalyan* guide).

By bicycle

It's rare to find bicyles for hire — and when you do, they are usually poor quality. An exception is a German firm, **Lykienbiker**, with a base at the Robinson Club Çamyuva (near Kemer), www.likienbiker.de (only in German). Otherwise, if you want to tour this area by bicycle, take your own bike — and a helmet as well (you must wear one by law). A Dog Dazer (see page 23) is also a good idea.

By hitchhiking

It's not common to hitchhike in Turkey, since public transport is so inexpensive, but in principle it's possible everywhere and once in a while is the best option at the end of a walk. But unaccompanied female travellers should *not* hitchhike on their own.

By chartered boat

The Lycian coast and the southern Aegean are among the most popular sailing waters of the Mediterranean. Boats can be chartered locally, with or without a skipper. The main yachting centre for tourists in the area covered by this book is Finike, but nearly all the other larger resorts have a marina. Or you can anchor in many secluded ports and bays.

By organised tour

Take a helicopter to Pamukkale, a bus to Ephesus or a boat to the 'Sunken City' at Kekova: whether by air, land or sea, all the tourist centres offer innumerable half-day, full-day and two- or three-day excursions to local and surrounding sights. If you haven't time to plan an independent excursion or you prefer not to travel on your own, these organised trips are an enjoyable way to learn more about Turkey. From the price point of view, they are most economical for those travelling on their own, since a couple could probably hire a car for the same money. Even better value are the boat trips to secluded bays which you cannot reach by car.

The big catch with many bus tours and boat trips, of course, is that most of the routes are nearly identical, so many bays and tourist attractions are inundated with huge crowds for a just few hours of the day. What's on offer, and where, is listed for each area in the section 'Practicalities A-Z'

'Blue cruises'
The 'blue cruise' business is booming on the Lycian coast. A blue cruise is an all-inclusive holiday on a *gulet*, a beautiful, broad-beamed wooden yacht. While they do have masts and sails, they are usually motor-powered, and the only sail which is always raised is the protective awning. *Gulets* are usually very comfortably equipped, since blue cruises don't cater for yachtsmen but for tourists who enjoy seeing the coast from the water, bathing in isolated coves ... and sharing the 'on-board' experience with others. The only disadvantage is that, once the initial excitement has worn off, sharing a confined space with strangers can be trying. Backpackers will be used to this kind of accommodation and have the right attitude, but for more mature travellers it's a good idea to book as a group and charter your own *gulet*.
Blue cruises are named after trips made by a famous circle of philosopher friends who gathered round the bohemian journalist Cevat Şakir Kabaağaçlı. This 'Turkish Jean-Paul Sartre' published his work under the alias 'Fisherman of Halicarnassus', after he had been exiled to Bodrum because of his anti-militaristic stance. He fell in love with the area and stayed on. In the early 1960s a group of his disciples joined him in Bodrum, where they all sailed along the Aegean coast on sponge-diving boats, trying to live as close to nature as possible and surviving primarily on fish and *rakı*. They called their soul-cleansing travels 'mavi yolculuk', or 'blue journeys'.

Aboard a wide-beamed gulet

under 'Boat trips' and 'Organised tours'.

Prices for these excursions do not vary greatly between tour operators. If you *do* find a tour that is substantially cheaper than that offered by the majority of operators … then you can expect far more shopping breaks for carpets than are normally in the programme! The tour guides of course earn commission on everything you buy.

Walking

In recent years the development of the Lycian Way, Turkey's first long-distance trail, has been widely publicised. If you hadn't read that this is one of the world's top walks, your first glimpse of the towering chain of mountains which runs the length of the peninsula might utterly discourage you from exploring the area on foot.

But you are in for a pleasant surprise. In spring and autumn there is no more beautiful way to discover Lycia than on foot. If you plan to tackle the 'Way', or just parts of it, there is information galore on the official website (see panel opposite). In contrast, this book describes **15 *day* walks**, with many variations, using local

Likya Yolu — The Lycian Way

The 509km long-distance footpath runs along the coast from Fethiye (Ölüdeniz) and through the steep Taurus Mountains almost as far as Antalya. The 'Sunday Times' described it as one of the most beautiful walks in the world. It takes about five weeks to complete the whole route — and a few months of training beforehand! Anyone who wants to complete the whole walk, or even parts of it, will find a wealth of details on the official website: www.lycianway. com. The official guide to the route is available from this site or from your usual supplier — it's a good read in any case.

transport — or a car if suitable. There are walks for all ages and abilities; all are graded. Several of the routes take in parts of the Lycian Way, but you will always return to the comfort of your base in the evening.

Seasons: **April/May** and **October** are the best months for walking in this part of Turkey. In **spring** the air temperature is moderate (although the sun is still very hot), and there is a delightful freshness in the mountains. But remember that there is always the danger of typical mountain weather. As the temperature climbs after the winter months, the warm maritime air rises to meet the coolness around the snow-covered mountain peaks and condenses to cloud. This does not happen so much when the drier winds from the north are blowing but, when the warm southerlies with their moist air are gently sweeping in on a bright, clear morning, then the first tell-tale signs appear as wispy cloud around the high peaks. Around midday the cloud thickens and spreads, sometimes covering the sun — only to disperse and vanish as the day cools.

Autumn in this part of the country is often long and warm and provides ideal conditions for walking, but you cannot always rely on this. **Winter** is even more variable and, although temperatures never fall very low at sea level, the number of rainy days increases, and the rain is invariably heavy. The sun remains strong and warm throughout the autumn and winter, and the spells of fine weather can create very clear

visibility which make for ideal walking conditions.

High **summer** provides the most difficult conditions for walkers; temperatures get very high and anything more than a short stroll to the nearest beach is not advisable because of the constant danger of heat exhaustion and dehydration.

Guidelines: The **time checks** given at certain points always refer to the total walking time from the starting point, based on an average walking rate of 4km per hour and allowing an extra 20 minutes for each 100m/330ft of ascent. These time checks are not intended to pre-determine your own pace but are meant to be useful reference points. Do bear in mind that they do not include any protracted breaks. Before tackling one of the longer hikes, compare your pace with the authors' on one of the shorter walks. Depending on your level of fitness, you may also consider some of their 'easy' walks to be 'easy-moderate' — or even 'moderate'.

Please accept some words of caution: keep to the routes described and do not try to make your own way in this vast, rugged and difficult terrain. Points that may look close can sometimes take many hours to reach. Except for the Lycian Way, there is virtually no sign-posting or waymarking, nor are there any accurate large-scale topographical maps. For any walks except those graded 'easy', it will help to have some walking experience, a good sense of direction, perseverance, stamina and *a little good will*.

If you are an **beginner walker** or

you are just looking for a gentle ramble, look for walks graded 'easy', and be sure to check all the short and alternative walks. Look, too, at the out-and-back walks: several walks return by the same route, since access into the hills is limited to paths through gorges. Points of interest part-way along are suggested as short walk goals, but you could turn back even sooner.

Experienced walkers should be able to tackle most of the walks in the book, taking into account the season and weather conditions of course. Quite a few full walks are very long, so be sure of your fitness before you attempt them. **Experts** will enjoy the challenge of Tahtalı Dağı (with 1400m of ascent) and perhaps the overgrown trail to Termessos. Make sure the weather conditions are perfect before you attempt either of these hikes. *It is never advisable to walk alone*, and this is especially true for women. If you must go alone, carry a mobile and a loud whistle to use as a distress signal in case of an accident. Whether you are alone or in a group, *do* inform a responsible person where you are going and what time you plan to be back.

Maps: The **maps** in this book have been drawn up from a wide variety of base maps — all very different, none of them accurate. Detailed large-scale maps for Turkey are not yet available, and it remains an area of some sensitivity. (Do *not* try to obtain large-scale maps in Turkey; at the very least you will be regarded with suspicion.) Before publication, we found a 1:250,000 military map (not on general sale).

Despite its small scale, we have overlaid the UTM grid from this map on most of our walking maps for GPS enthusiasts to puzzle over (details on the individual maps). If any volunteers send in edited tracks for these routes, we will post them on our website and use them to update future editions.

Equipment: Give careful thought to **basic gear** before you go. Many footpaths are steep and stony; comfortable **walking boots** with ankle protection and good grip are strongly recommended. Long (and fairly thick) **trousers**, tucked into **long socks**, will help you avoid being scratched by prickly bushes and will keep ticks at bay too. **Sun protection** is crucial: sunhat, suncream, sunglasses, and a long-sleeved shirt. Always carry **plenty of fluid and food**: depending on the length of the walk you will need 1-3 litres of liquid per person (many mountain springs are dry from mid-September until the winter rains). Your day **rucksack** should of course contain a **first-aid kit**, small **torch** and **mobile phone** (emergency numbers are shown on page 50). You may also want to take an **anti-venom kit** (available from specialist camping stockists); see 'snakes' below. If you are walking between October and May, you should also take a **windcheat** and **waterproofs**; in winter a **fleece** or two, **woollen hat** and **gloves**. Any other special gear will be listed under 'Equipment' at the top of each walk.

Nuisances: Nuisances: Most pet **dogs**, and even strays, are harmless, but take care around shepherds' dogs, which may be aggressive. (If dogs worry you, take a 'Dog Dazer', an ultrasonic device which persuades aggressive dogs to back off, available from the Sunflower website, www.sunflowerbooks.co.uk.) But you will have to be on your guard against **snakes**. Most are harmless and will move out of your way rapidly but, if they don't, the best advice is to quietly move out of their way. There are **vipers** around and, since it would be dangerous to step on a viper, it is *imperative* that you do not walk in the countryside in open sandals. Always have your feet and ankles well covered and, as a sensible precaution, wear your long trousers tucked into your long socks. Take special care near water, when you are about to sit down, or when you rest your hand, so unthinkingly, on a drystone wall. If you do have the misfortune to be bitten by a snake, seek medical help urgently — and if you cannot identify the species, kill it and take it with you!

In comparison with snakebite, the sting of the **scorpion** is painful, but not dangerous to most people. Again, as a precaution, don't leave any of your clothes on the ground. You can avoid **ticks** by keeping your body covered. If a tick does get to your skin, it is necessary to make it withdraw before taking it off; an easy way to do this is to touch them with a solvent such as methylated spirits or alcohol. **Bees** and **wasps** are around in summer, so make sure you carry the necessary medications if you are allergic to insect bites. In any case, always give beehives a wide berth!

Wild boar forage for food in the mountains, but they are nocturnal creatures, unlikely to be seen.

Accommodation

Accommodation in the area varies from up-market resorts where you will be handed cocktails in the jacuzzi down to places where you wouldn't go into the toilets without shoes. Most hotels and guest houses are located along the coast. There is a very welcome increase in the number of '**boutique hotels**' — small stylish places to stay (some marketed as guest houses), which are often housed in old, restored natural stone buildings. *This book places particular emphasis on this type of accommodation.* The standard of most hotels is in direct relation to the price, but the best value for money will be found out of season (September to June). The growing Turkish middle class all want to spend their July/August holidays by the sea. While Turkey is still a relatively inexpensive destination, during high season not only are prices higher, but it can be difficult to find a room — reserving in advance is essential. *All recommendations in this book mention facilities like air-conditioning or telephones only in establishments where you would not expect to find them. Average prices are quoted for high season, and include breakfast and private bathroom (unless stated otherwise) .*

All-inclusive resorts

The bulk of all-inclusive resorts in the area is clustered around

Antalya's Çalkaya Airport

Antalya and the Kemer coast. These places, often behind high-security fences and with up to 2000 beds, are not geared up to receive individual travellers at short notice, so booking is either impossible or very difficult. If you do manage it, the walk-in rate is often well above double the normal rate that you would have paid booking through a brochure. Note, too, that the term 'all-inclusive' is not clearly defined, and some hotels give themselves this accolade without actually earning it. So make sure in advance whether for example the drinks or the sports facilities on offer are included in the price. And even where everything *is* 'all-inclusive', it may not mean the same thing in different establishments. Is the orange juice freshly squeezed or out of a bottle? The greed of many holidaymakers is contributing to ever-diminishing standards of quality.

Prices for the all-inclusives depend on equipment, service, size of the buffet, sports facilities, number of hosts and hostesses, etc. and range from £60-£205 per night for a double room.

Hotels

All hotels are registered with the Ministry for Culture and Tourism and are assigned categories. If you choose your accommodation depending on the number of stars, be aware that the classification is based on *equipment* (mini-bar, television, lift, restaurant, air-conditioning, etc.); criteria like location, architecture, friendliness of the staff, and the like are not considered. Moreover the rating is often out of date, because many Turkish hotels were built 'on the cheap', so the equipment often wears out quickly. This applies particularly to three-star hotels. Luxury **boutique** hotels are not categorised by stars. In hotels at the bottom end of the market and in many guest houses you will just

have to accept the fact that there isn't always hot water and the amenities are often unreliable.
Prices: The larger, sophisticated hotels charge from £65 for a double in peak season. In simpler places (where private bath and air-conditioning are nevertheless standard), you can get a double for half that and a single for about £25. Prices are up to 50% lower between mid-September and mid-June. A room in really cheap accommodation, without bath or WC, starts from £8 per person.

Pansiyonlar (guest houses)

When comparing simpler hotels and small *pansiyonlar,* the latter are usually the better choice, since their operators usually care more about the well-being of their guests. Even when compared with some of the top hotels, the *pansiyon* may be preferable, because the friendliness of the owners makes up for the (rarely missed) luxuries. Air-conditioning and private baths are standard almost everywhere. A number of cosy *pansiyonlar* can be found along the coast in places like Simena/Üçağız, Kaş, Kalkan, Patara and Dalyan. Many campsites (see below) also let rooms; equipment is spartan, but the rooms (often in bungalows) are usually very well done.
Prices for *pansiyonlar:* a double room with shower/WC/AC starts about £25 in high season. Singles are usually given a double room at a reduced price.

Aparthotels

The number of aparthotels has been rising constantly in recent years. Basic equipment includes a kitchenette or small kitchen, a living room with a sofabed and TV and — depending on size — one or more bedrooms.
Prices vary substantially, depending on size, equipment and location. You should be able to get a good apartment for 4 people for about £290/week in high season.

Youth hostels

In the whole of Turkey there are very few youth hostels, not least because many private *pansiyonlar* offer inexpensive rooms. There is *no* youth hostel in the area covered by this book.

Tree houses

These are wonky huts on stilts or built in trees. Simple bungalows are also widely marketed as tree houses. Tree houses offer no comforts or amenities — just madly romantic nights starting from £8 per person. They are meeting places for international backpackers. If you want to stay in a tree house, head for Olympos.

Campsites

More and more campsites are disappearing, as hotels take over the prime beach sites. Those that remain, however, are very good — the better ones with warm showers, power sockets and restaurants, and perhaps camper kitchens. There's sometimes even a pool.
Several campsites also let bungalows and parking bays for tents and camper vans. The 'bungalows' are usually simple wooden huts without much in the way of creature comforts, but they usually have tiled floors, bath and WC, terrace, etc.
Camping in Forestry Department **picnic places** is also possible;

there are toilets, tables, rubbish containers and often barbecues. '**Wild camping**' isn't a problem on the Lycian Way or in the mountains (where there is no other option), but not otherwise recommended: between curious villagers and police checks it can be a very unnerving experience. **Prices:** For two people and a tent or caravan, reckon on paying £5-17; bungalows cost £12-£45, depending on equipment. **Opening times:** Many campsites are only open from May to October. They are only crowded in high summer. By the end of September you may be the only guest on the site … and find that the bar and restaurant have closed.

Food and drink

'The Iman fainted', when asked to taste 'women's thighs' and the 'lady's navel'. 'The ruler was pleased' when served the 'vizier's finger'… Whole dramas can be performed based on the names of Turkish dishes! They also hint at which tradition the recipe falls back on and how much fantasy the chef puts into his creations.

'Life comes from the stomach' is a Turkish proverb. And in fact Turkish cuisine can claim to be one of the best in the world. The basis for dishes is usually fresh vegetables, including some that are either unknown or seldom used in Britain and Europe (like chick peas, broad beans, okra, rocket and purslane). It's different with herbs and spices: they virtually never use Eastern exotica, but rather trusted classics like pepper, paprika or parsley. Garlic is also used, but not as much as you might imagine.

Where to eat

In the larger tourist centres you can of course find anything from Chinese restaurants to Italian pizzerias, Bavarian beer gardens, and cuisine from around the world. For Turkish specialities the choice is primarily between *lokantas* and *restorans*. Smoking is prohibited everywhere; you can only smoke on outside terraces. *Lokanta:* You eat in a *lokanta* to get a meal under your belt rather than to enjoy the 'dining out' experience. *Lokantas* are found on every street corner; they are simple, good and cheap (prices start at £3.50). The décor — tiled walls and cold neon lighting — is spartan to say the least. The pre-cooked meals are kept warm in glass cases, and you select from meat and vegetable dishes, soups and stews. The busier the *lokanta*, the fresher the meals usually are. There are many variations on the *lokanta*, too: depending on what the speciality of the house is, it may be called a *kebapçı*, *köfteci* or *pideci*. At an *işkembeci* they serve soup with entrails and other

---

Tipping

In simple lokantas no tip is expected, but in restaurants it is. If the service is not included in the total (note that quite often it is included), about 10% of the total bill is expected (15% in more expensive restaurants). In restaurants where they have no menus and prices on boards, it is advisable to enquire about the prices before ordering — some waiters are sly foxes…

Waiting for customers at a Beymelek Lagoon restaurant near Demre

innards. Most *lokantas* do not have an alcohol licence.

Restoran: Restaurants normally have an alcohol licence, more tasteful décor, better service and of course higher prices. But the menu does not always differ from that of the simpler *lokantas;* this applies in particular to mid-range restaurants. A full meal with a beverage starts at about £6.50. For the better restaurants there is no limit: a candlelit dinner at an elegant restaurant by the water's edge will cost about £20 or more per person (without wine).

Fish restaurants — those that serve netted or line-caught rather than farmed fish — rank price-wise with the more expensive restaurants, and for a three-course set menu expect to pay £17-26 per person.

Breakfast

In the larger tourist hotels, an 'international' breakfast is nearly always served as a buffet; how

sumptuous or otherwise depends on the grade of hotel. If you want something 'local', go to a *pastane* (pastry shop also serving hearty snacks).

Do try a traditional Turkish breakfast *(kahvaltı)!* You will be served fresh white bread, jam, eggs (usually hard boiled), olives, cucumbers/gherkins, tomatoes, butter and sheeps' cheese. Turks enjoy sheeps' cheese on bread with honey. With all this, tea is the drink of choice. Filter coffee is not usually available; those who want it will have to settle for *neskafe* or something similar. Turks also eat *pekmez* (thickened grape juice) as a spread with *tahini* (sesame paste) on bread for breakfast — and it's delicious!

Starters

You can choose from things like piquant creamy yogurt *(haydari)*, spicy vegetable purée *(ezme)*, cold vegetables in plenty of olive oil *(zeytinyağlı)*, stuffed vine leaves *(yaprak dolması)*, melon with sheeps' cheese *(peynirli karpuz)* and similar delicacies. The Turks call such starters *meze*, and display them in glass cabinets for you to take your pick. In the better restaurants, cold meats like chicken salad *(tavuk salatası)*, as well as fish and seafood like *tarama* (pink roe with lemon) or prawns *(karides)* may be part of the *meze*. It's also fairly common to do without the main course altogether and select only starters; in many restaurants it's no problem. Fresh white bread *(ekmek)* is always served on the side. Turks rarely choose **soup** as a starter. They have soup as a replacement for breakfast, occasionally in between meals … or to nurse a hangover. Many Turks swear by the Alka Seltzer effect of entrail soup *(işkembe çorbası)* … but this may not be to your taste! If you would like some hot soup as starter, try the hearty lentil soup *(merçimek çorbası)* — another speciality.

Meat

The most popular meat dishes are *kebaps* and *köfte*. **Kebap** is the generic term for meat dishes of any kind (usually lamb, sometimes calf or poultry), which can be baked, grilled, or roasted. There is probably no need to dwell on *döner kebaps*. *Şiş kebap* is a tender meat dish roasted on charcoal, served with rice or bulgar (cracked wheat). *Patlıcan kebaps* are skewered minced meat with aubergine. If the meat is arranged with yogurt and tomato sauce on roasted round flat bread it's known as a *bursa kebap* (or *ıskender kebap*). A *tandır*

kebap consists of pieces of mutton braised in a sealed clay pot. Try, too, the *adana kebap*, a strongly peppered mince meat kebab. Or *güveç*, a tender pot roast with vegetables cooked in a clay pot. **Köfte** are essentially meat patties or meatballs made from minced mutton, lamb or beef; they can be roasted or grilled. The tasty 'women's thighs' *(kadınbudu)*, with added rice and a coating of breadcrumbs, get their name from the elongated shape of the meatball.

Turks love offal — like roasted liver *(ciğer)* or kidneys *(böbrek)*. *Kokoreç* is a snack on offer at many street corners — grilled intestines with onions and tomato in bread. There are many, many other curiosities to try, like grilled sheep testicles *(koç yumurtası)*, stewed sheep heads *(kelle)* or feet *(paça)*.

Turkey for vegetarians

A tired smile is all that most Turks can offer a vegetarian — because those who voluntarily choose to do without delicacies like *şiş kebap*, *köfte* or entrail soup must be either ill or mad. Don't worry: even without meat one can enjoy delicacies in Turkey. The bulk of the starters are purely vegetarian, and there are plenty of tasty vegetable stews, creamy soups, salads and filled pastry dishes awaiting discovery. In order to avoid any nasty surprises, make sure by asking 'Etsiz mi?' ('Is it without meat?', pronounced 'Aytsis mee?') and follow this up by saying 'Et yemiyorum' ('I do not eat meat', pronounced 'Ayt yaymeeyorum').

Fresh market fare

Vegetables

Vegetables *(sebze)* are used as the base of Turkish dishes rather than as a supplement to a meal. The choice of pot-roasted, baked, and stewed vegetables is enormous. A particularly popular dish is *dolma:* this consists of stuffed vegetables, like zucchini *(kabak dolması)* or aubergines *(karnıyarık)* filled with minced meat or bite-sized pieces of lamb. It is usually eaten with yogurt. Various stews are also tasty; try *kıymalı ıspanak* (spinach with minced meat). Chick peas *(etli nohut)* or okra with lamb *(etli*

bamya) are also delicious. *Caution:* Take it easy, at least to start. The food is often swimming in olive oil — on stomachs unaccustomed to this diet, this can have the same effect as a dose of castor oil.

'Bio': Turkey is one of the world's largest exporters of 'bio' products. Organic foods are popular with Turkish young people, who find them cool. But when you see 'bio' or 'organik' on the menu in a coastal restaurant, it's just vegetables from their own garden!

Fish

Salt-water fish frequently on offer are sea perch *(levrek)* and gilthead sea bream *(çupra* or *çipura)* — both usually farmed and so relatively inexpensive. Among the more pricey fresh fish are turbot *(kalkan)*, Mediterranean mackerel *(kolyos)*,

Simit *street vendor at Olympos*

mackerel *(uskumru)* and sardines *(sardalya)*. These are usually priced by weight. Tuna *(palamut)* features on many menus, too, prepared in several different ways. Octopus *(ahtapot)* and squid *(kalamar)* are often on the starters menu. Trout is a particular fresh-water favourite, and there are many trout restaurants in the hinterland (some feature in our walks).

Sweets and fruit

One of the most popular **sweets** *(tatlı)* is *baklava*, a pastry made from several layers of dough, interspersed with almonds and pistachios. The small rectangles have a syrup of sugar, lemon juice and honey poured over them. *Helva* is just as sweet and sticky, a calorific 'bomb' made of white flour, sesame oil, honey and sugar. Easier perhaps on the British stomach (and conscience) are almond pudding *(keşkül)* or rice pudding *(sütlaç)*.

Those who enjoy experimenting should try *aşure* at least once — a jelly-like dessert: when prepared properly in a top-quality restaurant, this contains more than 40 ingredients, including rose water, nuts, cinnamon and even beans! It was inspired by the legend of Noah's ark — you mix all the left-overs together and boil them up.

The recipe for *tavuk göğüsü* is equally unusual — a mixture of chicken breast chopped into small pieces, rice flour, milk and sugar. All these and many others are on offer at the *muhallebici*, snack bars specialising in sweets. To end your meal with **fruit** *(meyve)*, there is a wide choice. Depending on the season, figs, melons, grapes, peaches, strawberries, cherries, pomegranates or citrus fruits are available. Washing all fruit thoroughly is good, but peeling it is better!

Snacks

Snacking is an art form in Turkey, and *börek* can almost

replace a complete meal; this speciality is a filo dough triangle filled with minced meat, spinach or sheeps' cheese. Similarly delicious fillings are hidden in *pide*, a crispy flat bread. Also worth sampling is *lahmacun*, the Turkish pizza topped with minced meat and herbs.

Mantı is known as the Turkish ravioli — so small that 30 fit on a single spoon; you eat it with garlic-flavoured yogurt, melted paprika butter and mint.

Simit salesmen are always around; their sesame rings are at their crispiest early in the morning. One often sees women in traditional dress beside them, preparing *gözleme*, a kind of pancake filled with different kinds of sweet or hearty ingredients. And try *kumpir*, if you get the chance, giant stuffed potatoes.

Soft drinks

Pepsi, Coke and all well-known brands are on sale everywhere. Water *(su)* is often placed on the table with the meal. If it comes from the tap, you should *avoid* drinking it. Freshly squeezed fruit juices *(meyve suyu)* are recommended. Delicious fruit juices are also sold everywhere in cans. *Ayran* is a refreshing

drink made from yogurt, salt and cold water — a little like buttermilk.

Hot drinks

The Turkish national drink is *çay*. This good black tea from plantations on the Black Sea coast is drunk at every opportunity. Whether at breakfast, business meetings, in carpet shops or at the hairdressers, the small bulbous glasses are found everywhere. Tourists seem to have taken a shine to *elma çayı*, apple tea. Turkish mocha *(Türk kahvesi)*, which can de ordered either sweet *(şekerli)*, slightly sweet *(orta şekerli)* or without sugar *(sade)*, is usually taken after a rich meal. Those who don't mind grit between their teeth order *neskafe*. In chic cafés you can of course also get cappuccinos, espressos or macchiatos.

Alcohol

Rakı is the favoured tipple — about 45 percent aniseed liquor — and tasting rather like the Greek *ouzo*. The Turks prefer to drink it diluted with ice and water from high, narrow 0.2 litre glasses. It then takes on a milky colouring and so is also called 'lion's-milk'. *Rakı* counts as a

digestive and medicinal aid against all possible ailments, and 70 million litres are consumed each year in the interests of keeping the population healthy. You can tell good quality *rakı* from inferior brands because it makes a film on the glass (the brand most highly prized is 'Tekirda').

Beer *(bira)* is popular with meals, the Efes brand being the most common. Danish Tuborg (brewed in Turkey) is available, too; it's somewhat drier than Efes.

Less known are Turkish wines *(şarap)*. The better varieties are normally excellent — especially the Dolucas and Kavaklideres. Turkish wines are stomach-friendly due to their modest acid content. But as wine is fairly pricey, even in supermarkets, Turks usually only drink it on special occasions.

Practicalities A-Z

Ancient sites — the most important terms

Acropolis: castle hill, also the upper part of town

Agora: market and meeting place in ancient Greece; the major part of a colonnade, surrounded by shops

Architrave: a main beam (usually stone) resting across the top of columns

Basilica: central Roman hall, in which the side aisles are lower than the main aisle (only later was the term used for churches)

Bouleuterion: council hall of the senate in Greek and Roman times

Cavea: auditorium of an ancient theatre, in Roman times usually semi-circular, in Greek times usually facing outwards

Cella: main hall of a temple, usually with one or several religious statues

Gymnasium: centre for athletic training, originally part of a school

Heroon: religious building in honour of a hero or dignitary

Capital: uppermost end of a column

Necropolis: graveyard

Nymphaeum: fountain

Odeon: theatre-like building for small cultural events

Orchestra: performance area of the theatre

Pantheon: a temple for all gods

Peristyle: a space surrounded by columns

Propylon: gate building

Stoa: roofed colonnade or portico

Beaches

The search for sun, sand and sea attracts millions to the Lycian coast every year. Some of the most beautiful and best-known long sandy beaches lie along the coast, but there is a multitude of idyllic 'hidden' bays as well. **Naturism** is forbidden in Turkey (although it is quite usual to see Turkish men bathing in their underpants). There have been quite a few police raids on beaches frequented by naturists.

Average water temperatures			
January	15°C	July	24°C
February	14°C	August	25°C
March	15°C	September	24°C
April	16°C	October	22°C
May	18°C	November	19°C
June	21°C	December	17°C

Books for background reading

John Julius Norwich, *A Short History of Byzantium* (Penguin, 1998)

Richard Stoneman, *A Traveller's History of Turkey* (Cassell, 1993), and *Alexander the Great* (Routledge, 2004)

Freya Stark, *Lycian Shore* (John Murray, 1956) and *Alexander's Path* (John Murray, 1958)

Kate Clow and Terry Richardson, *The Lycian Way* (Upcountry, 2005)

Chemists

Turkish pharmacies (*eczane;* open Mon.-Sat. 09.00-19.00) have more or less everything you would find at home. Many medicines are called by a different name, however, and are often available without prescription (for instance, antibiotics) — and they are cheaper too.

The nearest **24-hour chemist** (*nöbetçi*) will be shown in the window of the *eczane.*

Children

Turkey is paradise for those travelling with children. If your offspring plays sailboats with plates in the restaurant or cries on a long bus trip, nobody will get worked up over it, the pieces of broken glass will be removed with a smile, your child will even be comforted and probably given sweets.

You will be welcomed with children wherever you stay — whether in a simple *pansiyon* or a luxury hotel. The latter often provide babysitters who arrange an interesting children's programme, the former will welcome you with unbelievable warmth — with the host even taking the little ones fishing on his boat. Apart from building sand castles there are camel rides on the beach, aquaparks with giant water slides, etc.

For nappies, Ultra Prima have the best reputation, and for baby foods Ülker and Mılupa (both are available in pharmacies and some supermarkets).

Climate and weather

See 'When to go' on page 12 and the detailed information for walkers on page 21. Below some statistics.

Monthly averages		
air temperature*	hours of sun	rainy days
Jan. 10°C (7/16)	5	11
Feb. 11°C (7/17)	6	10
Mar. 13°C (8/18)	7	7
Apr. 16°C (11/21)	8.5	4
May 20°C (15/25)	10	3
Jun. 25°C (19/30)	12	0
Jul. 28°C (23/34)	13	0
Aug. 28°C (23/34)	12	0
Sep. 25°C (19/31)	10	1
Oct. 20°C (15/26)	8.5	5
Nov. 15°C (11/21)	6	7
Dec. 12°C (8/18)	4.5	11
*followed by minimum/maximum		

Consulate/embassies

Embassies for the English-speaking countries are located either in Istanbul ((prefix 0212) or Ankara ((prefix 0312).
UK (0312 455 3344
USA (0312 455 5555 (Ankara) and (0212 335 9000 (Istanbul)
Ireland (0212 246 6025
Australia (0312 459 9500
New Zealand (0312 467 9054
In case of emergencies, there is also a British consulate in Antalya:
British Vice-Consulate
Gürsu Mahallesi
324. Sokak No. 6, Konyaaltı, Antalya; (: 0242 228 2811

Crime

Thefts and robberies are relatively rare in Turkey. The country's worst crime is corruption, but that's another story and not a problem for tourists. Nevertheless, do be aware that, like everywhere else, there are cheats and con artists around — especially in the big cities and tourist centres. If you have a problem, contact the nearest police or tourist information office. They will help you because tourism is critical for the economy.

Of course it is a good idea to take the usual precautions of leaving valuables (including unneeded credit cards) in a hotel safe (*never* on view in a car or on the beach), carrying no more cash than you need, and keeping to well-lit streets at night.

Illegal drugs are on sale in Turkey: marijuana, hashish, opium and heroin. The punishments for bringing drugs into or out of the country, or drug use are severe — and Turkish prisons are known the world over for their dreadful conditions. *Never take a package out of the country without knowing what is in it.*

Currency

The currency is the Turkish lira (*Türk lirası* or TL). **Notes** to the value of 1, 5, 10, 20, 50, 100 and 200 TL are in circulation. One Turkish lira comprises 100 *kuruş* (KR), and **coins** have been issued for 1, 5, 10, 25 and 50 KR, as well as 1 TL. Inflation has fluctuated in the past few years at around 10%.

The prices quoted in this book were as accurate as possible at the time of writing (2011), but will no doubt differ greatly from the prices you find on the spot! This is partly due to the fact that prices in Turkey do not rise or fall in line with inflation, but

remain stable for longish periods and then jump steeply. But of course the chief factor is the instability of all exchange rates at present. **At the time of writing £1 = 2.36 TL.**

Turkey's **foreign exchange control regulations** require you to declare cash amounts to the value of US $5000 (about £3250) or more on departure.

You can **exchange currency** at banks (normally open Mon.-Fri. from 09.00-12.00 and 13.30-18.00) or the many exchange bureaus in the area. The difference in rates between the two is generally small.

Cash machines (ATMs) are thick on the ground, too, and the exchange rate on withdrawals using a debit card (*Maestro*) is often better than in an exchange bureau. But always taking out small amounts may eat up any advantage gained, so it's better to 'tank up'. With *Maestro* cards you can take out up to 800TL a day (but some ATMs only allow 400-600TL a day).

Credit cards are accepted in all of the better restaurants, hotels and shops.

Not every branch of a bank is authorised to redeem **travellers' cheques**. American Express travellers' cheques can be cashed free of charge (as long as it's by the person who signed them) at branches of Akbank, Türkiye Bankası and Yapı ve Kredi Bankası.

Tipping: in restaurants the rule is generally 10% of the bill; hairdressers, masseurs, chambermaids (per day) around 2TL. You needn't tip taxi drivers — round up the fare. In bars and cloakrooms leave some small change.

Students reductions and other **concessionary prices** are shown with the relevant entry fees.

Dress

Away from the holiday centres in Turkey, great importance is attached to cleanliness and proper dress. For what to pack check the table of monthly averages on page 34. For a bathing/beach holiday on the coast, light clothes — preferably cotton — are enough, but remember that in the spring a cool breeze blows off the water in the evening. For visits to mosques see under 'Mosque etiquette' on page 43.

Electricity

The power supply is 230 volts as in continental Europe, and two round-pin plugs are the norm, so take your continental or international adapter.

Festivals and holidays

The tourist centres on the coast have surprisingly little information about national holidays — probably because it's always 'holiday time' (but only for the tourist, not for them!).

1st January: New Year's Day
January or February: Kurban Bayramı (movable dates, four days); see page 43.
23 April: Independence Day, commemorating the first time the parliament sat in Ankara (on 23 April 1920). Is also celebrated today as 'Children's Day'.
1 May: Spring Festival (an unofficial holiday replacing the former Labour Day).
19 May: Youth and Sports Day; it marks the start of the Turkish

Shave ... or lose out

Whether bushy and magnificent or fine and delicate, they are always well trimmed: only a moustache makes a Turk a man — at least in Anatolia and in conservative circles. Even today village men who have worn moustaches for years keep an eye on the younger generation, to make sure that no young rascal grows a moustache before the 'proper' age.

But in many places on the south coast the young don't want to know about such antiquated traditions, so they are smoothly shaved or sport designer stubble. To them, the classical moustachioed male, with his standard grey department store jacket, has all the status of the village nincompoop from the Anatolian countryside. Even the young women see them as sleazy perverts with x-ray eyes. In some trendy clubs, the bouncers make sure that anyone with a moustache is barred.

Those who wear full beards also remain outsiders, at least when it comes to public offices and universities. In secular Turkey (see page 42) the full beard is seen as a symbol of the wearer's Islamic faith — the equivalent of women covering their heads.

War of Independence in 1919.
30 August: Victory Day, commemorating victory over the Greeks in 1922.
29 October: Republic Day; Turkey was proclaimed a republic on 29 April 1923. This festival is celebrated with parades.
October or November: Kadir

Gecesi (movable dates); see page 43 and Şeker Bayramı (moveable dates); see page 43.

10 November: while not an official holiday, the day of Atatürk's death (1938) is 'semi-official', since a large part of the population stays away from work.

See also 'religious holidays' on page 43.

Flora and fauna

The Lycian coast is characterised by typical Mediterranean vegetation, with forests of pine and cypress as well as bushy macchia comprised of oleander, holly, kermes oaks, box trees, myrtles, lavender, carob trees, etc. On the higher elevations, the prevailing tree is the Turkish pine *(Pinus brutia)*, but you will also find isolated firs, black pine *(Pinus nigra)* and the Lebanese cedar. Timber from the high Taurus Mountains was exported as far as Egypt in ancient times, for use in boat-building. The Taurus range stretches the length of the Lycian Peninsula, shielding the southern coast from the cool air mass coming off the central Anatolian highlands; below the mountains, olive groves and cotton fields flourish — as do greenhouses for growing vegetables. Everything from tomatos to melons is cultivated, including bananas, grapes, figs, citrus fruits and the like.

Uncontrolled hunting of wild game has led to the decimation of animal numbers roaming free. Stags and roe deer once played in the forests of the Taurus, today one only sees them rarely. With a bit of luck you can still come across foxes, wild boar, badgers, polecats, tree martens, stone martens and the almost-extinct porcupines or rodents like the cute ground squirrel. Wolves and bears are found only in the most secluded parts of the Taurus.

Fauna with 'lower profiles' can be seen darting or waddling along on the ground — lizards, geckos and turtles. When you're out hiking, you will also see snakes once in a while; 37

Cotton fields below the Taurus Mountains

different types of snake have been recorded in Turkey, including vipers and adders. Most are not dangerous but, if you are going out walking, read more about snakes on page 23. Chameleons are not uncommon, but hard to spot because of their camouflage.

Of the birds, the storks (under protection in Turkey) are fascinating. There are also many birds of prey such as eagles, falcons and buzzards. Further west (see the *Kaş to Dalyan* guide) ornithologists will be in their element on the beach at Patara and by the Dalyan Delta, where they can see grey and purple herons, kingfishers, white storks, songbirds, night swallows, and many more.

Finally, just another piece of advice regarding 'animal pests': mosquitoes, fleas and cockroaches don't only see the forests as their habitat!

Gays and lesbians

Behave discreetly! Homosexuality is frowned on in Turkey, where being outed leads to merciless discrimination. It's even one of the very few reasons accepted for avoiding military service. Only in the anonymity of Istanbul, with its millions of inhabitants, can Turkish gays and lesbians avoid discrimination and find the same variety of clubs and pubs as they would around the rest of Europe.

To find gay- and lesbian-friendly bars and hotels, see www.turkey-gay-travel.com.

Import and export regulations

You are allowed the following **duty-frees** for personal consumption when entering Turkey:
200 cigarettes (400 if bought in a Turkish duty-free shop before going through customs)
50 cigars or 200g of tobacco
0.7 litre spirits
gifts to the value of £165.

If you come into the country with anything extremely valuable (a high-carat diamond for example) it must be registered in your passport by the Turkish customs on entry.

To **export antique objects** from Turkey, one needs the written permission of a museum director. This also applies to old seals, medals, carpets, etc. Offenders are threatened with harsh punishments. The export of **minerals** also needs written permission (from MTA in Ankara, (0312 2873430). To take or ship out **carpets**, you must produce a receipt.

When you leave the country, items bought for private use (clothing, for instance) up to a value of ££390 can be brought back into the UK tax free (at time of writing). Check with the airlines before leaving about the latest regulations on bringing back duty-frees.

Information about Turkey

All the international branches of the Turkish Ministry of Tourism (www.gototurkey.co.uk or, in the USA, www.tourismturkey.org) have mouth-watering brochures that they will send on request (direct from their websites). Otherwise you can contact:

UK
Turkish Culture and Tourism Office
29-30 St James's Street
London SW1A 1HB

(020 7839 7778
(020 7925 1388

USA (New York)
Turkish Government Tourism
821 United Nations Plaza
New York, NY 10017
(212 687 2194/5/6
(212 599 7568
ny@tourismturkey.org

Inoculations

No inoculations are *required,* but
it is advisable to be vaccinated
against tetanus, diphtheria and
hepatitis A before your trip.
Double-check with your airline,
tour operator or the Department
of Health (www.dh.gov.uk), to
see if there are any changes.
By the way, if you are plagued by
a cold during your stay: blowing
your nose in public is considered
very unrefined in Turkey!

Internet access

There are plenty of internet cafés
in Turkey for those who want to
surf the web or send e-mails
during their stay. The more
stylish the café, the more
expensive it is to be on-line: half
an hour costs £0.45-0.80. The
addresses of internet cafés have
not been listed in this book,
because they change so
frequently. Many hotels and even
pansiyonlar also offer internet
access.

Invitations

The Turks are extremely hospitable. Those who enjoy mixing
with the locals, whether on bus
journeys or on visits to simple
restaurants, are frequently
spontaneously approached or
even invited to tea. Invitations to
their homes, on the other hand,
for example for the evening meal,

> **Tip on info**
> Compared with many other
> destinations, there's relatively
> little information on Turkey's
> 'official' web pages, so It's worth
> surfing the names of places in this
> book — from hotels to sites. For
> practicalities, a brilliant site is
> www.turkeytravelplanner.com

are much more rarely extended,
because of the sanctity of the
family. If you are ever invited
into anyone's home, you can take
it as a sign of special esteem.
Because of this, it is important to
remember some of the host's
customs and conventions
(although small breaches of
etiquette will obviously be
forgiven).
Guests usually bring a **gift** —
nothing lavish, just something
simple that would please the host
or family.
Shoes are removed at the
entrance. If there are no indoor
shoes ready, socks will do.
For a hearty welcome, one
traditionaly exchanges a double
kiss (right cheek, then left cheek)
— this is more common between
people of the same gender than
the opposite gender. If you are
uncertain, just politely offer your
hand and let your Turkish host
take the initiative before com-
mitting a *faux pas.*
Speaking loudly in the presence
of older people is considered
poor manners. Seniors are treated
very courteously. In traditional
families it is even usual to stand
when the head of the family
appears.
*To refuse something offered is
impolite.* The hosts have
undoubtedly made a great effort

to please you, possibly spending well beyond their means.

Islam

Islam (in English 'submission' or 'surrender') is the youngest of the major world religions. Like Judaism and Christianity, it is a strictly monotheistic religion, its followers believing in one omnipotent God. According to Islamic belief, Allah is the creator and guardian of all things and all life. He cares for, guides and judges human beings; on the day of the Last Judgement, 'the saved' enter paradise, while 'the condemned' descend to hell.

The religion's founder was Mohammed (around 570-632), who grew up as an orphan in Mecca. His religious and political work began around 610, after the Archangel Gabriel appeared to him in a vision, but his first sermons were received with scepticism in his home city. It was only when Mohammed moved to Medina in 622 (the start of the Islamic calendar) that he became established as a world and religious authority, generally accepted as a legislator and prophet. Some of Mohammed's messages were revolutionary for the times — for instance the condemnation of slavery in the name of God.

The role played by the Islamic faith in Turkey varies from region to region. For many inhabitants of the Westernised coastal towns, it means almost nothing. But just a few kilometres inland, things look very different. The swirling currents of Islam were a thorn in the side of pre-AKP governments, which chose the *imams* (who are government

employees) and prescribed both what they were allowed to preach and what they could teach in theological lessons based on the Koran. With the coming to power of the pro-Islamist AKP, this strict control has changed to mutual agreement.

The Koran and *Sunna* are the fundamental teachings of the Islamic faith. The **Koran** (Holy Book of Islam), which consists of 114 *suren* (chapters), is believed to be the true word of God, as told to Mohammed by the Archangel Gabriel. This explains the infallibility attributed to the Koran. The Sunna ('Tradition') is a collection of 9th-century stories *(hadith)* about the life of Mohammed and his followers, giving an insight into how some

The Five Pillars of Islam
The Koran dictates five obligations for all Muslims:
— profession of faith *(kelimei şahadet):* 'I testify that there is no God except Allah, and Mohammed is His prophet...')
— prayers *(namaz)* five times a day, washing before you pray
— extending charity to those in need *(zekat)*
— fasting during daylight hours during the month of Ramadan *(oruç)*
— a pilgrimage to Mecca *(hac)*
With some of the duties there is a bit of flexibility. Thus the Muslim need only make his pilgrimage to Mecca if he is healthy and can afford it; washing before prayer can be just done as a ritual, if no water is available; pregnant woman, the sick, and young children can postpone fasting.

Koran, with translation into modern Turkish (see page 53)

Mohammed's legal successor and the head of the Muslim world. For the Shiites (the name comes from the Arabic word *schia, or* 'party'), however, only a blood relative of the prophet could stake their claim to leadership. Since Mohammed left no surviving sons, the Shiites saw Ali (Mohammed's cousin and son-in-law) and his descendants as the legitimate successors *(imams)*.

Around 25 per cent of Turks (including many Kurds) are **Alevis**, who are Shias. But the only thing Alevis have in common with Iranian Shias is the belief in blood-line succession. For example Alevis reject the strict Islamic *Sharia* law: unchanged for more than 1000 years, this interpretation of the Koran and Sunna sets out the rights and obligations of individuals in the community and covers every conceivable aspect of life.

Mosques *(cami)* are not only intended for prayer; they are also used for community meetings,

of the Koran's more obscure chapters can be put into practice. In contrast to the Koran, the Sunna is *not* considered infallible.

Islam teaches that since human beings are morally weak and fallible, God sends **prophets** to them, who teach them how they should live. In Islam, Jesus also ranks among these prophets, beside Abraham and Moses. The Christian view, in which Jesus is seen as the son of God, is not shared by Islam. Muslims believe that the long line of prophets came to an end with Mohammed, and that the Koran is the final true word of God. Disputes after Mohammed's death about who should succeed him led to **a splitting of Muslims into two main groups: Sunnis and Shiites**. Over 70 per cent of Turks are Sunni. The Sunni saw the caliph as

Mosque etiquette
Turkish mosques can be visited by non-Muslims at any time, but follow some simple guidelines:
— non-Muslims should not visit during prayers
— men should wear long trousers and long-sleeved shirts
— women should cover their heads and shoulders, and their skirts should be at least knee length
— shoes must be removed
— maintain a respectful silence
— those at prayer should not be photographed

Laicism: separation of religion and state

'Islam will one day govern Turkey, the question is only whether the transition will be easy or hard, sweet or bloody.' Statements like this, from the former party chief Necmettin Erbakan, were one of the reasons for the banning of the Islamic Welfare Party (1998) and the Virtue Party that succeeded it (2001). From the broken pieces of the latter, the Party for Justice and Development (AKP) was formed, winner of the parliamentary elections in 2002. The banning of religious parties was justified on the grounds that Turkey had been a secular state, with a strict separation of state and religion, since Atatürk founded the republic ('any politician who needs the help of religion to run the government is an idiot').
For the revolutionary modernisers, supported by the military and Western-orientated politicians, Islam was the largest obstacle in the way of modernising the country. Atatürk rejected the Islamic calendar and withdrew Islam from its position as state

religion. The Turkish experiment was the first and most successful example in the world of the secularisation of an Islamic state.
But even after all these years laicism is still exposed to many dangers, as was pointed out by the former Turkish President Süleyman Demirel (1993-2000): 'Our state is laical, but its population is not'. The secular way presents a constant potential for conflict, insofar as the basic Islamic social philosophy is the principle that all spheres of life form an inseparable unit, whether spiritual, social, political or economic. While radical forces militate for a religious state, moderates look for ways to preserve traditional Islamic values in today's secularised world and not play off one side against the other. A popular advocate of this approach is Yaşar Nuri Öztürk, Dean of the Islamic Faculty at Istanbul University. His publications rank among Turkish best-sellers.

theological lessons, political meetings and temporary accommodation for pilgrims and the homeless.
Usually one enters a mosque via a forecourt (*avlu*), where the ritual washing is done at the cleansing well (*şadırvan*) before prayer. The prayer hall, spread with carpets, consists of a prayer niche (*mihrab*) which always points toward Mecca, a pulpit for the Friday sermon (*minbar*) and a chair or kind of throne (*kürsü*), from which the prayer leader (*imam*) reads out passages from

the Koran. Men and women pray separately, always however in the direction of Mecca. By kneeling and bending the head to the ground, one shows Allah humility and respect.
The muezzin calls followers to prayer five times a day from the mosque's minaret. Minarets were only introduced in the 8th century — before that the muezzins climbed onto the roof. But today the call to prayer, so alluring and 'Eastern-sounding' to the European ear, usually only comes from loudspeakers.

Men outside a mosque washing before prayer

The exact timing of **religious holidays** (see also 'Festivals and holidays' on page 36) is determined each year according to the Islamic moon calendar. In Islamic convention a holiday begins at sunset the evening before. When it comes to important holidays, all shops, offices, etc. will close at noon the day before. The following holidays are of particular importance.

Kadir Gecesi (Night of Power) falls on the 27th night of the fasting month of Ramadan. This holy night celebrates the Revelation of the Koran to Mohammed through the Archangel Gabriel. People believe that wishes and prayers expressed on this night will be granted.

Şeker Bayramı, the Sugar Festival, is the feast marking the end of Ramadan, the month of fasting. One visits relatives, and children go from house to house asking for sweets — hence the name. All businesses and public offices are closed for this three-day holiday.

Kurban Bayramı, the Sacrifice Festival, is the most important Islamic holy time and a four-day public holiday. This festival is rooted in the story of Abraham, who was willing to sacrifice his son Isaac, in order to prove his loyalty to God. At the last moment God provides a ram instead. The Turks follow in this tradition, with a lavish meal of newly slaughtered sheep for family and friends. All left-overs are donated to charity.

This is the time of year when pilgrims travel to Mecca, so that both domestic and international travel in Turkey is at a peak — be aware of this and try to avoid travelling on the first or last day. Remember, too, that banks will be closed and some ATMs will run out of money.

Ramazan

This is the name the Turks give the Islamic month of fasting, which is called Ramadan in most other Islamic countries. Followers may not eat, drink, smoke or have sexual intercourse between sunrise and sunset for 30 days. After darkness falls however … everything is possible. In conservative rural areas, you may find many restaurants closed during Ramazan, but of course In the holiday centres one hardly notices any difference.

Maps

The most reliable map of the area for general purposes is only for sale in Turkey itself: look for *A map of Ancient Lycia,* prepared and distributed by Sabri Aydal (scale 1:250,000), on sale in many shops. Large-scale topographical maps are impossible to find at present. Apart from the maps in this book (see notes on page 22), your best option is to use the maps published with the guide to the Lycian Way (see website, page 20), but they have little detail and no grids.

Medical care

There is no reciprocal health agreement between Turkey and the UK (or any other English-speaking country); it is strongly recommended that you take out **private health insurance** and read the conditions carefully if you intend to take part in any potentially dangerous sports like paragliding or rafting.

For minor ailments, it often suffices to visit one of the many chemists' shops and describe your symptoms to the pharmacist. Although they are very unlikely to speak English (use gestures), they have been dispensing remedies for the usual tourist problems for years. If by chance you are suffering from 'tourist tummy', straight away you might try drinking some black tea with a bit of salt in it.

Music and belly dance

To European ears, all Turkish music may sound the same, but it is in fact divided into different styles.

Folk music: With traditional Turkish folk music *(halk müziği,* also called *Türkü)* a *saz* (Turkish lute, usually with three strings) takes pride of place. Soloists or small combos sing about the simple things of countryside life — birth, love, death. After decades of absence, Kurdish folk music is also making a comeback. One hears this music mostly in cosy oriental taverns — ask for a *'Türkü-bar'.*

Classical (art) music: In contrast to folk music, *fasıl* or 'art music' is performed in restaurants. It had its origins in Ottoman palace music, but there are traces of more modern influences. The singers are usually accompanied by the *kanun* (zither), *darbuka* (hand drum), *tef* (tambourine) and *ud* (lute). One of the most successful interpreters on the Turkish art music scene is busty Bülent Ersoy: gaudily made up and clothed in mink and glitter, this corpulent 50-year-old Barbie Doll was a man until 1979.

Turkish **pop music** addresses the same topic as most English hits: love. 'Türkpop' mixes traditional Turkish melodies with modern influences, so the interpreter has a wide-ranging palette — from top songwriters like Sezen Aksu ('the Madonna of the Bosphorus') to trendy teen stars and even schmaltz.

Arabesque music, as the name suggests, has its roots in Arabian music: the topic is unrequited love. This rather monotonous oriental 'wailing' is often heard on the TRTint TV station … or on the *dolmuş*. Top among performers is Müslüm Gürses, who could be described as looking like a love-sick dachshund. There have been some notorious Arabesque concerts frequented by 50-year-olds (usually stoned) who fall about howling in ecstacy and

Play it again, Kemal!

cutting themselves with razor blades.

Many Europeans see **belly dancing** as the epitome of Turkish-oriental sensuality. But in Turkey itself, even today it is seen as somewhat indecent and is often attributed to other cultures. So for instance conservative Turks will tell you that these erotic shows originated in Egypt, whereas the Arabs are convinced that the dance was brought to Turkey by the Ottoman occupiers. Belly dance today is primarily put on for the tourist market.

Rock and electronic beats: Catchy guitar sounds are supplied by the female virtuosos Özlem Tekin and Şebnem Ferah, the soloist Teoman or the Duman Trio. Rashit's music is more punk. For grunge there's Mor ve Ötesi and for psychedelic Baba Zula. The percussionlist Burhan Öçal drummed his way into the international music scene, and the band Orient Expressions combined Anatolian folk music with electronic beats. For Turkish ska punk there's Athena. Among the country's most popular DJs are Emre and Murat Uncuoğlu. Arkın Allen, who lives between Montreal and Istanbul and is also known as Mercan Dede, pioneered links between Turkish Sufism and contemporary Western electronic music.

Newspapers and magazines

English newspapers and magazines are on sale in all the tourist centres along the Lycian coast, the papers usually being on sale the day after publication. The English-language *Daily News & Economic Review* prints background information and current news —politics, economics, sport and culture.

A new English-language daily newspaper, *Today's Zaman*, has appeared. It is very conservative (Islamic) editorially; if any

What Turkish names can mean

Imagine your butcher being called Etyemez ('he does not eat meat') or the drinks salesman Eck Suiçmez ('he does not drink water'). This can happen in Turkey.

The many strange, composite surnames go back to a law passed in 1934. In the course of Atatürk's reforms the Turks, who until that time had no surnames, had to give themselves one. Some could select a name, others were appointed one. Some made perhaps a suitable choice for their circumstances at that time, but didn't consider the legacy that would be left to their sons and daughters. And so the piano player at the hotel bar may be called Parmaksız ('without fingers')...

Unfortunately, today only the choice of first names remains. But these are in no way lacking in imagination either: the joy felt at the birth of a first child may be expressed by the name Devletgeldi ('the luck came') or Gündoğu ('the sun rose'). On the other hand, sometimes when the family is too large, they hope to be able to stop by naming the last-born (whether a boy or girl) Yeter ('this one's enough') or Dursun ('it ought to stop').

Western-thinking Turks see you reading it, you will be shunned.

Opening times

The Islamic day of rest is Friday, but the legal day of rest in Turkey has been **Sunday** since Atatürk's reforms.

Banks: see 'Currency', page 35.
Government offices: Mon.-Fri.

08.30-12.00 and 13.00-17.30; closed Sat./Sun.

Shops: The retail trade has no standard opening times; usually shops open Mon.-Fri. from 09.00-13.00 and from 14.00-19.00 and on Sat. from 09.00-13.00 only. But in tourist centres every day is shopping day. Large shopping centres are also usually open every day until late in the evening.

Post office: Mon.-Fri. 08.00-12.00 and 13.00-17.00; closed Sat./Sun.

Museums: 08.30-17.00; usually closed Mon., but see individual entries.

Restaurants: Usually open daily from 11.00 until at least 23.00. But small *lokantas* often close early in the evening.

Police

You'll see a lot of police about. Since they are very badly paid, they are usually bad tempered — except in their dealings with tourists, when they are generally very pleasant and courteous. The *jandarma* is another police force — a military unit in green uniforms, who ensure public order and security.

Post offices

Post offices (and post boxes) are instantly recognisable by their yellow signs with the three black letters PTT. The main post office *(merkez postane)* in larger cities is usually located near the main square or the bank and/or shopping district. A **postcard** takes about a week to arrive in the UK. Post offices usually have **telephones** (see page 50).

Prices

Compared with the UK, Turkey is an inexpensive destination,

Some tips for buying hand-knotted Turkish carpets are in the panel on page 48…
forewarned is forearmed.

even if prices in the tourist centres are higher than in the rest of the country. What a holiday will cost you depends on your requirements, but there is something for virtually every budget. Living very simply, for instance in a *pansiyon* with breakfast provided, picnic lunch and one restaurant meal, you could get by on well under £35 a day, including bus or *dolmuş* travel.

Shopping and bargaining

Leather goods, carpets, gold jewellery, ceramics, tea, spices, onyx, and all the other purchases that hint of the Orient are among the most popular souvenirs. Not forgetting T-shirts, jackets and trousers from the top designer labels — these are all imitations of course, but at least they fulfil their purpose: one can wear them. On the other hand, take

care with the deceptively packaged top-name perfumes, which are just ghastly.

It's best to buy from boutiques and shopping centres in the larger cities, where items are priced and you can compare prices.

Where there are **no fixed prices**, you must **bargain**. To bargain well, you must be able to estimate value and authenticity. Without wishing to get the better of you, unfortunately just about all Turkish dealers are as sly as foxes (like the waiters mentioned earlier). So don't let them sell you leather from pigs as fine napa lambskin and only believe a fraction of what you are told. If you know, when you first plan your trip to Turkey, that you may want to buy gold jewellery or carpets, check the value of what you want to buy in your own country before you leave.

Turkish **weekly markets** with stalls selling everything from vegetables and cheese to clothing and shoes are called *pazar*; **fixed markets**, like those at the bazaar in Antalya or the market quarter, with proper shops, are *çarşi*.

VAT: If you buy anything to the value of around £60 or more from shops or boutiques with a tax-free symbol in the shop window, you can get the VAT of 18% refunded in the airport departure lounge at so-called 'Cash Refund Offices' (in Antalya airport for example the counter is in the check-in hall). To claim the refund you need a completed tax-free receipt from the seller.

Sites and museums

Some of the most famous ancient sites in the world are to be found in the area covered by this book and the *Kaş to Dalyan* and *Bodrum to Marmaris* guides. You will also come upon a multitude of other sites, all indicated by brown signs. The most important of these are described, usually with accompanying site plans. Any site not described here is probably not worth the visit, unless you are a fanatic willing to walk a long, sweaty way through brambles just to stand next to a couple of weathered stones.

The **entrance prices** for ancient sites and museums are not uniform and are updated annually. Once in a while you find extreme jumps in price of 30-50% (up or down). However, as a rule of thumb, an entrance fee of up to £9 applies at the major sites. At time of writing only rarely were **concessions** available for students (with ISC)

Buying Turkish carpets

Turkey is well known for its low-priced carpets. But you have to know what you're doing and exactly what you want. Most tourists are talked into buying something on the spot — usually overpriced, too large, too small, or in unsuitable colours.

To negotiate a good price you must be able to distinguish high-quality workmanship from inferior goods. Forget everything you've ever heard about settling on one-third the asking price to guarantee a bargain; *everyone gets two-thirds off after the tenth tea*. The dealers know all about this rule of thumb, so who's to say that they don't start with a price magnified a hundredfold?

If you know next to nothing about carpets, by all means buy a small, cheap one as a souvenir (when you consign it to the loft the moths will be happy) — or go to a specialist back home, put up some security, and take a carpet home to try out.

If you *must* buy a carpet in Turkey, go with the advice of an expert: check the thickness of the knots and the number of knots per sq cm. Flex the carpet in natural light, dividing the pile with your fingers to make sure the colour goes straight through. Be careful not to burn a hole in the carpet with the infamous cigarette lighter test, or you'll fall straight through. Be sure to ask if the carpet can fly and, if not, immediately ask for a 50% discount. If you heed all this advice, the dealer won't take you for a fool. One more thing: *never* accept a dealer's offer to post your carpet home for you!

or seniors — this may change in future. **Photography** or filming (video) occasionally costs extra and then usually *quite a bit extra* (up to £8!). On the other hand there are many sites with free entry.

A word to the wise: often self-appointed 'guides' try to take money from tourists. Don't let yourself be taken in; only officially-authorised guides can hand over an entrance ticket!

Sport and leisure

The Turks are becoming more sports-orientated. Joggers, walkers and hikers will no longer find themselves conspicuous! But in places where the Turks themselves holiday, the sports on offer are meagre — after all, the precious holiday weeks are taken for recovery, which means lazing about. In the international tourist resorts, however, the trend is towards European-style active holidays, with plenty of leisure and sports programmes.

Naturally water sports dominate along the coast .

Diving: You can snorkel with mask and fins almost anywhere along the coast, but underwater hunting with tanks is forbidden — as is removing any historical and/or antique articles. Kaş, just west of the area covered in this guide, is the main diving centre.

Golf: Belek, about 45km east of Antalya, is the golfing centre of Turkey, with 16 courses, hotels and all-inclusive clubs. If you don't book an all-inclusive package, you will have to pay a green fee of £25-90. Information at www. bilyanagolf.com. Below just a a few of the courses:

— **Gloria**, US resort-style course designed by Michel Gayon, 6296m, several holes over lakes, men's handicap 28, women's 36, 18 holes, par 72. Nearby 9-hole **Gloria Verde** course, also designed by Gayon.

— **Robinson**, magnificent club-house, ingenious layout with a lot of optical tricks, designed by Dave Thomas, play over lakes, 5877m, men's handicap 28, women's 36, 18 holes, par 72.

— **National**, the oldest of the clubs, British in style, designed by David Feherty, 6109m, men's handicap 28, women's 36, 18 holes, par 72.

— **Antalya Golf Club Pasha**, designed by David Jones, 5731m, men's handicap 28, women's 36, 18 holes, par 72.

— **Antalya Golf Club Sultan**, for top players, also by David Jones, 6411m, men's handicap 24, women's 28, 18 holes, par 71.

Kayaking/Rafting: Various tour companies offer kayaking and rafting, especially in the Köprülü Canyon (see page 96). Sea kayaking is very popular around the Kekova area (or you can camp out; see 'Seven Capes Sea Kayak Centre' on page 9).

Paragliding isn't an option in the Antalya region, but very popular further west around the Ölüdeniz lagoon.

Riding: Most of the larger tourist centres have riding stables offering treks in the highlands; you can usually book through local tour companies.

Sailing: see page 19.

Skiing: The ski resort of **Saklı-kent** near Antalya (see page 104) has two lifts, but even in winter there's no guarentee of snow.

Surfing: In the tourist centres surfing schools offer courses and organise board rentals. But no experts surf in the Antalya region; the surf's better on the Bodrum Peninsula.

Tennis: Many of the larger hotels have tennis courts, at which non-guests can also pay to play.

Walking: One of the best ways to see Lycia; see pages 20-23.

Water sports: In the international resorts on the coast, various water-based activities are offered. Reckon on paying £20-£25 for 15 minutes on water skis, £25-£30 for 10 min. parasailing, £20-£25 for 10 min. jetskiing, £8 for 15 min. banana-boating, £60-£70 per hour in a speedboat with a 50 HP engine or £90-£100 for a 115 HP engine. The organisers are usually on the beaches.

Telephone

Making calls with a mobile is problem-free in nearly the entire area, but the roaming charges are expensive. If you make *a lot* of calls, or if you plan to stay in Turkey beyond a couple of weeks, it would pay to buy a SIM card from a Turkish network operator. But you will have to buy a new or used Turkish mobile as well (they're available everywhere), since Turkish SIM cards tend not to work in foreign mobiles after a week or so. Those who don't have a mobile or want to save money should make calls using a card phone.

Telephone cards (*telefon kartı*) are available from post offices, kiosks and small roadside stands. A good choice for international calls is the Arakart: 100 units for example (about £2.70) allows you to phone the UK for 15 minutes.

International dialling codes: for the UK first dial 00 44, for the USA 00 1, for the Irish Republic 00 353. This is followed by the local code (without the initial zero, if there is one), then the number.

Calls to Turkey: From outside the country dial 00-90, then the local code (without the initial zero), then the number.

Internet: Many hotels and guest houses now offer WIFI, whereby you can call free using Skype (www.skype.com). *Beware of making calls from your hotel room;* these are often charged at extremely high rates. Better to make a brief call and ask to be called back (directly to your hotel room).

Emergency numbers
Police ℂ 155
Traffic police ℂ 154
Ambulance ℂ 112
Fire brigade ℂ 110

Time

Turkey is on Eastern European Time, two hours ahead of Greenwich Mean Time, in both summer and winter (clocks go forward or back on the same days). At noon in Turkey, it's 10am in the UK, 5am in New York.

Toilets

Men's toilets have the label 'Bay', women's 'Bayan'. In tourist centres the facilities are usually up to European standards; otherwise is it not uncommon to find the stand-up 'hole in the floor', and no paper will be provided. *Take your own!* If a small bucket is provided in the toilet cubicle, please throw any paper in there and do not try to flush it away — the old-style thin sewage pipes simply cannot cope (and besides, toilet paper in the cesspits delays

The *hamam* — cleansing body and soul

The saying goes that the Ottoman past lives on in the *hamams*, the traditional Turkish communal steam baths which cater for all classes. Once inside, you're in a different world … enveloped by hot, moist air and the smell of soap, relaxing under the spell of splashing water and the murmurings of shining naked bodies lying on a huge marble slab.

The *hamam* is divided into three areas. The entrance hall *(came-kân)*, usually with a decorative fountain, is surrounded by the reception and changing rooms. On entering, you will be given a small robe *(peştamal)* and sandals. While it's usual for men to wear a towel around the loins and for women to bathe naked, you can bring a swimsuit if you prefer.

After changing you move through a passageway *(soğukluk)* into the main part of the *hamam*, the steam room *(hararet)*. The huge marble slab in the centre, which is warmed from below, is the *göbek taşı* (navel stone).

First you are expected to wash all over at the basins along the wall, then rise thoroughly (taking care to leave no suds behind, in case the water is used for ritual washing at the mosque). Then you lie on the marble slab, first to sweat for 15 minutes or so, and then to be massaged.

Women are usually massaged by a hefty masseuse, men by wiry muscle-men. Before the massage begins, the *tellaks* soap you down, then use a very rough flannel for exfoliation (a procedure called the *kese*). By this time your limbs are soft and rubbery, ready for the massage. Be warned: you will be pulled, twisted, kneaded and pummelled like a lump of dough; the massage is intended to loosen tight muscles and joints. Afterwards you will feel totally drained, totally relaxed.

Most *hamams* have separate sections for men *(erkekler)* and women *(kadınlar)*. At smaller baths men and women bathe at different times or on different days, but in tourist centres mixed bathing is sometimes offered.

---

decomposition). Naturally there are toilets in museums and at sites (small charge), and in restaurants. Otherwise you can usually find public toilets near a mosque.

Travel documents

Travelling from the UK or any English-speaking country you will need a **passport** and a **visa**. Package tour operators will arrange visas for you, otherwise you can buy one on the spot *for cash* at the airport or border when you enter Turkey.

While not strictly required, it is suggested that you also have a **ticket** for return or onward travel.

At time of writing you do not need any **inoculations**, but see page 39. Private **health insurance** is strongly recommended; see 'Medical care', page 44; **travel insurance** is mandatory.

If you plan to hire a car, you must have your **driver's licence**; if you are driving to Turkey in your own car, see page 13.

Turkish

In all the tourist centres you should be able to communicate in English with no difficulty. But in the countryside you may have problems if you don't know at least a few words of Turkish, since many schools there teach no foreign languages at all. Turkish is a very logical language and, once you have mastered a few of the rules you can progress quite rapidly, especially with pronunciation. A number of the letters in the Turkish language are unfamiliar to English speakers, but are easy to pronounce; one or two 'normal' letters are pronounced differently. **In Turkish, *usually* the first syllable is stressed.**

C/c	pronounced like the 'j' in 'jet'; *cami* (mosque) is pronounced **dja**mee
Ç/ç	pronunced 'ch'; *çam* (pine) is pronounced **cham**
Ğ/ğ	just elongates the previous vowel; *dağ* (mountain) is pronounced **daah**
İ/i	pronounced 'ee'; *iki* (two) is pronounced ee**kee**
I/ı	pronounced 'eh'; *altı* (six) is pronounced al**teh**
Ö/ö	pronounced like the 'ea' in 'learn'; *köprü* (bridge) is pronounced kurh**prew**
Ş/ş	pronounced 'sh'; *şeker* (sugar) is pronounced **sh**eker
Ü/ü	pronounced like the 'u' in 'lure'; *köprü* (bridge) is pronounced kurh**prew**

Basic words and phrases

Evet/hayır	Yes/No
Lütfen	Please
Teşekkür ederim	Thank you
Affedersiniz	Excuse me
Merhaba	Hello
Allaha ısmarladık (said by the person leaving)	See you later
Güle güle (said by the person staying)	See you later
Hoşça kal	So long, cheers
Günaydın	Good morning
İyi günler (as a greeting or when leaving)	Good day
İyi akşamlar	Good evening
İyi geceler	Good night
Nasılsın?	How are you (singlular)?
Nasılsınız?	How are you (plural)?
İyiyim	I'm fine.
... var mı?	Do you have…?
Saat kaç?	What time is it?
Büyük/küçük	Big/little
İyi/kötü	Good/bad

In towns

Tren istasyonu	Railway station
Garaj/otogar	Bus station
Havalimanı/ havaalanı	Airport
İskele	Ferry dock
Saray	Palace
Sokak	Alley
Cadde	Road
Meydan	Square
Cami	Mosque
Hisar	Fort
Kule	Tower
Kilise	Church
Müze	Museum
Banka	Bank
Hastane	Hospital
Köprü	Bridge
Ada	Island
Kütüphane	Library
Kitabevi	Bookshop
Eczane	Chemist
Bakkal	Grocer
Süpermarket	Supermarket
Pazar	Weekly market

Çarşı	Market
Postane	Post
Seyahat acentası	Travel agency

Directions/getting around

Nerede … ?	Where is … ?
Ne zaman?	When?
Sağ/sol	Right/left
Doğru	Straight ahead
Otobüs	Bus
Tren	Train
Araba	Car
Taksi	Taxi
Vapur	Ferry
Yaya	On foot
Bilet	Ticket
Varış	Arrival
Kalkıs	Departure
Giriş	Entrance
Çıkış	Exit
Tuvalet	Toilets
Bay/Bayan	Men's/Ladies'
Açık/kapalı	Open/closed
Polis	Police
Girilmez	No entry

Numbers

Bir	1	On sekiz	18	
İki	2	On dokuz	19	
Üç	3	Yirmi	20	
Dört	4	Yirmi bir	21	
Beş	5	Otuz	30	
Altı	6	Kırk	40	
Yedi	7	Elli	50	
Sekiz	8	Altmış	60	
Dokuz	9	Yetmiş	70	
On	10	Seksen	80	
On bir	11	Doksan	90	
On iki	12	Yüz	100	
On üç	13	Iki yüz	200	
On dört	14	Bin	1,000	
On beş	15	On bin	10,000	
On altı	16	Bir milyon		
On yedi	17		1,000,000	

Eating and drinking — general

Şerefe!	Cheers!
Yemek listesi	Menu
Bunu ısmarlamadım	I didn't order that
Hesap, lütfen	The bill, please
Kahvaltı	Breakfast
Öğle yemeği	Lunch
Akğam yemeği	Dinner
Tabak/çatal	Plate/fork
Bıçak/kaşık	Knife/spoon

Breakfast

Beyaz peynir	Sheep's cheese
Bal	Honey
Reçel	Marmalade
Ekmek/tereyağı	Bread/butter
Yumurta	Egg
Seker/tuz	Sugar/salt

Drinks

Çay/kahve	Tea/coffee
Türk kahvesi	Turkish mocca
Neskafe	Instant coffee
Süt	Milk
Meşrubat	Non-alcoholic
Su	Water
Soda	Sparkling water
Meyve suyu	Fruit juice
Ayran	Drink made of yogurt, water and salt
İçki	Alcoholic drink
Bira	Beer
Fıçı bira	Draught beer
Şarap	Wine
Beyaz şarap	White wine
Kırmızı şarap	red wine
Viski	Whisky
Votka	Vodka

Modern Turkish

Originally Turkish contained many Arabic and Persian words written in Arabic script. Despite Atatürk's language reforms (the Roman alphabet has been used since 1928), these influences remain. In his attempts to make the language more 'Turkish', the old words had to be transliterated into the Roman alphabet, leading to some inconsistencies that remain today.

Starters			
Meze	Turkish starters	*Tavuk*	Chicken
Ezme	Vegetable or	*Piliç*	Small chicken
	yogurt cream	*Sığır/dana*	Beef/veal
Haydari	Yogurt dip	*Kuzu*	Lamb
	with mint and	*Pirzola*	Cutlet
	garlic	*Karışık izgara*	Mixed grill
Humus	Hummus	*Şiş kebap*	Skewer
Patlıcan salatası	Aubergine salad	*Adana kebap*	Peppered
Zeytinyağlılar	Cold vegetables		mince kebab
	in olive oil	*Bursa kebap*	Döner kebab/
	(various types)		tomato sauce
Piyaz	Salad of beans,		and yogurt
	olive oil and	*Tas kebap*	Braised lamb
	lemon	*Arnavut çiğeri*	Pieces of liver

Fish and seafood

Alabalık	Trout
Balık	Fish
Barbunya	Mullet
Levrek	Sea bass
Lüfer	Blue bass
Kılıç	Sword fish
Sardalya	Sardines
Kalkan	Turbot
Hamsi	Anchovy
Uskumru	Mackerel
Dil balığı	Sole
Midye/yengeç	Mussels/crabs

Starters (cont.)	
Sigara böreği	Elongated fried pastry filled with sheep's cheese
Çerkes tavuğu	Chicken in walnut sauce
Beyin salatası	Salad of calves brains
Çiğ köfte	raw meatballs
Çorba	soup
Mercimek çorbası	Lentil soup
Yayla çorbasi	Yogurt soup with mint and lemon
Domates çorbası	Tomato soup
Tavuk çorbası	Chicken soup
İşkembe çorbası	Entrail soup

Vegetables and side dishes

Sebze	Vegetables
Bamya	Okra
Kuru fazulye	Dried beans
Taze fazulye	Green beans
Bezelye	Peas
Havuç	Carrots
Ispanak	Spinach
Karnıbahar	Cauliflower
Lahana	Cabbage
Domates	Tomatoes
Zeytin	Olives
Soğan	Onions
Salatalık	Cucumbers
Sarmısak	Garlic
Salata	Salad
Çoban salatası	Mixed salad with sheep's cheese
Yeşil salata	Green salad
Cacık	Yogurt/cucumber/garlic

Main courses

Dolma	Stuffed vegetables
Yaprak dolması	— vine leaves
Biber dolması	— peppers
Patlıcan dolması	— aubergines
Kabak dolması	— zucchini
İmam bayıldı (literally 'the iman fainted')	Baked aubergine with onions and tomatoes
Güveç	Braised vegetables, often with bits of meat
Köfte	Meatballs
Hindi	Turkey

Makarna	Noodles
Patates	Potatoes
Pilav	Rice
Bulgur	Cracked wheat
Yoğurt	Yogurt

Fruit

Meyve	Fruit
Armut/elma	Pear/apple
Karpuz	Watermelon
Kavun	Honeydew
Üzüm	Grapes
Muz	Banana
Portakal/limon	Orange/lemon
Çilek	Strawberries
İncir/kiraz	Figs/cherries
Şeftali/kayısı	Peach/apricots
Nar	Pomegranate

Desserts, sweet

Tatlı	Any sweet
Sütlaç	Rice pudding
Lokum	Turkish delight
Dondurma	Ice cream
Kek	Sweet biscuits
Pasta	Gâteau

Snacks

Börek	Stuffed filo triangle
Gözleme	'Turkish pancake' (filled)
Lahmacun	Turkish pizza
Simit	Sesame rings
Turşu	Pickled vegetables

Women

Thanks to the reforms of Atatürk in the 1920s (and Turkey's ambitions to join the EU), the position of women is nothing like that in most Islamic countries. Nevertheless there is a large discrepancy between their legal rights and reality in a country so long dominated by men. Naturally the divide is greatest between town and country. The increased literacy rate is mainly due to the education of women. On the Mediterranean coast and in the towns, over 50% of the female workforce are educated beyond the compulsory eight years (a third of all graduates are women), but in the countryside the figure falls to 5%, and one woman in three is illiterate.

On the other hand, more women are in managerial positions than in many other European countries: a third of the doctors are women, a quarter of the lawyers and a fifth of the judges.

Women travelling alone in this part of Turkey won't be treated any differently in the tourist areas than would be the case in, for instance, Italy or Spain. To avoid problems, it's sensible to dress decently and even wear a 'wedding ring' and carry photos of your 'husband' and 'children' (all can be fake). If you're approached, speak formally and avoid eye contact. Should you be out at night, it's best to get a taxi back to where you are staying.

Visiting or business cards
Turks seem to love them, and will sometimes honour you by handing you their card, or will ask for yours. Before a Turk hands you his card, he will usually make a squiggle on the back, thus 'invalidating' the card. This is because in the past people could go into a restaurant or shop, and it was understood that the bill would be settled by the person named on the card.

History

From about 150,000 BC (palaeolithic): Nomadic hunter/gatherers roam across the Turkish Mediterranean coast according to finds from caves like the Karain Cave near Antalya (see page 103).

8,000-5500 BC (neolithic): The cave paintings at Beldibi (see page 103) date from this period. Inland there are town-like settlements which today rank among the oldest 'cities' in the world. Loam is used in the building of dwellings. With the establishing of settlements, agriculture and cattle breeding also begin. Pottery is developed at about the same time — during excavations close to Konya (about 150km northeast of Antalya as the crow flies), archaeologists discovered small sculptures of full-breasted goddesses, symbols of fertility.

5500-3200 BC (chalcolithic): More finely-worked pottery and simple tools come into use, wrought from copper (found at the Hacılar excavations near Burdur, also some 150km north of Antalya).

3200-2000 BC: The Early Bronze Age sees the spread of spinning and weaving mills, as well as bronze jewellery work. Troy is founded, the oldest city on the Turkish coast. Traders from Assur (on the Tigris in what is today northern Iraq) meet with the central and eastern Anatolians, bringing them into contact with writing.

2000-1200 BC: The Hittites cross the Caucasus, and central Anatolia becomes part of the 'Old Kingdom', from which the 'Great Kingdom' is later formed.

Hattussas (some 170km east of Ankara) is made the capital. At the same time Mycenaeans expand their rule over the Aegean as far as Minoan Crete. Troy develops into a prosperous trading centre.

Around 1200 BC: The so-called 'Sea People', about whom little is known, invade from the north via Thrace. Among them are the Phrygians, who play a substantial role in the destruction of Troy and also put an end to the supremacy of the Hittites and Mycenaeans.

1200-700 BC: After the fall of Troy, Greek tribes (led by the seers Mopsos, Kalchas and Amphilochos) migrate from the west coast through Asia Minor to the south coast and found several cities, including Perge and Sillyon — or so ancient sources would lead us to believe, but these are now disputed. What is not in dispute is that, starting from about the 11th century BC, there is an increase in Greek colonisation (Aeolian, Ionian and Dorian) on the Mediterranean coast of Asia Minor. They come into direct competition with the local tribes (Lelegians, Carians, Lycians, and Lydians). By the 9th century BC many of these Greek settlements have grown into substantial ports.

690-550 BC: The Lydians found a large kingdom in the west of Asia Minor, with Sardis as its capital (about 90km east of İzmir); their king, Croesus, becomes legendary. They also conquer further parts of the south coast. Art, culture and science begin to flourish in the cities.

From 545 BC: Under Cyrus the Great, the Persians penetrate as far as western Anatolia and destroy the Lydian Kingdom. They use satraps (colonial governors) for the administration of Asia Minor. Regular rebellions against the Persians follow.

From 479 BC: The Persians withdraw from the Aegean coast. Cities and small towns come and go.

334-333 BC. Alexander the Great conquers Asia Minor; he spends the winter in Phaselis (see page 140). This is the beginning of the Hellenistic period, which lasts until the era of the Roman Caesars and brings enormous cultural developement.

From 323 BC: After Alexander's death the Macedonian Kingdom disintegrates; its army leaders divide it among themselves. The most important of these Diadochian realms are those of Ptolemy (in Egypt), incorporating Lycia and other parts of the south coast, the Attalid Kingdom of Pergamon in western Anatolia, and the Seleucid Empire — the largest part of Alexander's former kingdom, with Antioch (modern Antakya) as the capital.

197 BC: Under Antiochus III (the Great) the Seleucids conquer Lycia.

190 BC: The Attalids, with the support of Rome and Rhodes, defeat the Seleucids in the battle of Magnesia (today's Manisa). Nearly the whole Seleucid Empire falls to the Kingdom of Pergamon, which is allied with Rome. Only Lycia goes to Rhodes.

The Tomb of Xantabura at Limyra (see pages 168-170)

From 167 BC: The Lycian cities separate from Rhodes and form a federation, retaining their independence for about two centuries, thanks to skillful, Rome-friendly diplomacy.

From 133 BC: On the death of Attalus III, the kingdom of Pergamon passes to Rome and becomes the Roman province of Asia. Several cities on the south coast ignore Roman law, however, and indulge in piracy.

63-67 BC: The Roman Commander Pompey (the Great) brings the piracy to an end. Four years later he creates the Roman province of Syria.

42 BC: With Caesar's murder, the eastern part of the Roman Empire falls to Mark Antony.

31 BC: Octavian (later Emperor Augustus) is victorious over Mark Antony's fleet in the battle of Actium. Beginning of the 'Pax Romana', lasting nearly 250 years. Roman culture penetrates all cities in Asia Minor. Temples, boulevards, theatres, aqueducts and the like still bear witness today to the glory of the age.

43 AD: Lycia is merged with Pamphylia into a Roman province, but the Lycian League continues to exist under the Romans.

45-60 AD: St. Paul the Apostle stops off in different cities on the Lycian coast during his missionary journeys. The first Christian communities are formed.

Around 290: A child is born in Patara, who later becomes world-famous as St. Nicholas.

330: Emperor Constantine (the Great) names the former Byzantium (Istanbul today) Nea Roma (New Rome) and makes it the new capital of the Roman Empire. Soon after his death, Constantinople becomes the generally accepted name.

380: Christianity becomes the state religion; all pagan cults are forbidden.

395: The final division of the Roman Empire into west and east. The latter, later known as the Byzantine Empire, becomes the heartland of Christianity, with Roman law and Greek as the language.

527-565: Under Emperor Justinian I, Byzantium expands and blooms. It extends from southern Italy over the Balkan Peninsula and the whole of Asia Minor to the edge of the Iranian highlands. All building activity is concentrated in Constantinople. The coastal towns play a subordinate role from now on, even though many of them are made diocesan towns.

622: Mohammed and his followers emigrate to Medina (the *Hijra*, or 'Flight'); this is later designated the first year of the Islamic calendar.

From 636: Eastern Byzantium is conquered by the Arabs. Trained by Syrian sailors, seaborne invaders plunder the Byzantine coastal towns. Coastal fortresses are rebuilt or strengthened for protection — often using ancient stonework for the building materials.

860: Arabs occupy Antalya.

1054: Schism of the Roman Catholic and the Greek Orthodox churches.

From 1071: Seljuk Muslims penetrate west from the Kirgistan steppes and attack Byzantine troops in the battle of Manzikert. They bring Islam with them, and spread throughout central Anatolia, making Konya their capital and holding the remnants of the Byzantine Empire in fear.

From 1096: Help comes to Byzantium from the Occident: the Crusades begin, to free the lost holy cities from Islamic rule.

1204-1261: The Fourth Crusade is organised against Constantinople itself, with the intention of reviving the Roman Catholic faith. After taking the city, the Knights establish a Latin (Roman Catholic) Empire. The Greek

Byzantines withdraw to Nicea (İznik); it is not until 1261 that, under Michael VIII Palaeologos, the Greeks take Constantinople back from the Latins.

1226: The Seljuks conquer further parts of the coastal region. Venetians and Genoese receive permission to establish future trade.

From 1243: The Seljuk Sultanate is crushed by the Mongols. In its place several small principalities are established in Anatolia by Turkmen dynasties.

From 1309: The Order of Knights of St. John found a sovereign state on Rhodes; in the following years they establish various fortresses in the Aegean.

1326: Osman I (1281-1326), army leader and chieftain of a Turkmen tribe, conquers the west Anatolian city of Bursa, later called the cradle of the Ottoman Empire. Since Mongolian armies control the east, Osman's successors look to the north and west.

1354: Gallipoli is conquered by the Ottomans, providing them with their first foothold in Europe.

1402-1406: The Mongolian ruler Timur Lenk (1365-1405; also known as Tamerlane) makes a short and bloody appearance in Anatolia, devastating many cities. This however has little effect on the ascent of the Ottoman Empire.

1453: The Ottomans conquer Constantinople, the only remaining stronghold of the Byzantine Empire, thereby

Sultanate of Women

Süleyman the Magnificent (1520-1566) and his main wife Roxelane initiated the so-called 'Sultanate of Women' — a transfer of power from men to women and an explanation for the slow decline of the Ottoman Empire lasting over three centuries.

With her intrigues and murderous plots, Roxelane brought her own son Selim II (1566-1574) to the throne. He went down in history as 'Selim the Sot'. Even before he slipped and drowned in the bathtub, the Ottoman Empire lost its entire fleet.

Selim II had five sons, four of whom were murdered by his wife Nurbanu, so that her own offspring could be crowned Sultan Murat III (1574-1595). Like so many sultans, he proved to be more active in the harem than in politics. This rewarded him with over 100 children, of whom his wife Safiye contrived to have 19 murdered, so that their son took the throne as Sultan Mehmet III (1595-1603)…

One could go on and on about the history of female influence on the successors to the Ottoman throne. And the fact that the budding sultans grew up in the harems, pampered and spoilt, in a world completely out of touch with reality. Flattered by courtiers scheming to see their own interests satisfied, the regents were for the most part incapable of acting for themselves. Many were not even strong enough to govern to the natural end of their lives. They were either strangled, poisoned or so weak-willed that they were driven out of office.

wiping it off the map. From now on Constantiniya, the future Istanbul, is capital of the Ottoman Empire, and its sphere of influence grows steadily. Less than 20 years later the Ottomans take the Turkish south coast.

1517: Selim I (1512-1520) conquers Syria and Egypt, thus bringing the Caliphate to the Bosphorus.

1520-1566: Süleyman I, known as the Magnificent, conquers Bagdad, Belgrade, Rhodes, Hungary, Georgia, Azerbajan and parts of North Africa. In 1529 he besieges Vienna for the first time. He leads the Ottomans to the zenith of their powers, when it takes 75 minutes for the sun to set over their Empire. Süleyman and his successors have little interest in the development of Asia Minor's coastal towns.

From 1683: Defeat after the second siege of Vienna means the end of expansion and heralds the gradual decline of the Ottoman Empire. There are repeated flashes of unrest on the domestic front.

From 1808: Under Mahmut II (1808-1839) the first attempts take place to gradually reform the Empire. He eliminates the Janissaries (an elite military unit who resist all progressive currents), probably by the ruse of inciting them to revolt, leading to their massacre or exile. He outlaws the turban and introduces the fez in its place.

1853-1856: The Crimean War; Russian-occupied territories are recaptured. Florence Nightingale gains fame for her nursing work in Istanbul.

1875: The 'Sick Man of the Bosphorus' receives the bill for its failure to join the Industrial Revolution and its many expensive wars: the consequence is national bankruptcy.

1876-1909: During the reign of Abdül Hamit II the Muslim population instigate pogroms against the Christian Armenians. At the start of the Young Turk movement, officers force the resignation of the sultan. True power now lies in the hands of the military.

1912-13: The First Balkan War; the Ottoman Empire loses its remaining European territories.

1914-1918: During the First World War the Turks side with Germany and lose. The winners divide the spoils: Greek troops march on Ankara; Italy occupies the coastal strip around Antalya; France occupies Cilicia; English troops control the Bosphorus. The Ottoman Empire now only consists of central Anatolia.

1919-20: Istanbul is forced to accept the Treaty of Sèvres on behalf of the Ottoman Empire, however the nationalists do not. April 1920 sees the first meeting of the Grand National Assembly in Ankara and the formation of a new government under Mustafa Kemal, later Atatürk (see panel opposite). Military resistance is organised.

1921-22: Kemal's troops strike the Greek army at the Sakarya River. The Italians and French retreat.

1923: With the Treaty of Lausanne the Allies recognise the independence and sovereignty of the new Turkey. In Ankara, the new capital, the National

Atatürk, father of the Turks

Atatürk's likeness greets you in every office, shop and restaurant; he bids you goodbye from every lira you hand out. He excites the imagination of Turkish sculptors, too — because with the exception of Atatürk, public statues are rarely commissioned. Hardly any other statesman is assigned such cult status.

As Mustafa Kemal (born around 1881) he was elected the first President of the new Republic of Turkey in 1923. He secularised and Europeanised the new state in an enormous act of will. For his services to the country, in 1934 Parliament gave him the name Atatürk, 'Father of the Turks'. Four years later he died in Istanbul from cirrhosis of the liver. His remains rest in the Atatürk Mausoleum in Ankara.

Assembly proclaims the Republic and selects Mustafa Kemal as President. In the same year, the Norwegian Fritjof Nansen, working on behalf of the League of Nations, suggests a population exchange between Greeks and Turks. Ankara agrees immediately. This effectively ends the 3000 years' history of the Greeks in Asia Minor.

1924: A new constitution comes into force, incorporating the separation of state and religion. Islamic Sharia law is replaced by Swiss civil law, Italian criminal law and German commercial law.

1925-1938: Up until Atatürk's death numerous reforms are brought in to Europeanise Turkey: education and writing reform (transition from Arabic script to the Roman alphabet), the introduction of surnames, changing of the rest day from Friday to Sunday, etc.

1945: Having remained neutral for most of the Second World War, Turkey declares war on Germany. In the same year it becomes a founding member of the United Nations.

1952: Turkey joins NATO.

From 1960: Long periods of political and social unrest, with several interventions by the military. 1960: Kemalistic officers stage a *coup d'état* and allow the execution of the Prime Minister Adnan Menderes. 1971: The cabinet is forced to resign. 1980: The military take power again and dissolve Parliament. The military sees itself as the guardian of Laicism (see page 42) and of Atatürk's legacy. It stands in clear opposition to Islamic fundamentalism and radical left-wing groups.

1974: Turkish troops occupy northern Cyprus.

1984-1999: The Kurdish fight for autonomy claims roughly 25,000 victims in the east and southeast. The situation eases in February 1999 with the arrest of Kurdish Workers' Party boss Abdullah Öcalan; a truce is agreed.

1999: On 17th August a devastating earthquake hits northwest Turkey; approximately 18,000 people die.

From 2002: The AKP emerge as clear winners in the government elections; many small parties lose seats due to a clause requiring a 10% minimum threshhold for a party to gain entry to Parliament. Party leader Recep Tayyip Erdoğan becomes the head of government one year later. Under his leadership there is a full-on push for much-needed reforms. Laws are passed to meet the Copenhagen criteria for EU membership. But Islamic extremists do not want to see a successful democracy in an Islamic land: to destabilise the country and make Europe fear Turkish EU membership, a Turkish terrorist cell with supposed Al-Qaida connections commits several atrocities. The bloodiest of these shake Istanbul in November 2003: explosions at the British Consulate, two synagogues and the HSBC Bank kill 64 people (including the British Consul) and wound 750.

From 2005: The PKK brings more terror to the land, having ended their five-year armistice in 2004. Splinter groups cause atrocities in several Mediterranean tourist resorts, including Antalya.

2006: The long-awaited EU negotiations begin. But any joy in finally getting to the table is quickly swept aside by the unwelcoming attitude of the EU member states. EU euphoria in Turkey decreases correspondingly: in 2004, 70% of the population were in favour of joining, by 2006 the figure is down to only 30%. Orhan Pamuk becomes the first Turk to win a Nobel Prize; his novels typically deal with the clashes of identity between East and West.

2007: Gül, a member of the conservative AKP, becomes President. The fact that his wife wears a headscarf almost precipitates a military coup

2008-2012: The international financial crisis hits Turkey. In six months the Turkish lira loses 30% of its value. National bankruptcy can't be ruled out. By the first quarter of 2010 the Turkish economy had bounced back, with growth of over 11%. In the list of the world's largest economies, Turkey ranks 17th.

1 ANTALYA

Orientation • History • Accommodation/camping • Food and drink • Nightlife • Beaches and diving • Sights • Practicalities A-Z

Area code: (0242
Information: the official Tourist Office is at Güllük Cad. 31 (also called Anafartalar Cad.); open daily from 08.30-18.30, in winter 08.00-17.00; (2411747, antalya@kulturturizm.gov.tr; see also www.antalyaguide.org.
Connections: Çalkaya, Antalya's international airport, is about 15km east of the city. It has three terminals, two international (Terminals 1 and 2) and one domestic (İç Hatlar). Terminal 1 is within walking distance of the domestic terminal, Teminal 2 about 2km away — and there is *no shuttle bus* between the terminals! In the arrivals hall of both international terminals there are **exchange bureaus** (bad rates!) and cash machines, in both the arrivals and departure halls **duty-free shops** (cheaper than home). **Car hire** companies are located in the domestic terminal and Terminal 2.
Airport transfers: It's easiest to take a **taxi** from or to the airport (about £14.50), but there are also **buses** (something taxi drivers will deny). They run from the *domestic* terminal (turn right from Terminal 1 to walk there; not accessible from Terminal 2) into the centre about hourly from 06.00-22.00 (£4.20 per person, 30-45min.; operator Havaş). It's best to ask the driver to let you off at the station called 'Eski Otogar' ('Old Bus Station') about 10min. on foot (or two tram stops) north of the old town. After that the bus passes the minibus station on Akdeniz Bul. by the Migros Shopping Centre, from where there are *dolmuşes* to Kemer,

Çıralı and Kumluca. The final stop is the bus station ('Otogar'). It is cheaper, but more time-consuming, to take **town bus 202** from the airport past the centre to the main bus station. This runs every two hours from 06.00-22.00, from both the domestic terminal and Terminal 2; £0.55. If you want to be near the centre, ask the driver to let you off at Şarampol Cad., about 10min. on foot (or two tram stops) north of the old town.
Travelling out to the airport from Antalya (remember, only to the *domestic* terminal), Havaş buses leaves from the Yavuz Özcan Parkı by the main post office on Konyaaltı Cad.; www.havas. com.tr. If you're taking town bus 202, this leaves from in front of the İlçeler Terminal; look for the sign 'Havaalanı' (Airport).
Buses: The bus station ('Otogar') is about 8km outside the city on the road to Burdur. You get to and from the centre with the AntRay tram (underground at this point; look for the 'Tramvay' signs. The tram terminus in the centre is called İsmetpaşa. From the bus station get on trams heading for 'Meydan'. A taxi from the station to the centre costs £8.50.
From the bus station you can travel along the coast to all larger Turkish cities and to smaller locations in the area (e.g. take the Serik bus for Aspendos). Some journey times and prices: Selçuk (8-9 hours; £12.50), Pamukkale (4 hours; £11), Istanbul (12 hours; £21) and Fethiye (via the inland route 3 hours; £8.50, along the

coast via Finike, Kaş and Kalkan 7-8 hours; £11.70).

Dolmuş/**minibus:** For **Kemer, Çıralı, Olympos** and **Kumluca** get on either at the bus station or on Akdeniz Bul. between the Migros Shopping Centre and Aqualand. You can get to these pick-up places from İsmet Paşa Cad. in the centre with minibuses or buses signed 'Liman', 'Marina' or 'Konyaaltı Plajı' (buses 43, 48, 56 and 65). *Warning: Departure points can change on account of roadworks!* For **Perge** you take a bus or minibus to Aksu and then continue from there on foot (2km). Aksu buses (like 93 and 106) pass Atatürk Cad. (also called İsıklar Cad.) on their way past the old town. Minibuses also serve as **city transport**, with stops everywhere.

Parking: There is a paid, super-vised car park at the marina in the old town (£2.25 for however long) as well as at the stadium near the old town (same price); in addition there is a multi-storey car park opposite the post office on Güllük Cad. (£1.25 for 2h; £2.50 a day).

Trams: There are two tramlines, one old, one new. The old one, which was a gift to Antalya from its twinned city of Nürnberg, starts from the Archaeological Museum and runs parallel with the coast along Konyaaltı Cad. (later Cumhuriyet Cad.) into the heart of the old town, then south along Atatürk Cad. to the end of Işıklar Cad. Service every half hour from 07.00-21.00; tickets (bought on the tram) cost £0.50. The new AntRay tram runs from the bus station via Abdi İpekçi Cad. and Şarampol Cad. to İsmet Paşa Cad. (the place to alight for the old town) and then along Ali Çetinkaya Cad. and Aspendos Bul. to Meydan (the extension towards the airport having been torpedoed by the taxi mafia). Lines to the western harbour and towards Lara are being planned. Tickets for this tram (£0.55) are bought before boarding at special ticket stalls or kiosks.

Taxis: Rates are fixed for all well-known destinations, both local and further afield. If you're travelling outside the centre, try haggling (except in high season). Examples of some return trips: Termessos £42, Perge/Aspendos (combined) £50, Phaselis/Olympos (combined) £58, Belek or Kemer £42.

Ferry: A ferry to North Cyprus has been in planning for years.

The metropolis of Antalya (with about 1-1.5 million inhabitants) rises above abrupt cliffs — the setting framed by the mighty Taurus Mountains with peaks above 3000m. The city's old town, often praised for its beauty, is today flooded with tourists.

There's hardly a travel agency shop window in Europe that doesn't advertise a special deal to Antalya, the number one Turkish holiday airport. If you book via a brochure, as most tourists do, no doubt you'll end up somewhere near the beaches to the east or west of the city and only go to Antalya on a day trip. In that case be sure to visit the charming old part of town, to see the narrow,

The clock tower at the entrance to the old town and the Tekeli Mehmet Paşa Mosque during rush hour

shady lanes and Ottoman timber buildings with pretty oriels, roofs and gardens full of orange trees and hibiscus. Or stroll along the palm-lined boulevards through the adjacent modern city centre, with its chic boutiques and large shopping centres.

The province of Antalya, which extends east to Alanya, is the most visited holiday region in Turkey, and the city itself is also a vibrant business centre. Boomtown Antalya doesn't just rely on tourism; industry and trade have also contributed to the upturn. Chromate factories and textile mills ship their goods around the world from a large new port a few kilometres to the west. In the surrounding countryside, the rich soil encourages the cultivation of fruit and vegetables, cotton, peanuts and sesame, adding to the city's prosperity. In line with this continuing growth, a modern congress and conference centre has been built, the Sabancı Congress Centre, housed in a glass pyramid on 100 Yıl (Yüzüncü Yıl) Bulvarı. The intention is to attract professionals from the worlds of science and commerce.

Orientation

The labyrinthine old part of town with its *pansiyonlar* and souvenir shops rises steeply in a semicircle from the small port. Inland it is surrounded for five kilometres by what was originally a Hellenistic town wall. Atatürk Caddesi runs south along the battlement's reinforced ramparts, which were rebuilt again and again by the Seljuks and

Shopping
1 Özdilek Park
2 Handmade Turkish goods

Accommodation
4 Uygulama Oteli
9 Bambus

Food & drink
3 Parlak Restaurant
5 Zeynep'in Mutfağı
6 Salman
7 Paşa Bey Kebapçısı
8 Lara Balık Evi

Ⓢ Tram stop

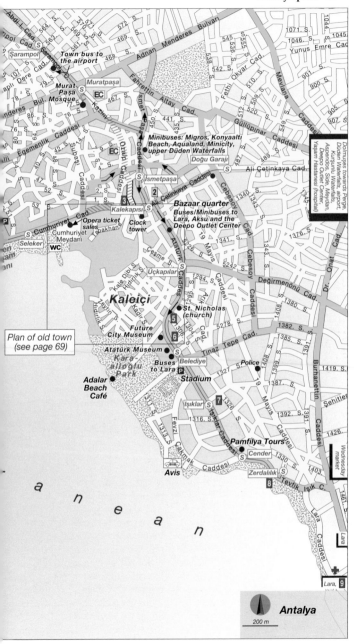

Şarampol

Town bus to
the airport

Murat
Paşa
Mosque

Muratpaşa

EC

Minibuses: Migros, Konyaaltı
Beach, Aqualand, Minicity,
upper Düden Waterfalls

Doğu Garajı

Ali Çetinkaya Cad.

EC

İsmetpaşa

Kalekapısı

Bazaar quarter
Buses/Minibuses to
Lara, Aksu and the
Deepo Outlet Center

Opera ticket
sales

Cumhuriyet
Meydanı

Clock
tower

WC

Seleker

Uçkapılar

Kaleiçi

St. Nicholas
(church)

Plan of old town
(see page 69)

Future
City Museum

Atatürk Museum

Kara-
alioğlu
Park

Buses
to Lara

Belediye

Police

Adalar
Beach
Café

Stadium

Işıklar

Pamfilya Tours

Cender

Avis

Zerdalılık

Dolmuşes towards Perge,
Düden Waterfalls, airport,
Kurşunlu Waterfalls,
Aspendos, Side, Meyxan,
Deepo Outlet Center,
Yaşam Hastanesi (hospital)

Wednesday
market

Lara

Lara, 9

Antalya

200 m

Driving in the old town — chaos!

To stop gridlock in the alleys of the old town, new rules were put in place. You can take your car in free — as long as you leave again within two hours. If you stay longer, you have to pay — a mere £2 for 2-6 hours, but £42 for over 12 hours! Some car rental firms have licenses giving free access; hotels must pay the fees as soon as their guests arrive, so that they can leave the next morning without paying.

The entrance to and exit from the old town are separate: traffic enters either by the clock tower (take İsmet Paşa Cad. to the old town and go right shortly before the tram lines) or along Kocatepe Sok. by the Patio Restaurant. Cars leave along Mescit and Yenikapı Sok. The entrances and exit are part of a confusing one-way system. To avoid the stress, park outside, perhaps by the stadium.

Ottomans. Cumhuriyet Caddesi defines the northern edge of the old town and leads west towards the Archaeological Museum and Konyaaltı Beach. Antalya's geriatric tram also bumps its way along these two streets, while a modern line runs from the centre north to the bus station. The old town is encircled by modern Antalya, the bustling business centre, full of shops. The further one goes away from the sea, the less swanky the façades.

History

For Turkey, Antalya is a young city. It was founded in 158 BC as *Attaleia* by King Attalus II of Pergamon (159-138 BC), after he had tried in vain to conquer Side.

In the year 36 BC the city came under Roman rule. Under Emperor Hadrian (117-138 AD) it received the status of an independent province with a senator as governor. The city made a name for itself within the Roman Empire because of its fine wines — one wonders if this is what attracted pirates again and again over the following centuries. In Byzantine times *Adalia* (as it was then called) became a diocesan town. In the 12th century the city served the Crusaders as a supply port, in 1207 the Seljuks conquered it, and 100 years later it fell under the sphere of influence of the Emirs of Eğirdir. In 1387, under Sultan Murat I, Adalia was finally incorporated into the Ottoman Empire. Subjected to Islamic law, the tradition of winemaking was lost, replaced by the cultivation of roses. For the next few centuries one of the main sources of income was rose oil, used in the making of fine perfumes. Silkworm farming was another 'replacement crop'.

In 1918 Italian troops occupied the local coastal strip, but left in 1921. Two years later the Greek inhabitants of what was by then called *Antalya* had to leave their homes during the population exchange. In the 1970s the sleepy town of 40,000 inhabitants began to develop into a modern economic metropolis. There followed a rapid rise in the population, as the city attracted masses of immigrants from eastern Anatolia who saw a chance to better their lot: at the beginning of the 1990s there were 450,000 inhabitants, by the mid-1990s 800,000. Mostly tourism is responsible for the last explosive rise. The current population (1-1.5 million) can only be estimated to the nearest half million, thousands of whom are foreigners who have bought themselves a place in the sun. All the bypass roads will become inner-city highways before too long — it's estimated that Antalya will have 10 million inhabitants by 2030!

Accommodation/camping

(see plans on pages 66-67 and opposite)

There are about 80 pensions and small hotels in the old town and, no matter how simple the establishment, almost all rooms have climate control. But remember that the nearer you are to the port, the louder the racket from the Ally nightclub! In the westernmost part of Antalya,

behind Konyaaltı Beach and the four-lane boulevard along the coast, there are several mid-range hotels, as well as simple pensions and all-inclusive resorts. There are hotels in all price ranges at (see under 'Beaches' on page 75).

In the old town

Otel Tuvana (12), a quiet place to stay. Beautiful rooms with wooden ceilings, antiques and reproduction furniture. Pleasant garden with orange trees and pool. Doubles £110. Somewhat hidden away on Karanlık Sok. 18, (2476015, (2411981, www. tuvanahotel.com.

Hotel Alp Paşa (19), an old Ottoman house converted into a first-class hotel. The rooms vary, but range from comfortable to elegant, decorated in the old Turkish style and named for

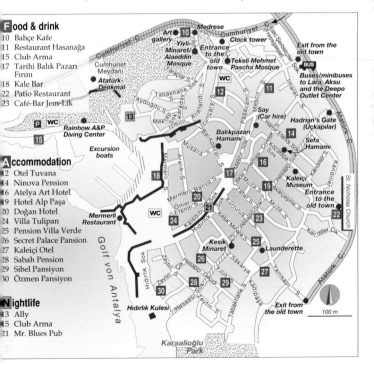

F ood & drink
10 Bahçe Kafe
11 Restaurant Hasanağa
15 Club Arma
17 Tarihi Balık Pazarı Fırını
18 Kale Bar
22 Patio Restaurant
23 Café-Bar Jem-Lik

A ccommodation
12 Otel Tuvana
14 Ninova Pension
16 Atelya Art Hotel
19 Hotel Alp Paşa
20 Doğan Hotel
24 Villa Tulipan
25 Pension Villa Verde
26 Secret Palace Pansion
27 Kaleiçi Otel
28 Sabah Pension
29 Sibel Pansiyon
30 Özmen Pansiyon

N ightlife
13 Ally
15 Club Arma
21 Mr. Blues Pub

Ottoman paschas. Small pool area (where dinner is served in the evenings). Doubles with H/B £75. Hesapçı Sok. 30, (2475676, (2485074, www.alppasa.com.

Doğan Hotel (20), another attractive place in Ottoman style. 41 comfortable rooms, many with delightful views. Pretty garden, pool. Good restaurant. Singles £42, doubles £63. Mermerli Banyo Sok. 5, (2474654, (2474006, www.doganhotel.com.

Villa Tulipan (24), Dutch run; 5 rooms, 1 suite, 2 apartments — all individually decorated with taste, some with large balconies and fine views. If you have a room without a view, go up to the fantastic roof terrace. Doubles from £33, apartment £50. Kaledibi Sok. 6, (2449258, www.villatulipan.com.

Pension Villa Verde (25), a well-kept, comfortable place, fairly new. Well equipped, amply large rooms with lovely wooden floors and good baths. Quiet location, a lot of greenery. Accent on good service; breakfast with a view to the Kesik Minaret. Singles £33, doubles £46-50. Seferoğlu Sok. 8, (2482559, (2484231, www. villaverde.com.

Atelya Art Hotel (16), well-run hotel with 30 individually-styled rooms divided between several historic city buildings. Ultra-high ceilings, creaky wooden floors, oriental decorations. Chic but very charming; many rooms with balconies. Guests love the idyllic, jasmin-scented courtyard. Doubles from £33-42. Civelek Sok. 21, (2416416, (2412848, www.atelyahotel.com.

Secret Palace Pansion (26), once Antalya's first gay pension. Since then ownership has changed, but the image remains. Small, charmingly laid out, with well-kept rooms and friendly courtyard with a cosy pool area. Singles £33, doubles £42. Fırın Sok. 10, (2441060, (2412062, www.secretpalacepansion.com.

Ninova Pension (14), family-run little pension, very clean. The 19 colourful rooms (usually with parquet floors) are divided between two 200-year-old mansions. Lovingly equipped; pretty garden. Really quiet area. Good value for money. Doubles or singles £33. Hamit Efendi Sok. 9, (2486114, (2489684, www.ninova-pension.com.

Kaleiçi Otel (27), 11 very comfortable rooms with solid furniture, stone floors, fridge, phone, baths with shower cubicles. Small pool. Helpful host. Singles £25, doubles £33. Sakarya Sok. 11, (2447146, (2448053, www. kaleiciotel.net.

Sibel Pansiyon (29), a readers' tip, located in tranquil Fırın Sok. at number 30. Run by a friendly French lady called Sylvie. 9 very well kept and spotless rooms with marble floors; some of the rooms are really large. Pleasant, shady inner courtyard. Family atmosphere. Doubles with tasty breakfast £25, singles £21. (2411316, (2413656, www. sibelpansiyon.com

Sabah Pension (28), near Hıdırlık Kulesi on the pedestrian precinct through the old town. 24 rooms (some large, some tiny, so look first!) divided between an old building and annexe, all with air-conditioning. In summer very pleasant terrace courtyard. Popular with backpackers. Cars can be hired or tours to the surrounding area organised.

Good food. Doubles from £21, singles £17. Hesapçı Sok. 60, (2475345, (2475347, www.sabahpansiyon.8m.com.

Özmen Pansiyon (30), near Hıdırlık Kulesi. Large guest house with 25 spotless rooms, 8 with balconies. Delightful roof terrace with a view over half the town and the sea — popular meeting place in the evening. Recommended by many readers. All rooms with air-conditioning. Doubles £24, singles £17. Zeytin Çıkmazı 5, (2416505, (2481534, www.ozmenpension.com.

Behind Konyaaltı Beach

Uygulama Oteli (4), a sterile, elderly 8-story purpose-built block, today used as a hotel school (so you should get perfect service!). 94 very clean, generous rooms with frumpy/kitschy decorations. About 3-star level, all with balconies, some with good views to the beach. Pool. A pretty unattractive setting, but good for those with hire cars who don't want to fight their way through the old town (it has a large car park). Singles £19, doubles £33. 100. Yıl Bul. Müze Arkası (opposite the Falez Hotel), (2385130, (2385135.

Camping: There are no campsites in or around Antalya. If you come with a caravan, you park it on the paved but shady car park at the simple **Bambus fish restaurant (9**; also called **South Shield Bistro & Bar)** southeast of the centre. The restaurant has a bathing platform. Eski Lara Yolu 1, (3111401. To get there, head along Atatürk Cad. towards Lara, following the coast; it's 3km along, on the right.

There's a proper campsite near Termessos (see page 00).

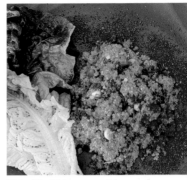

Kısır (Turkish couscous) is a good choice for vegetarians; the main ingredients are bulgar, tomatoes, onions, dill, mint and red pepper flakes — although of course there are variations.

Food and drink

Many romantic restaurants with wonderful views are clustered around the old port and the cliffs above, most of them quite good. The prices are what one would expect given the location. Hidden in the narrow lanes of the old town are more good restaurants, sometimes in cosy *pansiyonlar* and hotel gardens. Good and convenient fast-food restaurants are located east of Hadrian's Gate in the alleys off Atatürk Cad. The trendiest and best restaurants are at Konyaaltı Beach (see 'Nightlife' and 'Beaches' below) and above the coast on the way to Lara, where Antalya's 'high society' lives.

Club Arma (15), restaurant and open-air dance club at the marina, meeting place for the young members of the upper crust. Inside a rustic room with wrought-iron candelabras and open fireplace, outside lovely terrace. Fish and international cuisine. Pricey, but very good quality. (2449710.

Antalya: old town and port

Lara Balık Evi (8), the best central fish restaurant— right above the cliffs, with a spectacular terrace. Large windows through which you choose your fish (charged by the kilo). Reckon on spending £60 for 2 people, with drinks. Get there by taking the old tram south; it's shortly before the terminus, on the right. ℂ 2298015.

Restaurant Hasanağa (11), in an old, renovated town house at Mescit Sok. 15 in the old town. Lovely courtyard with orange trees, friendly service, and almost daily folk music. House speciality is the *Osmanlı tabağı*, tender meat in a tasty thick sauce served in a bubbling stoneware pot (£8). ℂ 2428105.

Patio Restaurant (22), well-appointed, modern but cosy. Pretty garden with lemon and orange trees. Mediterranean dishes like *spaghetti aglio oglio* or saffron chicken. Good service.

Mains £4.25-8.50. Kocatepe Sok., ℂ 2489558.

Parlak Restaurant (3), somewhat hidden away at the start of Kazım Özalp Cad. In business over 50 years. Large choice of Turkish food, delicious grilled baby chicken. Covered terrace area. Middle price class. Kazım Özalp Cad. 7, ℂ 2419160.

Paşa Bey Kebapçısı (7), a well-kept kebab house with terrace and garden. They serve southern Anatolian starters at no extra charge — like *ayran çorbası* (yoghurt soup with barley), *ezme* (spicy paprika sauce) und *çig köfte* (raw meatballs). This is followed by *pide* and tasty meat dishes with fresh pita bread from the stone oven. Very helpful service. Mains £3.50-7 — most reasonable for what's offered. No alcohol. Işıklar Cad. 1319 Sok. 4, ℂ 2449690. To get there from the old town follow Işıklar Cad. south. When you come to the

Kâmil Koç bus office on your left, turn left, then take the alley on the right.

Zeynep'in Mutfağı (5), a small simple restaurant with a couple of tables out front. Top-class home cooking. A meal with *cacık* and soup £3.50, without soup £2.50. Only open in the day. To get there, from Hadrian's Gate follow Atatürk. Cad. (the tram side) south until it heads left and becomes 1304 Sok. Now it's only a few steps along to the right.

Outside town

Arkadaş, north of Antalya near the Düden Waterfalls (see page 82). This popular trout restaurant is idyllically situated in a wildly romantic valley beside a tumbling river. The trout comes from the restaurant's own breeding farm. Fair prices. Signposted from the road to the falls and can even be reached by minibus. From the car park about five minutes on foot: take the steps down and then head upstream. (3610165.

Çakırlar, not a restaurant, but a collection of several grill restaurants west of Antalya on the road to Saklıkent. From the cosy gardens you choose your meat yourself (usually priced by weight). There's also *meze*, beer or *rakı*. Not expensive, a lot of fun, and almost free of tourists! By car use the instructions to Saklıkent (page 104), and you will automatically pass the restaurants. If several people share the cost, it's worth taking a taxi (agree price in advance).

Tünektepe Döner Restaurant (also called Club Maji), where they do *not* sell *döner* kebabs. *Döner* means more or less 'turning around' — and that's very appropriate for this panorama restaurant high on a cliff above the bay of Antalya. It sounds great, but unfortunately both service and cooking have been rated 'poor' by readers in recent years. Mains £11-19.50, plus a stiff parking fee. Should you want to try it, drive towards Kemer and, at the southern end of the bay, where the road goes left to 'Yat Limanı/Marina', head right for 'Tünektepe Döner Restaurant' (the sign is easily missed). From here it's a steep 7km-long drive up the mountainside.

Cafés/Bars

Bahçe Kafe (10), by the Yivli Minaret. Attractive, shady spot away from the tourist crowds, with local clientele; no alcohol.

Kale Bar (18), the café/bar of the C & H Hotel (formerly Tütav Türk Evi Otelleri). Gorgeous hotel terrace with turquoise-coloured cast-iron chairs and a beautiful view over the harbour. Very cosy; friendly service. Relatively expensive, but not a rip-off.

Café-Bar Jem-Lik (23), an oasis in the old town. Idyllic, shady garden café with mandarin trees and bright flower borders. Lovingly decorated. Middle price range. Snacks. Hesapçı Sok.

Salman (6), cake shop and café. All kinds of sweets, pastries, tortes and *börek*. Good place for breakfast, too. Fevzi Çakmak Cad. 7.

Tea garden:
The **Çağdaş Yaşamı Kültür Alanı** and **Atatürk Park** stretch out high above the cliffs west of the old town. Both have tea gardens and cafée with lovely views. Reasonable prices.

Bakery:
Tarihi Balık Pazarı Fırını (17), small, old-established bakery on the corner of Mescit

Sok. and Balıkpazarı Sok. Praised by readers. Bread and pastries.

Nightlife

At Konyaaltı Beach: There are innumerable restaurants, taverns, disco bars and clubs on the well-kept strip of greenery just behind this beach. The whole area has become Antalya's No. 1 night-spot, where you can relax on comfy sofas, watch the sunset while listening to quiet background music and, later, party on the beach with DJs from Istanbul or abroad — or listen to live Turkish music at an open-air bar with a romantic garden. There's something for every taste.

In the old town: Since the scene has moved to Konyaaltı, evenings here are relatively dead. But a few clubs still make enough noise to keep you awake at night, if you're in a nearby *pansiyon*. Among these is **Ally (13)**, a kind of amusement park for the palate and ear, with several restaurants offering food from all over the world and a lot of music. It's pretty expensive and only open in the summer. There's also **Club Arma (15)** at the old port, mentioned above under restaurants, with pricey drinks.

If you just want a beer, try **Mr. Blues Pub (21)**, a little bar right out of the blues and jazz era. By the second visit you feel like a regular. Really nice host, who plans to offer sizzle up some steaks for his guests in the future. Hıdırlık Sok.

Between Antalya and Lara: The **Jolly Joker Pub** is the latest venue for local partygoers — a 3-storey pleasure palace with a Starbucks on the ground floor and the Jolly Joker upstairs (live music all night — a lot of retro and no dance floor, so you dance between the crowded tables). In the basement there's the Club Soho (usually also with live music). It's southeast of Antalya on Özgürlük Bul., the road to Lara (just near the Dedeman Hotel).

Beaches and diving

When founding the city, Attalus did not plan for beach-orientated tourism and positioned Antalya up on cliffs above the sea. So you'll have to go further afield to swim. The only exceptions are the small sandy area less than 100m south of the old port (access via the Mermerli Restaurant) and the **Adalar Beach Café** in the town centre (access via Karaalioğlu Park near the Deniz Restaurant); this latter has a wooden deck with chairs. Otherwise, the nearest beaches are:

Konyaaltı Beach, with a breathtaking backdrop

Konyaaltı (also known as **Antalya Beach Park**): the long sand and shingle beach shown opposite, which begins about 2km west of town. It's easily reached: take the old tram to the last stop at the Archaeological Museum, from where it's a five-minute walk downhill. A taxi costs about £6.50 one way. The bars and beach clubs mentioned under 'Nightlife' rent loungers and umbrellas; there are changing rooms and showers … and of course good cocktails (if you have one too many and go under, there are also lifeguards). Various watersports are on offer from banana-riding to para-sailing.

Lara: see page 00.
There are **other beaches** between Altalya and Kemer, mostly in large or small bays close to the (built-up and hardly idyllic) coast road. Usually there is a charge for these beaches (about £3.50 for a car and £1.25 per person). Coming from Antalya, you pass first **Topçam** (with a super picnic place, only accessible when driving west towards Kemer), then **Küçük Çaltıcak** and finally **Büyük Çaltıcak**, which is really quite large.

Diving: The **Rainbow A&P Diving Centre**, in the old port near the car park, organises boat-based dives to an old wreck (£29). A 'taster' course for £42 and various other diving courses starting from £250. (0532 7641409 (mobile); www.apdivers.de (English pages).

Aquaparks: AquaLand is set back from Konyaaltı Beach, well to the west of the maintained section of beach. Mega-slides, several pools, etc. Entrance fee

£10.50, children £6.50. To get there take a bus or minibus with the sign 'Liman', 'Konyaaltı Plajı' or 'Marina' from İsmet Paşa Cad. (Nos. 43, 48, 56 and 65). The same sort of facilities are on offer (same prices) at the **Dedeman Aqua-park** between Antalya and Lara (reached from Atatürk Cad. with Lara buses) or by car along the coastal road.

Sights
Most of Antalya's sights lie within or close to the old town (**Kaleiçi**). You can easily take them in by walking, but they are in a bewildering tangle of narrow and sloping lanes, making them difficult to find on first attempt. No town plan can give a truly accurate picture of these chaotic lanes, which are partially an inheritance from the Greeks. The Greeks were followed in the 1920s by many Sinto gypsies; some of them have since moved on, but those that remain rank among the poorest inhabitants of the old town. In some places you'll see their crumbling houses standing in stark contrast to the restored *pansiyonlar*, but there are fewer every year. The city fathers want to turn Kaleiçi into a picture-book village (thereby losing much of its former slightly morbid charm). On our last visit Hesapçı Sokak, which runs from Hadrian's Gate to the Hıdırlık Kulesi, had been turned into a marble-surfaced pedestrian zone.

Yivli Minaret and Alaeddin Mosque: The Seljuk **Yivli Minaret** of the **Alaeddin Mosque** dates from the early 13th century and is Antalya's main landmark. It rises skywards not far south of Cumhuriyet

Caddesi. The brick tower, shaped like a bundle of asparagus stalks and known as the 'Fluted Minaret', was used by sailors as an orientation point for centuries. The adjacent mosque was built over the foundations of a Byzantine church. The 12 columns which support the six domes are from the previous building, and the bases of some columns were used as capitals. Sultan Alaeddin Keykobat I, one of the best-known Seljuk leaders, was responsible for building both the mosque and the minaret. Opposite the minaret, the ruins of the **Karatay Medrese** (a Seljuk theological college) are today covered by a steel and glass enclosure housing stalls selling arts and crafts and spices. Next door is the former convent of the Mevlana Dervishes; today, totally restored, it's the **Güzel Sanatlar Galerisi** (art gallery), with regular exhibitions.

Clock tower and Murat Paşa Mosque: A huge **clock tower** stands on Cumhuriyet Caddesi, at the entrance to the old town; its foundations are part of the old town's fortifications. Just next to it is the Tekeli Mehmet Paşa Mosque, an uninspiring building architecturally, but with a fine silhouette. If you walk from the clock tower along Kazim Özalp Caddesi, one of the most vibrant shopping streets in the new part of the city, you come to the **Murat Paşa Mosque** in a small park. This mosque, dating from the second half of the 16th century, is well worth a visit; the interior has beautiful glazed tiles.

Port: The first ships sailed from here in the 2nd century BC; the impressive walls date from Roman times. For over 2000 years this port was Antalya's gateway to the world, until it was replaced by the new port west of the city. Now only tour boats, fishing boats and a few yachts moor here (it's quite fun to watch the yachtsmen having dinner with their families on their boats).

Kesik Minaret: located on a lane with the same name. There was once a round temple on this spot, dedicated to the Egyptian god Serapis, followed by a Byzantine church in the 5th century and a mosque 800 years later. When the mosque burned down in 1851 (during a major fire in the old town) only a the base of the minaret remained. Since then it's been called the Kesik ('Truncated') Minaret. Today weeds grow between the fenced ruins of the walls.

Suna ve Inan Kıraş Kaleiçi Museum: Located in an Ottoman manor house, this three-room, air-conditioned museum has some old photographs of the city, as well as tableaux depicting life in the 1900s (coffee being served, bridegroom being shaved, henna-dying session the evening before the wedding). If you don't think that sounds very exciting, you're right. A Greek Orthodox church from the second half of the 19th century also belongs to the museum complex, which puts on regular exhibitions and some indoor concerts. *Address/opening times: Kocatepe Sok. 25. Daily (except Wed.) 09.00-12.00 and 13.00-18.00; entrance fee £0.90, concessions half price.*

Hadrian's Gate: This splendid marble triumphal arch, with its two massive towers, was built in

130 AD to welcome Emperor Hadrian when he visited the city. It is still the pedestrian entrance from Atatürk Caddesi into the old town. The grooves at the base below the chic new footbridge were probably made by Roman carts. What can be clearly seen is that the level of the old, Roman city was a few metres below today's old town; one wonders what ruins still lie undiscovered there.

Hıdırlık Kulesi and Karaalioğlu Park:

The 17m-high tower (**Hıdırlık Kulesi**) in the south of the old town dates from Roman times. Whether it was built as a mausoleum or as part of an old citadel, nobody knows. It was used later as a lighthouse and a platform for cannons protecting the port. In any case, climbing it is a pleasure. **Karaalioğlu Park** continues south from the tower — a sea of flowers beside the sea, a delightful place to take a break in one of the tea gardens or restaurants. For children there is a small adventure playground with a suspension bridge and slides. *Tip:* come here to watch the sun set.

Atatürk Museum and City Museum:

The **Atatürk Evi Müzesi**, housed in a reproduction of the Ottoman mansion where Atatürk spent the nights of 6-12 March 1930, displays memorabilia of his stay in the city, from photographs to his old socks. A few steps further along is the old city hall *(Belediye)*, soon to become the **City Museum**. *Address/opening times: Atatürk Museum, İşıklar Cad. (east of Karaalioğlu Park). Daily (except Mon.) 09.00-17.00 (19.00 in summer). Free entry.*

Çağdaş Yaşam Kültür Alanı and Atatürk Kültür Parkı:

West of the old town, stretched out between the steep coast and Cumhuriyet Caddesi (later Konyaaltı Caddesi), two parks are worth a visit: **Çağdaş Yaşam Kültür Alanı** and, a bit further west, **Atatürk Kültür Parkı**. Delightful cafés and tea gardens are dotted about, with fine views over the whole of Antalya's bay: to the west you can see the mountains near Kemer, to the east the steep coastline at Lara. Both parks have cultural events fairly frequently. A small entrance fee is charged for some areas.

Archaeological Museum:

One of the most important museums of its kind in Turkey and well worth a visit. Finds from Lycia and Pamphylia — some so spectacular that it's more exciting than visiting a site — are arranged in chronological order. The circuit begins with a collection dating from prehistoric times and ends in a section devoted to ethnography. The museum's main attractions are the statues of gods and emperors from Perge, among them Hadrian, Trajan, Zeus, etc. There are also richly ornamented sarcophagi (also originating predominantly from Perge), with marble friezes depicting the Labours of Hercules. These sarcophagi are from the 2nd and 3rd centuries, when sarcophagus production reached its height — virtually mass produced. There is gold jewellery from Patara, small metal figures from Arykanda, mosaics from the Seleucid Empire and a huge coin collection (of which the latest source of pride is the 'Elmalı Treasure' mentioned on page

Statue of Hermes in the Archaeological Museum

173). There are delightful surprises, too: among the Byzantine icons, for example, is a little box covered with red velvet with some bone fragments (including a jaw) inside. The accompanying text reads: Holy St. Nicholas.
Address/opening times: in the western part of the city, just before the road down to Konyaaltı Beach; easily reached on the old tramline (last stop). In summer daily (except Mon.) 09.00-1900, in winter 08.00-17.00; entry £6.50.
Minicity: This leisure park features over 70 famous Turkish architectural monuments in miniature format (scale 1:25). A free brochure helps you tell your children about all the things they mustn't touch…
Address/opening times: in the west of Antalya behind Konyaaltı Beach. Coming from the centre, you first pass AquaLand (watch for it on the left), then Minicity (on the right). Easily reached by buses or minibuses signed 'Liman', 'Konyaaltı Plajı' or 'Marina' from İsmet Paşa Cad. (Nos. 43, 48, 56,65). Open daily 09.00-22.00; entry £2.25.

Practicalities A-Z

Boat trips: There are trips east and west along the coast, for instance: short 1h trip £4.20; 2h trip to the lower Düden Falls (see page 82) and Pirates' Cave £8.50; 6h trip visiting Rat Island (an islet west of Antalya, usually with a 1h stop for bathing) and Çaltıcak Bay further west £29.
Car hire: For many years users have recommended **Say**, Barbaros Mah. Mescit Sok. 37, (2430923. The company has mostly German clientele (and their website is in German: www.say-autovermietung.de, but at least you can see the cars and prices). Say has been recommended by English visitors as well and can be found via www.carhiremarket.com. 24h service number (0532 2645054 (mobile). In 2010 their cheapest model was £21 per day. Cheaper or more expensive cars can be found by walking along Fevzi Çakmak Cad., where there are several firms, like Avis (at No. 30, in the Talya Oteli, (2481772, airport number (3303008, www.avis.com.tr).
Childrens' attractions: In summer there are carousels, dodgems and other attractions at the Atatürk Kültür Parkı and

behind Konyaaltı Beach. The city's **Aktur Fun Fair** (opposite the Migros Shopping Center, see below) is open year-round.

Church services in English: St. Paul Union Church, with Sunday service at 11.00, even has a website: www.stpaulcc-turkey.com.

Consulate: There is a British Vice-Consulate in Antalya; see page 34.

Doctors and dentists, English-speaking: the small private **Özel Antalya Yaşam Hastanesi** near the Dedeman Hotel in Lara, with English-speaking doctors, has a good reputation. Şirinyalı Mah. 1487 Sok. 4, ℂ 3108080. Dr. A. Faik Güven is a dentist at Konyaaltı Cad. 46, ℂ 2476070.

Events: At the beginning of October the traditional **Antalya Film Festival** is held in the Antalya Cultural Centre (on 100 Yıl Bul. between the Sheraton and the glass pyramid); the best films are awarded the 'Golden Orange' (*Altın Portakal*). Turkish films are the focal point. Performances of **opera and ballet** are held in June/July at the **open-air theatre at Aspendos (see page 90)**. Tickets can be bought in advance from kiosks or at the Archaeological Museum (about £21). There is also usually a transport service. See www.aspendosfestival.gov.tr. *Another tip:* ask at the Tourist Office when the **Altın Kiraz Yağlı Pehlivan Güreşleri** is taking place. This display of Turkish oil wrestling is held in Korkuteli, a town of some 17,000 inhabitants about 60km to the northwest of Antalya. Although the small mountain town itself is conservative and boring, the

wrestling matches are *not*.

Football: Antalya Spor plays in the stadium near the old town, usually on Saturday or Sunday.

Launderette: Sempatik Laundry in the old town near the Kesik Minaret, opposite the Villa Verde pension. £6.50 per load.

Markets: The **Wednesday market** on Portakal Çiçeği Bul. southeast of the old town, always has a lot of fruit, vegetables, cheese and clothing on sale, but no souvenirs. To get there follow Işıklar Cad. and all its continuations. There's also a large **Friday market** at the Murat Paşa Mosque, while the huge **Saturday market** in Lara (near the Marmara Hotel) has become a tourist attraction. ℂ

Newspapers: Daily and weekly English papers are available from some kiosks on Cumhuriyet Cad. and Ali Çetinkaya Cad.

Opera/ballet: The Antalya Devlet Opera ve Balesi (City Opera and Ballet) stages productions in the Haşim İşcan Cultural Centre on Mevlana Cad. Tickets can be bought in advance from a kiosk on Cumhuriyet Meydanı (about £45). To see what's on, go to www.antdob.gov.tr.

Organised tours: Most travel agencies organising tours have their offices on Atatürk Cad., Cumhuriyet Cad. or in the old town, but there are not that many offers around. Day trips to Perge, Aspendos and the Kurşunlu Waterfalls, to Kekova and Myra (with boat trip) or to Termessos and the Düden Waterfalls from about £25. No matter where you book, there will always be a lot of stops at jewellery and leather goods shops.

Police: There are several police

At the bazaars you can find anything from colourfully woven bags to dried chilli peppers; barbers' and shoe-shine shops are usually tucked away on side-streets.

more trendy things in **shopping malls** (see below) or in the boutiques on Atatürk Cad., İsıklar Cad. and Cumhuriyet Cad. **Silver and gold jewellery** is sold in the many small jewellers' shops in the northern part of Atatürk Cad. A whole range of **handmade Turkish goods**, especially copper and brass (good for gifts) can be found in artisans' shops between Çetinkaya Cad. and İsmetpaşa Cad; sometimes

stations scattered around the city. In the old town there is one at 19 Mayıs Cad, (155.
Post: The main post office is on Güllük Cad. (also called Anafartalar Cad.), a side-street off Cumhuriyet Cad.
Shopping in town: There are quite a few **leather** and **fashion shops** in the bazaar around Ali Çetinkaya Cad., but you'll find

you can watch the craftsmen at work.

Shopping malls: **Migros Alışveriş Merkezi** is a modern mall with over 100 shops — from Adidas to Tommy Hilfiger and Zara. Offers a stress-free stroll, and tax-free purchases are possible in most shops. At 100 Yıl Bul. (take any bus signed for 'Migros' from İsmet Paşa Cad.

Özdilek Park, the city's newest shopping centre, is a bit to the north, on the way to the bus station. About 110 shops, lots of restaurants. From İsmetpaşa in the centre take the AntRay tram

and alight at Dokuma station.

Deepo Outlet Center is the largest factory outlet on the Mediterranean coast, with about 90 shops. A lot of goods (many from last season's collections). On the road to Alanya near the airport. Buses from Atatürk Cad. (signed 'Deepo', for instance Nos. 49 and 52).

Travel Agency: Pamfilya Tours can sell you airline tickets, arrange tours, and even cash American Express travellers' cheques (3% commission). Işıklar Cad 57, (2431500, www. pamfilya.com.tr.

Two-wheel hire: There are some **motorbike** hire places in the old town and on Fevzi Çakmak Cad. You can rent anything from a 125cc Yamaha scooter (from about £14.50 per day) to a 600cc Honda Enduro (about £83/day). Be sure to note all scratches and/or defects in the rental contract, just as you would with a car. **Bicycles**, on the other hand, are a problem. Very few places rent them out because it's too much hassle for the rental firms compared with what they can charge. Once in a while you will find a car hire firm that keeps a bike or two to rent; prices start at about £8.50 per day.

Turkish baths (hamamı): Hidden away on Kocatepe Sok. in the old town is the **Sefa Hamamı** (mixed bathing), only open in summer, daily 09.30-22.00, entry £10 including massage and *kese*. There's also the **Balıkpazarı Hamamı** at the corner of Balıkpazarı Sok. and Paşa Cami Sok.: a restored Ottoman bath, large and beautiful, with separate sections for men and women, open daily from 08.00-23.00, 'the works' for £15.

2 EXCURSIONS EAST OF ANTALYA

Düden Waterfalls • Kurşunlu Waterfalls • Perge • Sillyon •
Aspendos • Zeytintaşı Cave • (Belek • Köprülü Canyon • Alarahan)

Area code: (0242
Walks: 1-4

Access/opening times/prices:
see individual attractions

The three ancient ruined cities of Perge, Aspendos and Sillyon are the main attractions east of Antalya. Perge can boast the largest stadium and Aspendos the best-preserved Roman theatre in Asia Minor. By comparison Sillyon is just a small morsel of history and culture, but its landscape makes it an especially tasty one.

These three cities flourished in Pamphylia (the 'land of all tribes' according to the ancient Greeks), just to the east of Lycia. You can visit all three on a day trip — and there should even be time to take a detour via the Düden and Kurşunlu waterfalls, explore the two-level Zeytintaşı Mağarası cave or gawp at the gigantic Kundu club hotels. Other possible excursions include the coastal resort of Belek, Köprülü Canyon or even Alarahan (130km away) — for a round of golf or some walking.

Perge, Aspendos and Sillyon follow the same pattern as other early cities above the Gulf of Antalya, each sited on a precipitous, steep-sided, easily defended 'table' mountain. The area had to be good for agriculture as well, and easily accessible by river from the sea (no towns were established on the coast itself, because of pirate raids). Today these cities are surrounded by greenhouses.

Düden Waterfalls

The **upper falls** are located in a small park (Düdenbaşı Piknik Alanı) to the northeast of Antalya. On Sundays the park is a popular place for families, with picnic and dancing areas, tea gardens and restaurants (see also 'Arkadaş' on page 73). Caves allow you to penetrate the misty area behind the falls ... but in summer you may not hear or see very much, because the Düden River sometimes dries up.
The **lower waterfalls** are near Lara on the coast and are a popular destination for many boat trips. The Düden has been carrying lime deposits from the springs downriver for thousands of years, creating some interesting rock formations where the falls plunge into the sea.

Getting there/opening times/prices: The upper falls are signed 'Düden Şelalesi' from the west-east ring road (Gazi Bul.). Buses and minibuses leave regularly from İsmet Paşa Cad. until 21.00 (Nos. 14, 78, 80, 85). Open daily from 08.00-20.00 (17.30 in winter); entry £1. The lower falls are not signposted. From Işıklar Cad.) head south on the road closest to the coast. If you pass a little wood and cross a bridge, you've gone too far. Minibus No. 77 from Işıklar Cad. passes the falls. The area is always accessible, and no entry fee is charged.

Lara and Kundu

Lara, 12km southeast of the city, is just a strip of faceless hotels and apartments below the airport flight path. But there is good swimming. A 5km-long stretch of beach begins east of the Sera Club Hotel — at first it's fine shingle, then sand and about 50-100m wide. The further east you go, the less crowded it is, but you'll never have it to yourself. Behind the beach there's room for about 20 new resorts; until they're built, there are paid beach clubs with sunbathing lawns, but they are not as harmonious as Konyaaltı Beach west of Antalya. East of here, on the far side of a river, is **Kundu Beach**, also 5km long. It's all happening behind this beach: 10-storey apartments, shopping centres, and colossal five-star spa hotels in Disneyland style (with the Topkapi Palace and the Kremlin facing each other). The end of this beach is punctuated by the 560-room Mardan Palace Hotel (opened 2009; www.mardanpalace.com), reputedly the most costly ever built in Europe: the white sand comes from Egypt, 1200 staff care for the guests (mostly Russian), and gondolas ferry them about. Seeingis believing!
Getting there: Buses and minibuses from Işıklar Cad. to Lara (Nos. 16, 25, 56, 77, 85); Bus No. 6 to Kundu.

Kurşunlu Waterfalls

Larger and more impressive than the Düden falls, the Kurşunlu Şelalesi were declared a natural park in 1991. But don't expect *too* much; the river that plunges into the valley is not that impressive. What does draw the crowds is the turquoise basin below the main fall. Otherwise, walkers can easily escape the crowds on the narrow paths through 'tunnels' of vegetation. Walk 1 would show you the best of the area.
Getting there/opening times/prices: Signposted 'Kurşunlu Şelalesi' off the D400 about 10km east of Antalya (from where it's a further 8km). Minibuses 230 and 231 from İsmet Paşa Cad. and Bus 79 call here. Open daily 07.00-20.00 (earlier in winter); entry fee £1.

The upper falls at Düden

Walk 1: Kurşunlu Waterfalls

Time: 3h20min
Grade: easy; a small amount of climbing, but much of the walk follows riverside paths.
Equipment: see page 22.
Travel: 🚗 car or 🚐 minibus 230 or 231 to Kurşunlu Şelalesi; depart from İsmet Paşa Cad., or bus 79, usually four times a day in summer; journey time 1h; return on the same service.
Short walk: Kurşunlu Waterfalls — the highlights (35min; easy). There are two special things to see at Kurşunlu— the waterfalls and lagoon. Follow the main walk to the lagoon, then return to the bridge, cross it, and follow the main walk again from the 3h10min-point to the end.

There are two waterfalls (şelalesi) to the east of Antalya — Düden and Kurşunlu. Düden is certainly the better known among tourists. The two waterfalls are roughly the same height, but they differ remarkably in character. Düden is more rugged, with caves that allow you to get behind the falls, whereas Kurşunlu is a study in soft greens.

Start the walk at the entrance to the **Kurşunlu Şelalesi**, where you alight from the bus and pay the small entrance charge of about £1. Walk ahead towards the **picnic area**, then swing left down the steps to see first the **wheelrace** and then the **main falls**. From here walk in the direction indicated by the sign for the plant tunnel — **'Bitki Tüneli'**. (If this route is closed because the summer house ahead is occupied, go back to a footpath marked 'Patika' on the right-hand side of the river and follow this until you can turn left on a path and cross a bridge to the other side of the river. You rejoin the route described below just before a weir.)

Plant 'tunnel' is exactly the right description, as the path follows the left side of the river. Pink splashes of oleander add a touch of colour, and the plane trees, enjoying the constant source of water, spread their large leaves for a share of the sun. In five minutes or so descend steps, to pass a summer house and continue along the river bank on a cobbled path which quickly reverts to footpath. When the path appears to end, locate the overgrown continuation just before the river bank. Soon the way is clear again and you arrive at a **weir** (**15min**).

Stay on the left-hand side of the river, passing the beautiful

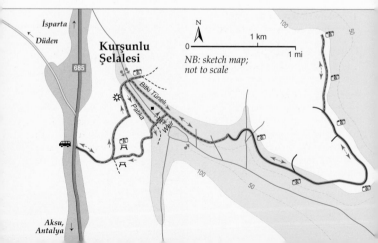

lagoon, then turning slightly away from the river, to cross a small stream. Now you head away from the narrow confines of the wooded valley into more open woodland. Oleander borders the river, which is sufficiently tranquil to allow water lilies to find a perfect home and add their own touch of charm and grace to this green oasis. The woodland thins quickly, and the path leads through a meadow splashed red with poppies and anemones in spring, before dipping through a hollow to cross a dry stream bed. When you join a track, turn right to continue through an open meadow. Very shortly, as the river sweeps away to the right, stay with the track as it ascends left into a wooded valley. A small stream is on the right. A minute later, cross this stream and then a second one, on stepping-stones.

Continue along the gently ascending track, which heads back down the small valley towards the river. Eventually you reach a '**plateau**' (under **50min**). Eucalyptus trees dot the way as you continue along the track at this higher level. Keep straight on at the junction of tracks a few minutes later. Soon you can see the plain down on the right stretching out towards the sea, past ancient Perge, which eventually comes into view. The track swings around to the left, into an area of cultivation and comes to another junction. Go right here, then watch out, a few minutes later, for a red arrow directing you onto a trail off to the right, by a wall. This rather overgrown trail ends at a fine **viewpoint** (100m; **1h40min**).

Falls and lagoon at Kurşunlu

Return the same way until you have passed the lagoon and weir, then cross the **bridge (3h10min)** to the other side of the river. Continue along the gently ascending path which winds up the hillside through pines and strangely shaped rocks (with fresh water taps). Return via the **picnic area** to the **main gates** (**3h20min**).

Perge

The Perge site is a large, shade-less field of rubble: 1000 stones, but they no longer conjure up this ancient city's famous Temple of Artemis. If we can believe old travellers' tales, then the ruins of Perge were still in extraordin-arily good condition at the beginning of the 20th century. But in the 1920s the inhabitants of nearby Murtuna restored and enlarged their village by plundering Perge, creating irreparable damage. Turkish-led excavations began in 1946 and are on-going, with impressive finds from Hellenistic, Roman and Byzantine times.

History

Perge was founded in about 1000 BC — legend has it by the Trojan seers Kalkhas and Mopsos. But the truth is probably more banal, and it is likely that it was founded by keen settlers from Sparta. The first centuries of urban history do not differ substantially from those of other cities in the Gulf of Antalya: in the 7th century BC Perge became Lydian, and later Persian. Only in 333 BC did Perge begin to make its own way: the city fell to Alexander the Great without a fight and, because of their bad relations with the neighbouring cities of Aspendos and Side, the citizens put themselves at his disposal. 'Pathfinders' from Perge led his troops quickly and safely over the difficult trails through the Taurus Mountains.

After the death of Alexander, the city was incorporated into the Seleucid Empire. In 188 BC the Romans conquered Perge and

Artemis of Perge — mother goddess and Virgin Mary

The cult of Artemis was practiced in Perge as well as Ephesus. The Temple of Artemis, goddess of the hunt and archery, the giver of fertility, defender of wild animals, children and all the weak, was a famous place of pilgrimage and asylum located outside the city. Artemis of Perge was also the dominant motif on Pergamon coins. On the oldest coins she is still called Vanassa Preiia, 'Queen of Perge', and is represented as a square stone block with a human bust. What was really being depicted was an old Anatolian mother-goddess with a Greek name. The cult of Artemis lived on under early Christianity: the Virgin Mary, before becoming generally accepted as a goddess in Perge, was only seen as a further incarnation of the age-old divine mother.

entrusted it to Eumenes II of Pergamon. On his death the city fell back under Roman rule, as did Pergamon. During the era of the Roman emperors, Perge was famous for its Artemis cult (see above). In 48 St. Paul the Apostle arrived in Perge with his companion Barnabas. The missionaries were welcomed cordially — above all because they were considered personifi-cations of the gods Zeus and Hermes. Soon after, Perge became one of the first Christian cities in Asia Minor, although for a few centuries the local cult of Artemis was more prevalent. That finally changed under Byzantine rule. With the elevation of Perge to a bishopric,

The Hellenistic gate at Perge

three basilicas were built, and the famous Artemis Temple and all related religious symbols were destroyed.

During the attacks by the Saracens in the 7th century, the inhabitants abandoned their city in favour of more safely sited Attaleia (Antalya) — so that by the time the Seljuks arrived, only the wind swept along the empty streets.

Getting there/opening times/prices: Perge is signposted from the D400 at Aksu (also called Çalkaya, part of greater Antalya), 16km east of Antalya; from there it's another 2km. If you take a bus from Antalya (see page 63), you have to get out in Aksu and walk the rest of the way (about 20min). The site is open May-Oct., daily from 09.30-19.30, Nov.-Apr. shorter hours; entry fee £6.50.

Sights
Theatre: You pass the theatre (not always accessible) on the approach road to the paid-entry part of the site. The original Greek building was extended in the 2nd century AD by the Romans and provided with a three storey fly tower and a decorative nymphaeum. Located on a hillside southwest of the city, it had space for 14,000 closely packed spectators. Evidently quite a few people held 'season tickets', since some seats are engraved with names.

Stadium: Just past the theatre on the approach road, the 234m-long stadium stretches out on the right; it was one of the largest in Asia Minor. It was used for sports and bloody gladiatorial fights. Since it was built on one level, enormous foundations had to be created for the 12,000 spectators; these can still be seen today, supporting the surviving rows of seats. There were once shops in the inter-connected, solid vaults of these foundations. The Perge car park is just past the curving north end of the stadium.

Late Roman and Hellenistic town gate: After passing the site

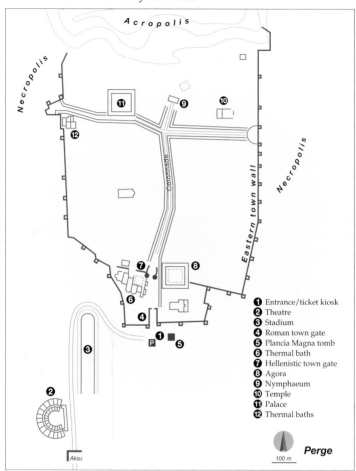

1 Entrance/ticket kiosk
2 Theatre
3 Stadium
4 Roman town gate
5 Plancia Magna tomb
6 Thermal bath
7 Hellenistic town gate
8 Agora
9 Nymphaeum
10 Temple
11 Palace
12 Thermal baths

Perge

100 m

Aksu

entrance, the first thing you see is the pincer-shaped **late Roman town gate**; it was once decorated with marble columns and was probably built in the early 4th century, when the town area was extended to the south. Behind, on the left, was a **nymphaeum** and **thermal bath**. Bathing pools and floor mosaics can still be made out.

The monumental dressed stone-work of the **Hellenistic town gate** with its two striking round **towers** led to a horseshoe-shaped **courtyard**. Statues were set on marked bases in the rows of niches in the walls: below were gods, above the legendary Trojan city founders. The statues were donated in the year 120 by Plancia Magna, a rich patroness-philanthropist from the city who made nearly her entire fortune available for urban buildings. In thanks, various statues were dedicated to her. Her tomb can be seen near the car park.

Agora: At the right of the Hellenistic town gate is the agora, once the focal point of social life. In its centre stood a round temple dedicated to the Goddess of Luck, Tyche. In the northeastern corner of the agora you can see a '**gaming stone**', where the old people passed time and hoped Tyche would bring them luck.

Colonnade: From the Hellenistic town gate, a 20m-wide colonnade (some of its columns have been rebuilt) leads north towards a **nymphaeum** at the foot of the **acropolis**, which was crowned by a statue of the river god Kestros. A 2m-wide marble water channel cascaded down the middle of the road. Cart tracks are visible to the right and left, worn into the stone. Behind the row of columns people once strolled along mosaic pavements past a line of shops. This road was the main thoroughfare; large parts of the city off both sides of the colonnade still await excavation.

Other sights: If you walk along the colonnade to the nymphaeum (past four **columns** on the right with reliefs of Apollo, Artemis, Kalchas and Tyche), you come to a crossroads once graced with a triumphal arch. Turning left here, you arrive at the remains of the **palace** and more **thermal baths** at the **western necropolis**, which lay outside the city walls. The most beautiful sarcophagus found here is now on display in Antalya's Archaeological Museum.

Sillyon

Sillyon is a setting straight out of a picture book: it rises on a steep table-top mountain in the middle of the flat coastal plain, with views to the sea and to nearby Perge. The city was founded by Greek colonists around 1000 BC, at about the same time as Aspendos and Perge. In Hellenistic and Roman times, Sillyon was an important trading centre; later, under Byzantine rule, it became a bishopric. But Sillyon never made the historical headlines. Today it's a small, quiet, ruined town, only partly excavated and little visited by tourists. While the remains will probably not impress you, the location surely will.

Sights: From the car park in the hamlet of Asar at the foot of the flat-topped mountain, it's only a few steps uphill to the **stadium**, its foundations still visible. Above are the ruins of a **gymnasium** and, at the same level, to the right, the **lower city gate** with round towers and a horseshoe-shaped atrium. Somewhat further along lie the remains of a **military tower**, from which a five metre wide (once covered) ramp leads to the **upper gate** to the acropolis. On the plateau you can still easily make out the ruins of a **palace**, Hellenistic buildings and a **temple**. There is also a small **mosque** dating from the time of the Seljuks and a Byzantine **church** with three naves. There is an inscription in Greek letters on the church doorway; while it has still not been deciphered, it's thought to be proof that Pamphylia had its own language — something long suspected. The **theatre** at the southeastern edge of the plateau is the most impressive of the remains. In

1969 it lost its fly tower in an earthquake. If you didn't know this, you might think that the theatre was built just for the spectacle of watching the sunrise — the sight is simply breath-taking. The odeon next door to the theatre disappeared completely after the quake.

Getting there/opening times/prices: Signposted off the D400 between Aksu and Serik, from where it's another 12km. There's a second turn-off 5km west of Serik, opposite the turning to 'Belek Turizm Merkezi'; from here it's another 9km. Park at the (overpriced) Sillyon Café, where the path to the mountain ruins begins. Not accessible by public transport. The site is open round the clock and officially free (though this doesn't stop self-proclaimed 'warders' trying to extract money. Watch out for hidden holes in the ground (cisterns)! Strong footwear is advisable.

Aspendos

A visit to Aspendos is most rewarding in the context of the Antalya Festival (see 'Events' on page 79) — the atmosphere at the performances is even more moving than in Verona. For those who don't need opera or ballet to be stimulated, the best time to come is early in the morning, before the coach tours arrive — see Walk 2 on page 93.

History

The city's history hardly differs from those of its neighbours, but it was far more wealthy. This explains why, for example, the Aspendians were able to stop the advancing army of Alexander the Great: they paid 100 gold talents (1 talent = 20kg gold ingot) to stop their city being destroyed. The Aspendians owed their success mainly to salt deposits from nearby Lake Capria, which drained during the summer months. Aspendos was also famous for breeding horses and for its wines, and both of those trades flourished.

Aspendos reached its zenith in Roman times; most buildings still remaining today originate from that epoch. The silting-up of its port at the mouth of the Eurymedon River during the Byzantine period brought about its fall. In Seljuk times Aspendos was still a small principality, with its theatre serving as a caravanserai. The Seljuks can be thanked for the fact that the theatre is in such good condition today — they repaired damage from earlier times.

Getting there/opening times/prices: Aspendos is signposted some 3km east of Serik off the D400 highway. Depending on the season, there is a dolmuş *connection from Serik to Aspendos every 1-2 hours ('Belkıs Aspendos Baraj' service; departs opposite the* jandarma *in the centre). Virtually all buses travelling east from the Antalya bus station stop at Serik. The site is open May-Oct. daily from 09.00-19.30, Nov.-Apr. from 08.00-17.00. Entrance fee £6.50.*

Sights

Seljuk bridge: See photograph and caption on pages 92-93.
Theatre: The 2nd-century AD theatre next to the car park is certainly the most impressive building in Aspendos. An inscription above the two outer stage entrances proclaims that it was a gift from the generous

Aspendos — the best-preserved Roman theatre in Asia Minor

Curtius brothers to the country's gods and the emperor — and that it was built by the architect Zenoi to their satisfaction. From the outside, the theatre (which held about 20,000 spectators) appears to be a completely closed structure, with the fly tower and seating the same height. On the upper rows of seats, as at Perge, there are reserved places engraved with the names of 'season ticket' holders. Look at the curve of the theatre from here! The facade of the 30m-high fly tower was clad with marble and decorated with 40 columns, statues and reliefs; a relief of Dionyses still stands in the central pediment.

Ancient city: Most coach groups limit their tour to looking at just the theatre and save themselves the effort of walking on into the nearby ancient city — a big mistake. Aspendos extends above the theatre over what is today a mountain plateau over-grown with shrubs and bristling with crickets. Walk 2 takes you around the site; some of the highlights are mentioned below. North of the theatre, the way leads up to the little-visited **agora**, its western side lined by a 70m-long two-storey market hall.

Parts of the square stone-block walls still stand. The north side dominated a **nymphaeum** with a façade full of niches richly fitted out with statues. The eastern side bordered a **market hall**, from which the Christian **basilica** later

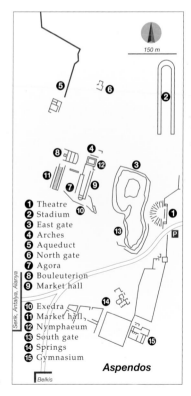

1 Theatre
2 Stadium
3 East gate
4 Arches
5 Aqueduct
6 North gate
7 Agora
8 Bouleuterion
9 Market hall
10 Exedra
11 Market hall
12 Nymphaeum
13 South gate
14 Springs
15 Gymnasium

150 m

Aspendos

Serik, Antalya, Alanya

Belkis

The massive aqueduct at Aspendos

developed. Some 15m-high walls still remain from the northern entrance hall.

Aqueduct: From the northern edge of the hill the remains of a Roman aqueduct can be seen on the intensively cultivated land; some of the walls still rise to their original 30m height. (If you have your own vehicle, you can get there by simply continuing along the road past the theatre). The waterway was once over 15km long; the last three kilometres crossed the plateau on arches. The water flowed through clay pipes. The towers in places where the aqueduct bends served to air the pipes and prevent the hydrostatic pressure from dropping.

Zeytintaşı Cave
In contrast to the Beldibi or Karain caves (see page 103) the Zeytintaşı Mağarası, discovered during blasting in 1997, was never inhabited. This cave is worth a visit on account of its impressive stalactite and stalagmite formations, which

formed over a 14 million year period. The cave is on two levels, but to date only the upper level, 138m long, is open to the public. *Getting there/opening times/prices: The cave is signposted from the D400 highway at Serik, from where you continue 16km inland. It is also signposted from the car park at Aspendos, but this signage runs out. There is no public transport. Open daily from 09.00-18:00; entry fee £1.70, concessions £1.25.*

Belek
A beautiful, 12km-long beach begins about 35km east of Antalya. The sand — partly fine, partly coarse — is interrupted here and there with bits of pebble. The coastline here, shaded by forests of pine and eucalyptus, boasts around 50 magnificent all-inclusive resorts, some of them huge. These are among the best-kept and most popular in all Turkey. All year round it's 'the season' here. The Belek area is a popular beach resort in summer, but equally popular in winter — with both golfers (16 courses; see page 49) and football teams from the top European leagues who come here to train.

But for independent traveller Belek is of little interest, since the club resorts can only be booked from home before you travel, and strangers are not welcomed on their private beaches. And since visitors dine in their all-inclusive resorts, there are few restaurants. Behind the rows of hotels lie the little town of **Kadriye** (to the west) and the coastal village of **Belek** (to the east), with car rental offices, souvenir shops and regular *dolmuses* to Antalya.

Time: 4h15min
Grade: easy; after a visit to the site, the walk ends on a quiet country road. Dean comments: 'There is a confusion of paths in the overgrown site — one wonders how the fairly high entrance fee is spent!' *Note:* This walk originally ran from the hilltop site straight to Belkis and the aqueduct, then on to Serik. A 3m-high fence now surrounds the base of the site, meaning out-and-back legs to the viewpoint over the aqueduct from the clifftop and to the aqueduct itself. If you are doing the full walk, you may prefer to omit the leg along the track into Belis and back, since you will pass under the aqueduct further north. This would save 30min.
Equipment: see page 22.
Travel: 🚌 bus from Antalya bus station to Serik (almost any east-bound bus, journey time about 40min), then *dolmuş* to Aspendos (every one-two hours, depending on season); return on the same bus from Serik (half-hourly).
Short walk: Aspendos (1h35min; easy, but some of the paths in the site are overgrown). This short walk takes in the theatre, agora, odeon and aqueduct, before returning to the theatre. Follow the main walk to the aqueduct and Belkis (1h05min), then retrace your steps to the theatre/ entrance. See plan on page 91.

The plain to the east of Antalya is rich and fertile. The winter rain shed from the surrounding Taurus Mountains filters its way down to feed the rivers which cross the plain to the sea. With such an abundance of water available for irrigation, high average temperatures the year

round, and a summer full of sunshine, the crops grown in the region are boundless. Fresh vegetables are constantly available, including (apart from the usual lettuce and tomatoes) cucumbers, courgettes, beans, and aubergines. This last is the basis for the dish called imam bayıldı *('the iman fainted'). The more exotic crops grown include oranges, cotton and bananas, the latter particularly so in the east of the region around Alanya. The ancient Pamphylians also found it a good region to support their civilisation, and there is a scattering of important sites in the area — Perge, Aspendos and Side (the last not covered in this book). In many ways they vie for the splendour of their theatres, all of which are worth a visit, but the most famous and best preserved is at Aspendos. So advanced were the people of Aspendos in architecture that their buildings have withstood the ravages of the natural elements including the most destructive of all, earthquakes. The theatre, described on page 90, has magnificent acoustics. Most people simply visit the theatre without realising that there are more significant remains to be seen on the hill behind it — including the best-preserved Roman aqueduct in Turkey, shown opposite.*

This walk is designed take you through the ancient site (see plan on page 91) and bring you back to Serik through quiet pastoral countryside. It is said that the finest horses in the world were raised in these rich pastures around Aspendos, and that Alexander the Great bought 4000 of them here. Unfortunately, the horses are no longer bred in the area, ousted perhaps by the growth of the farming industry and the increasing demand for food.

As you start to explore behind the theatre, you may be dogged by young lads keen guide you or sell you ancient coins. Be equally persistent if you don't require their services, and try 'Çekil!' ('go away') if politeness fails.

The **theatre at Aspendos** will keep you enthralled for quite some time. After your visit, **start the walk** by taking the path up the hillside between the theatre and the toilets. Views across the plain open up the moment you gain some elevation, but nearer at hand are some interesting shrubs including Christ's thorn, *Paliurus spina-christi*, from which Christ's crown of thorns was supposedly made. It is easily picked out by its spiny, zigzag, slender branches. On the left, just five-six minutes along the path, is the site of the agora, but the way to it is rather overgrown with yellow-flowered Jerusalem sage. It is better to stay with the main path until you reach a junction a few minutes later, where you could take the small path off left to wander around the remains of the **odeon** and the **agora**.

From the junction continue straight ahead for a minute or so to a fork, then go left, to pass through some ruins ahead. From here, head right towards the aqueduct which you can see on the plain below; very quickly you arrive at an excellent **viewpoint** overlooking it. The path leads to the edge of the cliff, from where you might spot a narrow path down to the nearby village of Belkis. But unless you fancy tackling the three metre-high fence surrounding the base of the site, you now have to retrace your steps to the theatre before seeing the aqueduct at close range.

Back at the theatre, follow the road north for about 1km, then turn left on a track. This takes you beneath the **aqueduct** and into the typical rural community of **Belkis (1h05min)**.

Again you have to retrace your steps to the the road — from where there is a fine view of the aqueduct and also of the Aspendos site, where you can see the theatre nestling against the side of the low hill. Turn left on the road *(but for for the Short walk, turn right, back to the theatre)*. A few minutes later, turn left again, this time along a narrow tarmac road — now with the accompaniment of a **canal** on the right and with pleasing views all around.

As you turn off the D400 highway en route to Aspendos, look right to see this ancient Seljuk bridge across the river Köprü (the Eurymedon River of antiquity). The river was navigable before its mouth silted up, and the previous bridge was higher, to allow entrance for taller ships.

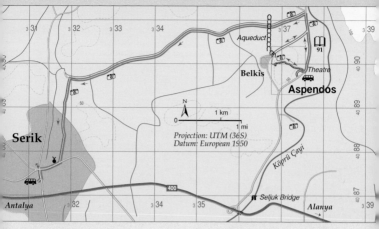

Soon you again walk underneath the **aqueduct** again; Belkıs is now over to your left and your destination, Serik, lies almost directly ahead. An easy stroll on this quiet country road now takes you across the plain. Bent figures tend the fields of tomatoes and acres of wheat sparkle golden in the sunlight.

Eventually the road rises a little above the canal and you reach a **junction (3h25min)**. Turn left here and glimpse the red roofs of Serik ahead. It is a very pleasing and pastoral approach to the town as you follow a raised ridge, enjoying views of the gentle rolling mountains around. Turn right when you meet the main road in **Serik (4h)** and continue past the **mosque** to a roundabout with a **fountain**. Turn left here. The **station** where you can catch the bus back to Antalya is down a side street on the right, reached a minute later (**4h15min**).

Köprülü Canyon

The 360 sq km Köprülü Canyon National Park (Milli Parkı) is about 50km northwest of Side. Its highest mountains reach 2500m, still powdered with snow in spring. The landscape is wild with pines, cedars and cypress woods. Supposedly there are even bears around.

The park is famous for rafting trips on the Köprü Çayı (the Eurymedon River of antiquity). The turquoise-green water snakes through a gorge — in places 100m high — carved out of the karst Taurus Mountains millions of years ago. Rafting trips up to 12km long (Level 3) are possible all year round — such a beautiful

Alara Castle, glimpsed through the gate of the caravanserai at Alarahan (Walk 4)

adventure that this canyon is one of the most visited in the world: in the high season there are 'traffic jams' as up to 4000 people a day make the trip!

When you reach the area there are fish restaurants, tea gardens and fairly basic campsites. But it's not a good idea to swim in the river because of the strong currents. You could rent a kayak if you have the necessary experience — there have been some fatal accidents. What you *can* do, in more peace and quiet, is enjoy Walk 3!

Getting there/prices: This is a popular organised tour from many holiday centres between Antalya (see page 79) and Alanya; prices vary between £13-21, including rafting, travel and food). Otherwise, you need a hired car: take the D400 highway towards Alanya and head inland at Taşağıl (between Serik and Manavgat); the turn is signposted. (Taking a bus from Antalya and then dolmuş from Taşağıl is not recommended; there are few departures and you won't see the best spots.)

Alarahan

While Alarahan is outside the scope of this book (and not shown on the touring map), it is an easy drive from Antalya, signposted off the D400 highway at Okurçallar, then a further 8km inland. Park at the caravanserai shown opposite (han in Turkish) or at the Alarahan Restaurant opposite (recommended for the welcome, the food and helpfulness to walkers). See some notes about the area in Walk 4. There is a fascinating website about the caravanserai under www.turkishhan.org/alara.htm.

Walk 3: Köprülü Canyon

Time: 2h25min
Grade: difficult; you must be as sure-footed as a mountain goat and have a head for heights. You might prefer to do the walk with a local guide; if so, contact 'Adem', the spokesman for the villagers to the national park and goverment authorities. He guides walks in the Selge area, speaks English and is a mine of information. He also can arrange a meal at his house in the village of Altınkaya. His mobile number is 0535 7628116 — be sure to phone in advance.
Equipment: see page 22.
Travel: 🚌 leave the D400 highway at Taşağıl (see opposite) and drive via Beşkonak; park 8km further north, near the trout restaurant at the side of the Köprü River.
Short walk: Two bridges (50min; easy). Omit the difficult scramble along the gorge and just visit the two bridges. Follow the main walk from the start to the first bridge and then pick up the walk again at the 1h45min-point and follow it to the end.

Köprülü Canyon Milli Parkı is a region of very great natural beauty. White-water rafting is the big attraction, with thousands of people attempting the rapids every day throughout the summer season. There are numerous companies with centres along the river bank, and you can just turn up to make the plunge if you fancy it. Fortunately the area is not spoilt with too many tourist facilities.
As an alternative to rafting, this is a spectacular walk into the canyon along the wide rocky ledges that extend part-way down one side of the gorge. There are two interesting

bridges to challenge the photographer, the Roman Oluk Bridge over the canyon and the Bügrüm Bridge over the nearby Kocadere stream.

Start the walk from the **trout restaurant** by the Köprü River: head up the road along which you arrived. It swings briefly away from, then back towards the river, before reaching a junction a few minutes later, where you go left downhill, to the **Roman Oluk Bridge**. It is a narrow bridge, but wide enough to take a car over — and you must do so if you intend to drive on to Selge. But it's better to walk over it and look down into the Köprü — the same river that flows past Aspendos.
Just over the bridge, on the right, is the start of the footpath into the canyon. The narrow footpath follows rocky ledges above the

NB: sketch map; not to scale

Rafting on the Köprü River

river, which runs very deep —
5m in winter and 3m in summer.
Make your way along the path (a
bit of a scramble at times) and
clamber behind the rock pillar
you meet early on. Rock faces
tower all around, enfolding you
in the arms of the canyon. But the
vegetation, which makes the best
of every niche, softens the hard
lines and adds a touch of colour.
The purple flowers of the Judas
tree, *Cercis siliquastrum,*
displayed on leafless branches,
contrast sharply with the limestone rocks, while the Anatolian
orchid, *Orchis anatolica,* so much
at home on small ledges, gives a
display unrivalled in any alpine
garden. Look back occasionally,
for some good views back to the
Roman bridge.

This is hardly a walk, you might
think, as you clamber over the
rocks, but there is the reward of
fast-changing spectacular
scenery. Soon a chasm up on the
left attracts your attention and, a
few minutes later, a **waterfall**
cascading down on the right.
Make a mental note of this waterfall, to use as a waymarker on the
return journey.

A minute or so past the waterfall,
take note of a **cave** under the
overhanging rocks on the left and
then head right, down to the
river. Once down on the bank,
keep under the rock face to make
further progress up the canyon.
Water rushes over the rocks
beneath your feet to cascade into
the river here. If you look ahead
and over to the right, you can see
where a smaller canyon joins the
main one.

Some 10 minutes along the bank
you have a fairly easy scramble

over the rocks ahead. Once over this outcrop, the path is again visible. If you stop to catch your breath, there are plenty of interesting flowers around, like the striking *Arum dioscorides*. Those interested in natural cures might like to know that the root of this plant applied in admixture with bullocks' dung is supposedly good for gout…

The path continues above the river, leading you towards a narrower section of the gorge. Climb up some rocks to regain the path. It leads you beneath a rock overhang before ending at a heap of **rocks and brushwood** (just over **50min**) — indicating that not even the average mountain goat should continue beyond here.

Retrace your steps to the Roman bridge, remembering, when you are back down at river level, to use the **waterfall on the other side of the gorge as a waymark**: here you ascend to the higher level. As you near the Roman bridge, small paths proliferate, but they all seem to reach the road near the bridge. The return

scramble takes about the same time as the outward one.

Once back at the **Roman bridge** (**1h45min**) continue ahead (right) to a fork in the road. Keep left here (the right-hand fork continues up to Selge, 11.5km away). From here you can see the trout farm across the river and, below it, the aqueduct and castle you passed on the way to the canyon.

Continue down the road, past some ruins on the right, before meeting the **modern bridge** over the river (**2h**), at the point where the road swings sharp left. Just upstream from the new bridge stands ancient **Bügrüm Bridge** — a slender, almost delicate arch across deep green waters tumbling through the gorge below. If you want to inspect it closely, it takes a few minutes to scramble up to it. Downstream from the new bridge is a picnic site with one or two benches enjoying the shade offered by the plane trees. From here return to your car at the **restaurant** (**2h25min**) … and perhaps a lunch of fresh trout.

The beautiful Kocadere stream near Büğrüm Bridge

Walk 4: Alarahan • Alara Castle • Alarahan

Time: 2h10min
Grade: difficult; you must be sure-footed and have a head for heights (there is quite a lot of scrambling and walking up steeply-inclined rock faces — more difficult on the descent).

Equipment: see page 22; each member of the party should have a *good torch*.
Travel: 🚗 to/from Alarahan (see page 96); park by the river as you come into the village, opposite the caravanserai.

The walls of Alara Castle give the impression of lace draped over the hill.

Alara is a fairy-tale castle built around the summit of a hill at the head of a plain next to the Alara River. The river at one time provided an important access to the castle and was a key element in its defence. If you think that it looks impregnable, with the castle walls built part-way up the steep, rocky mountain — well it very nearly is, and it is probably better to describe this as an assault course than a walk.

*It is **imperative** that you have a reliable torch even to start the walk, preferably one for each member of the party, or one between two people as a minimum, in order to negotiate the 100m-long dark tunnel which provides the initial entrance to the castle. The steps inside the tunnel are in a state of decay, full of rubble or simply missing, and there are very few port-holes for natural light. It is such a challenge, that it really is satisfying to make it to the very top and, when you are finally there, you will enjoy splendid views. One final point: there are usually some young lads near the castle who will offer to show you the way. If asked, they usually say that there is no charge, but they do expect to be paid. With these notes, you should have no need of their services.*

Think in this batter'd
   Caravanserai
Whose Doorways are alternate
   day and night
How Sultan after Sultan with his
   Pomp
Abode his hour or two, and went
   his way.
*(Rubaiyat of Omar Khayyam by
   Edward Fitzgerald)*

A caravanserai, or *han* in Turkish, is simply an unfurnished inn or an extensive closed courtyard, where caravans could stop, and the one at Alarahan is an excel-lent example. It was built by the Seljuk sultan Alaeddin Keykubat, who was also responsible for building the present-day castle at Alanya (part of a chain of castles stretching from Alanya to Konya and marking an important medieval trading route).

Start the walk opposite the **caravanserai** by continuing along the road, with the river on your left. Alara Castle is so well-integrated into the pinnacle of rock on which it is built, that you may be quite unaware of it until you get fairly close. At the end of the road, reached in only a few minutes, there is a covered seating area *(kosk)* where guides are usually waiting, but continue on here to join a well-defined footpath which leads around to the left through an area of cultivation. Ignoring a path on the left down to the river, pass behind the glasshouses and by the old cistern (also on the left).

Continue ahead through the wheat field towards the base of the castle hill, to some old, narrow steps. Climb these, and suddenly it is steep going, as you scramble over a rocky ledge to arrive at the entrance to the **tunnel (20min)**. Duck down to enter the tunnel, and stand still for a minute or two, until your eyes adjust to the darkness and you can see the steps rising in front of you. Switch on your torch now and start up the steps, keeping over to the left (the stairs on the right have been destroyed in places). Go slowly and steadily, making sure of each step before you proceed until, a good five-six minutes later, you are back in daylight. The steps continue for a little way and then

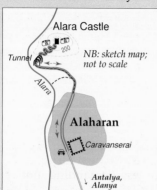

Alara Castle

Tunnel

200

NB: sketch map; not to scale

Alara

Alaharan

Caravanserai

Antalya, Alanya

end at the walls of **Alara Castle (30min)**. Looking back along the line of the tunnel, you can see its direct connection with the river and, looking around, you already enjoy some good views down the river valley to the sea.

Carry on through what was probably the lower entrance gate, following the path from the tunnel, gradually working your way uphill and to the right. There are a few rocks and boulders to surmount on the way, before you reach the small archway where you look for steps ahead and to the left, before the next building. From here it is a steep ascent over boulders which block the way — to find yet more rock-cut steps. As you wind up more steps behind a high wall, it is worth stopping to enjoy the superb scenery and catch your breath. Three-four minutes later you walk through a gap in a covered wall, watching out for a deep hole.

From here do *not* follow the path alongside the wall, but go up to the left — across the rocks — where you should see traces of steps. Ascending these 'steps' is largely another scramble. *It is*

important to stop at this point and consider the onward route. Ahead of you, at the top of the hill, is a high wall with square turrets. No entrance or gateway can be seen. There *is* an entrance, but it is out of sight for the moment. It is located on the right-hand side of the first complete rectangular tower from the left.

Zigzag up over the rocks, heading first towards the left side of the tower, until you are fairly close. Then swing right, across the front of the tower, and finally turn left up to the **tower entrance (55min)**. After passing through, watch out for more deep holes. Climb the steps inside and then (with difficulty) the wall ahead, to finally haul yourself to the very top — where there are yet more deep holes to avoid. As you stand here, looking down on the cultivated plain and at the wild and wooded landscape inland, it's is easy to imagine yourself 'king of the castle'.

When you are ready to return, retrace your steps, *taking even more care on the way down*. Back at the **caravanserai (2h10min)**, take an opportunity to inspect it. Did you see the film *Sharpe's Mission* with Sean Bean? Dean Livesley, who checked all the walks in this book (see pages 8-9), reminisced when reporting on this one: 'My 30 seconds of fame — as an extra, playing Pierre, the French deserter — took place on the battlements of Alarahan caravanserai, with Sean Bean throttling me round the neck as I squawked 'I surrender, I surrender' in my cheesy French accent' …

Beldibi Cave • Karain Cave • Saklıkent • Güver Canyon • Termessos

Area code: (0242
Walks: 5, 6

Access/opening times/prices: see individual attractions

The ancient ruined city of Termessos, caves settled back in the palaeolithic age, deep ravines, and mountains rising high above the tree line are the focal points west of Antalya.

Termessos, located in the Güllük Dağı National Park, is one of the most beautifully located sites in all Turkey. But to really explore it, you need to be quite agile. The Beldibi and Karain caves are less demanding, but are usually only visited by dedicated archaeologists (who come in droves). Lovers of landscape and nature will no doubt head for the mountainous region around the skiing area of Saklıkent and the impressive Güver Canyon.

Beldibi Cave

This cave, near the eponymous holiday resort (see page 120), is well known for its cave paintings. But unfortunately most of them have been lost through decomposition and erosion. It is estimated that they were created in the 7th millennium before Christ, so date from the neolithic era. Archaeologists are entranced by the faded designs, but laymen are likely to consider their children's drawings of matchstick men more exciting. The ceramic finds from the cave are in Antalya's Archaeological Museum.

Getting there/parking: From Antalya take the D400 highway towards Kemer; after about 20km you go through two tunnels. Just after the second tunnel a narrow path leads down to the coast. The cave lies on the left, surrounded by a fence which can be climbed without too much difficulty. If you just stand in front of the fence, you'll see nothing at all. The only parking possibilities are in Beldibi itself, some 500m past the tunnel.

Karain cave

This cave was once an interesting discovery for science, today it means little for tourists other than somewhere to escape the sun. There is nothing unusual to be seen in the cave itself, but the little museum that lies 300m below the cave is worth a visit. Inside the finds are displayed, in particular arrowheads and ancient tools that date back to about 150,000 BC.

Getting there/opening times/prices: From central Antalya, first head in the direction of Kemer, then turn right towards Burdur. About 13km further on turn left towards 'Yeniköy/Karain'. The cave is signposted from here, another 19km away. It's also possible to reach the cave directly from Termessos (see page 107), since the turn-off to Karain is signposted from the Termessos/ Antalya road, from where it's 12km. The cave and museum are open May-Oct daily from 07.30-18.00, Nov.-Apr. from 08.00-17.00; entry fee £1.25.

Landscape en route to Saklıkent

Saklıkent

Saklıkent lies inland some 50km west of Antalya at a height of 1800m. There's no idyllic mountain village; like so many other ski resorts, it's characterised by its drab and sterile accommodation. The slopes (1890-2400m; www.saklıkent.com.tr) are well known simply because there are a couple of lifts ... whereas the main ingredient, snow, is sometimes missing. So the marketing ploy 'ski in the morning, sunbathe on the beach in the afternoon' is a bit of a misrepresentation.

On the other hand, the drive up into this mountainous countryside *is* certainly worth the trip, because the route is through simply beautiful landscape. Pack a picnic to eat on the slopes below the village!

Getting there: From Antalya, first head for Kemer, and then follow the road towards Burdur; from here on the way is signposted.

Güver Canyon

Lycia's 'Grand Canyon', 'Güver Ucurumu', lies in the **Güver Kanyon Tabiat Parkı** (Natural Park), southeast of the Termessos road. The park has game enclosures and plenty of places for picnics. Walk 5 is an excellent tour of the area, and you will pass several viewpoints: not only is the outlook over the canyon impressive, but in fine weather there are far-reaching views to Antalya and the sea.

Getting there/opening times/prices: From Antalya, first head for Kemer, and then follow the road towards Burdur. About 10km along, turn left towards 'Denizli/Korkuteli'. After another 7km, at the exit from Döşemealtı (also the signposted exit from greater Antalya), the entrance is on the left. Or hourly bus from Antalya (bus station) to Korkuteli; warn the driver to let you off at the entrance. Daily from 08.00-21.00 (shorter hours in winter); entry fee £0.90 per person, cars with passengers £2.

Walk 5: Güver Canyon

Time: just over 3h
Grade: easy — level walking on good tracks
Equipment: see page 22
Travel: 🚌 from Antalya to the Güver Kanyon Tabiat Parkı, (Antalya/Korkuteli service), journey time 25min; return with the same service. Or by 🚗: see 'Getting there' opposite.
Shorter walk: Güver Canyon out-and-back (2h40min; easy). You can shorten the walk a little by missing off the circuit at the end. Follow the main walk for the first 1h20min, to reach the third and final viewpoint; then return the same way.

Güver Canyon is located within the Güver Kanyon Natural Park, on the Korkuteli road just outside Antalya. The canyon itself — one million years old — is quite a staggering formation and well worth visiting. It is at its most photogenic around the

middle of the day, when the sun is at a high point over the north-south axis of the gorge. The views are splendid.
There is a small charge to enter the park (£0.90, or £2 for a car and its passengers), but it is well equipped, with a picnic site, tables and other facilities — including a children's play area, car parking, water and toilets. It's best avoided on weekends, when half Antalya is there! Once beyond the picnic area immediately inside the entrance, you will come upon a small community of forestry workers where you might see some of the aspects of village life, including the preparation of yufka bread and börek.

Leave the bus at the stop for the **Güver Kanyon Tabiat Parkı** and walk along the short road across the road from where the bus stops. **Start the walk** as you enter the park by continuing along the

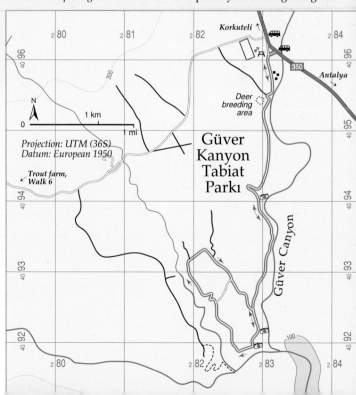

Güver Canyon

the left, to see the shallow beginnings of a minor canyon. Eventually you come to a **first viewing platform (55min)** over the grand canyon. You can walk out to get a good view into the very depths of this narrow gorge, some 115m deep. Despite the steep sides of the canyon, the forest trees manage to get a foothold and enjoy the protected environment. Looking to the south you can see the mountains in the distance which are part of the Beydağları range.

Continue in the same direction to a **second viewpoint (1h15min)**. Antalya comes into view here, as does the end of the canyon. A **third and final viewpoint** is reached a few minutes later, where you see two canyons join. This viewpoint is perhaps the most interesting, with its far-reaching outlook to the right towards the pine-clad mountains which hide the ancient city of Termessos and the distant snow-capped peaks.

From here continue ahead along another wide track which swings away to the right, following the line of the second canyon for a short while. One of the botanical finds of the day along this stretch may be *Ophrys iricolour*, a beautiful bee orchid with lip markings in iridescent blue — like the closed wings of an insect. Ignore a wide junction on the right (a short-cut); 1km further on, the track bends right, then right again (just before the woods). After just over 1km you rejoin the main **outward track** near the second viewpoint (**2h 10min**). Turn left here, back to the **park entrance** (just over **3h**) and the main road.

motorable track ahead, skirting the picnic area on your right. Very soon you are passing the small community of forestry workers, on the left. Just a little further on is a breeding station for wild goats (*yaban keçi*, prized for their horns) and red and fallow deer, all of which are under protection here. There is a sign indicating the current state of the population, giving the numbers (*adet*) of males (*erkek*), females (*dişi*), and young (*yavru*). On such level ground you might wonder about the nature of the canyon but, as the track swings sharply left, keep a watch out on

Termessos

A visit to the ruins of Termessos is a must for any visitor to the Lycian coast. Located at a height of over 1000m, they are breathtaking.

As impressive as the site itself is its setting in the species-rich animal world around Güllük Dağı ('Rose Mountain'), which was declared the Güllük Dağı National Park in 1970. Besides eagles, falcons and hawks, you can see wild goats and, with some luck, red and fallow deer. You may even see a wild *Capra aegagrus*, a relative of the ibex (called *yaban keçi* in Turkish); they are bred in the Güver Kanyon Tabiat Parkı. Even bears have supposedly moved back again in recent years. (In the 19th century the British adventurer Charles Texier reported a still-large leopard population, but the last ones were hunted to extinction in 1938.)

The flora resembles that of typical alpine regions with low trees. An exceptional flower is the lady's slipper orchid (*Cypripedium calceolus*), which shows its pale, rose-coloured blooms in April and May.

There is a small museum at the entrance to the park — nothing spectacular, just a few faded photographs of landscapes, some stuffed animals, a few small finds from the ruins and the like.

Getting there/opening times/prices: Termessos lies about about 35km northwest of Antalya. The only easy way to get there is by car: from the centre of Antalya, head towards Kemer, then turn right towards Burdur. About 10km further on, turn left on the main 350 road in the direction of Denizli/Korkuteli. The site is signposted from here (another 23km). Travelling by public transport or on foot, there are two other ways to get there, both difficult! You can either reach it by following Walk 6 (highly recommended for adventurous walkers; see page 114) or via the 'King's Road'. For the latter, take the Korkuteli bus from Antalya bus station. Alight at the top of Yenice Pass by the 'Termessos' sign, across from the entrance to the national park. From here it's a long climb of about 9km, with an ascent of 700m up a steep road (the 'King's Road'), exposed to the sun — brutal in hot weather. Allow well over two hours for this, and only attempt it early in the morning. In summer, if you arrive early, you have a good chance of hitching a ride to the top, or there may well be taxis waiting at the turn-off. In the summer the site is open daily from 08.00-17.00, in the winter from 08.00-16.00. Entry fee £4.20. Allow almost three hours for your visit to the site, and be sure to bring along plenty to drink, since sometimes there are no local drink- or snack-sellers around. A picnic is also recommended, and the theatre would be a wonderful place to unpack it!

History

The history of Termessos probably goes back to the 2nd millennium BC. The city developed from an impenetrable Pisidian mountain fortress at the foot of the Güllük Dağı, which at the time was known as Solymos. According to Homer's *Iliad*, the people of Solymos were extremely courageous fighters. Neither Alexander the Great nor any other potential conquerors could ever take the city. The

1. Hadrian's Gate
2. Town wall
3. Towan gate
4. Upper wall
5. Gymnasium
6. Osbaros Stoa
7. Theatre
8. Smaller Temple of Artemis
9. Heroon
10. Cisterns
11. Temple of Corinth and Attalos Stoa
12. Larger Temple of Artemis
13. Odeon
14. Temple of Zeus Solymeus
15. Colonnade
16. Tomb of Alketas
17. House-like rock tombs

Entrance, Museum

Soldiers' cemetery

King's Road

Agora

Walk 6

Southern necropolis

Termessos

100 m

success that remained out of reach of human beings came in the mythological form of Bellerophon and then nature — the first destroyed the city, the latter took her back.

Termessos reached its zenith from the 1st century BC up until the 2nd century AD, particularly once it had allied itself with Rome against the Pontiac King Mithridate. The Romans knew how to show appreciation and how to profit from treaties. Termessos was granted numerous privileges and legal freedoms which contributed to the prosperity of the city. Most of the ruined buildings seen today originate from this time. How close the connection with Rome must have been is illustrated by the fact that the Termessians started a new calendar with the signing of the treaty.

During the period of the Eastern

Roman Empire the city gradually lost its status and was destroyed by an earthquake and abandoned (probably around the end of the 4th century or beginning of the 5th century). Termessos was rediscovered in 1842 by English archaeologists. But systematic research and measurements were only begun some 40 years later, under a team led by the Viennese Count Karol Lanckoronski (1848-1933). Their work is still of great importance today, since many building remains which collapsed in the last hundred years could only be reconstructed on the basis of the sketches and photographs made by Lanckoronski and his co-workers.

Sights

The ruins are best visited in the order described if you approach

---

Bellerophon — a hero who fell from heaven

Bellerophon, son of the King of Corinth, is one of mythology's heroes, along with Heracles (Hercules), Jason and Theseus. He was the one who tamed the winged horse Pegasus, but he also inadvertently killed his brother Deliades and so was exiled from Corinth. He looked for refuge in Argos, with King Proetus. There Bellerophon was made more than welcome — Proetus's wife fell in love with him.

When Bellerophon spurned her, she accused him of rape. Proetus naturally wished him dead, but risked the wrath of the erinyes (furies) if he murdered a guest. So rather than carry out the killing himself, he sent Bellerophon to his father-in-law, King Iobates of Lycia. He gave Bellerophon a sealed letter for the king, which contained the request to kill the deliverer.

But Iobates also feared vengeance if he killed a guest. So he gave Bellerophon three tasks, one of which was sure to bring about his death. First he had to kill the Chimera: Bellerophon slew the fire-breathing monster. Then he had to destroy Solymos, Lycia's enemy. Which Bellerophon also succeeded in doing. Finally he had to fight the Amazons — those warrior women, who cut off their right breasts in order to hold a bow more easily (amazon = chestless). Bellerophon returned from this task as well, still alive.

At this point Iobates relented, made Bellerophon his ally, married him to his daughter Philonoe and gave them half his kingdom. Iobates also showed the courageous hero the letter which should have meant his death.

Bellerophon swore revenge on Proetus's wife, rode to her, flattered her and suggested they flee together. She consented, and they rode off on his winged horse. He pushed her into the sea from a great height, and she drowned.

Bellerophon would experience a similar fate later. His hubris led him to believe that he could ride Pegasus to Mount Olympos, realm of the gods. This presumption so infuriated Zeus that he sent a fly to sting Pegasus. The horse threw its rider off and back down to earth. Bellerophon survived the fall, but was left a blind cripple. Euripides immortalised the life of the tragic hero in his Bellerophon tragedy.

from the park entrance; there is some signposting to help with orientation. If you are combining a visit with Walk 6, pick up the description at the gymnasium (see facing page). Before arriving at the site, as you drive or walk up from the park entrance you will pass the remains of some walls (after about 5km, on a curve to the right) and then the foundations of a **fortified tower**. A large entrance gate probably once stood here, a kind of tollgate for caravans travelling over the Yenice Pass. The road continues to wind uphill, in many places following the ancient '**King's Road**' which ran from the gate to the city. The road ends at a car park near an ancient **soldiers' cemetery** with some sarcophagi. From the car park a footpath leads up to Hadrian's Propylon, the first of the sights.

Hadrian's Gate: The clearly

Hadrian's Gate (Hadrian's Propylon)

legible inscription in the four metres high and nearly two metres wide marble gateway states that behind it once stood a temple dedicated to the Emperor Hadrian. Except for a few architectural fragments, however, nothing remains. One can assume that the temple probably had Corinthian columns about eight metres high. From Hadrian's Propylon a footpath leads past a necropolis with plundered stone sarcophagi and well-preserved rock tombs and into the centre of the city. Choose this *for your return route*; the easier way uphill from the car park is via the 'King's Road' (signposted 'Giriş Yolu Ruins'), which is very well preserved in places.

Town wall and gate: King Attalus II, the founder of Antalya, once rode along the King's Road into the centre of Termessos. As you follow this ancient road, remains of the lower town wall soon emerge on the left — sufficient to give a good impression of the protection afforded by the original six metre high defences. Nothing much remains of the city gateway, or of the **dice oracle** which once bordered it. It worked with seven dice, making a possible 120 answers, all of which were engraved on a board. A little further along there are the ruins of an **observation tower**, its square stone blocks over ten layers high.

Gymnasium and upper walls: The road now leads past the ruins of the gymnasium — 91m long but only 14m wide. Thick undergrowth unfortunately makes access fairly difficult. The southwest front is the best-preserved part of the ruin, where baths and classrooms were grouped around an inner courtyard approximately 50m long. The large niches and gates in the front and the entrance gateway, still intact, are worth a pause. A Roman bath, clearly added at a later date, takes up the eastern end of the gymnasium. It's still recognisable from the two column gates, still standing, and the collapsed water channel.

The gymnasium lies at the foot of the upper walls, the inner ramparts. Walk 6 comes in from a path southeast of the gymnasium.

Colonnade: If you carry on to the next terrace up, on the way to the theatre you pass the colonnade, once a boulevard flanked by 47 columns and quite a few statues. Behind it were shops, columned halls and smaller buildings, but nothing remains of this except some overgrown foundations. The colonnade is no longer a place for strolling — only for clambering.

Osbaros stoa: Further uphill is the city's former market complex. At its northern side you can still make out the foundations of the Osbaros stoa (named after a city dignitary). The 100m long, 11m wide building was divided lengthwise down the centre by a wall.

Theatre: This is Termessos's most beautiful and imposing ruin. Parts of the seating and stage building (underneath are two gates) are still standing. The unique, grandiose location of this theatre can only be compared with that of Taormina in Sicily. Your views sweep unhindered across the mountains, through the valley, to Antalya and the Mediterranean beaches. Because of its shape (the stands range beyond the typical semi-circle of Roman theatres) it must have been built originally to Greek design. The theatre was relatively small and seated only 4200 spectators. Its radius amounted to 33m, the height from the orchestra up to the highest stands scarcely 13m, holding 26 rows of seats. The auditorium is interestingly divided into two parts: eight upper and 18 lower rows of seats. While for the upper (cheaper) seats one entered from the side, the lower seats were accessible through a tunnel, which has since collapsed. During the time of the Empire there were also gladiatorial fights on the bill here. Bets were placed, and one man's victory meant another's death.

Odeon: Further south is the powerful back wall of the once enormous odeon, nearly 23m wide and 10m high. It had a roof and served at the same time as the city hall. The names of successful athletes are chiselled between the pilasters, although worn away and hardly recognisable. One can enter the Odeon via the nearby Artemis Temple (see below), but once inside, there are only a few bits of rubble strewn about in the undergrowth.

Artemis Temples: Two temples dedicated to Artemis stood near the Odeon. The larger of them lies completely in rubble. The smaller and younger probably originates from the 3rd century BC. The beautiful portal walls are

These house-like rock tombs are near the Tomb of Alketas.

found in Termessos bear witness to its importance.

Agora, heroon and cisterns: The ancient market place in the city centre is today almost completely overgrown: you need a lot of imagination to visualise that this was once the heart of Termessos. Above all, fruit and grain, as well as horses and cattle, were bought and exchanged here. In those times a sacrifice was usually made to signal the end of business. At Termessos this was done right in the agora. The place of sacrifice was atop the heroon (tomb) resting on a large rock. It is not known for certain who was assigned the extraordinary honour of being buried here. Under the agora there is also a five-part, ten metre deep cistern. The city suffered again and again from water shortages, particularly when it was being besieged.

Attalus stoa and Temple of Corinth: From the cistern, a path leads down to the Attalus stoa, which was a gift from King Attalus II of Pergamon. Just beside it stood Termessos's largest temple. Its inner hall measured some 10 x 10 metres, with walls over a metre thick. The temple takes its name from the Corinthian capitals on the external columns; it is still not known to whom it was dedicated. From here a few steps further south you come to a path signposted to the tomb of Alketas and the southern necropolis.

Tomb of Alketas: The most prominent tomb in Termessos is documented in the following account by the Greek historian Diodor (1st century BC). The Pisidian Commander Alketas,

completely intact and bear inscriptions confirming that a certain Aurelia Amasta donated the temple.

Temple of Zeus Solymeus: Behind the Odeon, four metrehigh external walls still enclose an area of 6 x 7 metres. This small temple was dedicated to the local god, Zeus Solymeus. The Termessians took the Zeus cult from their Greek neighbours, but merged it here with worship of their local Anatolian god, Solymeus. Numerous statues outlawed after murdering the Macedonian Meleandros, found refuge in Termessos during the Wars of the Diadochi. The Termessians promised to protect him from his Macedonian rival Antigonos. Antigonos waited with a large army (40,00 infantry, 7000 cavalry and numerous elephants) in front of the city and requested the handing over of Alketas.

In order to avoid armed conflict, the city elders wanted to accede to the request, but the young were ready for a fight. By means of a ruse — promising to continue the fight — the elders lured the youth out of the city, so that Antigonos could walk in — something which even Alexander had failed to do! When Alketas realised the betrayal, he committed suicide. His body was violated by Antigonos and left unburied. The young people, full of resentment and shame, buried Alketas with full honours. Nothing remains of the front of the tomb, but on the back wall there is the relief of a mounted warrior, and over the body an eagle with a snake in its bill — the symbol of a king. The two niches on the left and right of the tomb were where the burial gifts (wine, grain and the like) were placed.

Southern necropolis: The climb from the upper terrace to the southern necropolis is tough but worthwhile — as it is one of the best-preserved necropoli of the ancient world. You'll probably have the place to yourself; very few visitors come up here. Unfortunately, some of the tombs mentioned below are not easily found; with luck there will be a warder on duty, who can point them out.

One of the most interesting tombs is the temple-like **Lion Tomb**, with a hardly damaged stone sarcophagus bearing the relief of two lions. Similarly built, but less well preserved, is the **Mamastis Mausoleum**, an approximately four metre wide temple tomb fronted by four Corinthian columns; inside three large sarcophagi hold the mortal remains of the Mamastis family.

The **Agethemeros Mausoleum** lies under pine trees at highest point of the necropolis and is visible from far away, but is almost inaccessible. The sarcophagus rests on a high base and has withstood the attacks of grave robbers quite well — apart from a hole in the side panel, through which the tomb's treasures have disappeared.

If you follow the main path all the way to the highest point, you'll come to a fire-watch tower, from where there's a great view over the site, the mountains and forests to the south and the sea to the west.

Walk 6: Termessos via the ancient trail

Time: 7h, plus almost 3h to explore the site

Grade: strenuous and difficult, with an ascent of over 750m; *only for the adventurous, and not to be attempted alone!* The walk should *never* be tackled after rain and is unsuitable for children. You must be absolutely sure-footed and have a head for heights, as well as a very good sense of direction. Despite red dot waymarking and occasional cairns, the trail is often hard to follow, with fallen trees making major obstructions and overgrown prickly vegetation blocking the way. *With luck, the pair of friendly dogs at the trout farm will guide you to Termessos!*

Equipment: see page 22; take plenty of food and liquid. You may collect ticks in the dense shrubbery; keep all parts of your body are well covered.

Travel: 🚗 to the trout breeding farm at the start of the walk: head out of Antalya towards Kemer, then turn right towards Burdur. About 10km along, turn left towards Denizli/Korkuteli. After

7km, shortly after the sign denoting the end of greater Antalya (just past the entrance to the Güver Kanyon Tabiat Parkı), turn left on a motorable track signposted 'Ayalar Alabalık Restaurant'. (The Korkuteli 🚌 also stops here.) It's another 7km to the trout farm; en route you pass the Alageyik Yaşam Sahası (brown/yellow signpost), where red deer are under protection. *Note: the restaurant at the trout farm is not always open!*

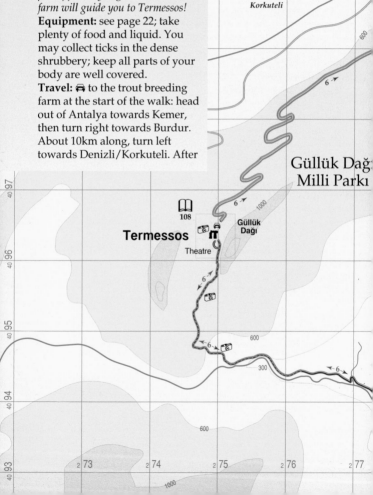

Shorter walks

1 Ascent to Termessos (4h; grade as main walk). By only doing the walk one way you can almost halve the walking time. Ideally, hire a 🚕 taxi for a day and ask the driver to drop you off at the trout farm and collect you at Termessos later. Another option is to drive to the trout farm and hope that when you get to Termessos you can either hitch a lift or pick up a taxi who has recently dropped visitors at the site and will be glad of the extra fare. But they may only be willing to take you as far as the turn-off to the trout farm, leaving you to walk the 7km back to your car.

2 Descent from Termessos (3h; grade as main walk). Take a 🚕 taxi to the upper car park at Termessos and walk down to the trout farm, arranging for the taxi to meet you there. But the route is slightly harder to follow in this direction, since the waymarking is designed for the *ascent*. The

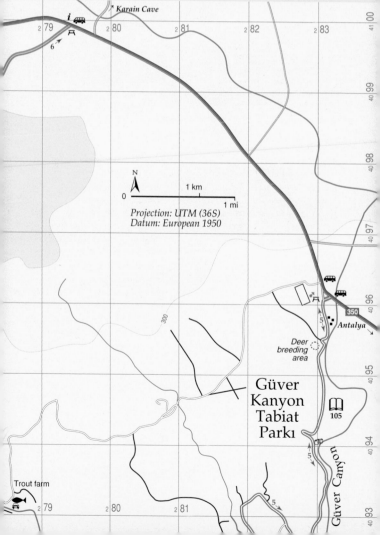

path down starts beside the gymnasium; very soon you pass a sarcophagus.

Alernative walk: trout farm — Termessos — Antalya road (6h; grade as main walk). Take a 🚕 taxi to the trout farm and follow the main walk to Termessos. Return on the access road downhill from the site. On reaching the park gates and the main road you can catch a 🚐 to Antalya.

This exhilarating walk uses a little-known old trail up to Termessos. It was probably the direct link between the ancient city and Antalya. It approaches by using the natural lie of the land, ascending though a magnificent wooded gorge with steep-sided stark mountains, to emerge at Termessos by the gymnasium. At some stages you are constantly brushing through prickly bushes and shrubs, often at head-height (beware of ticks!).

The ancient Psidian city of Termessos is located in a setting of indescribable beauty among the mountain peaks of Güllük, blending into a stark landscape which hints only at hostility. It is said that the Termessians were warlike, fiercely independent spartans, but one can imagine that this description owes as much to a knowledge of the site as it does to the poorly-recorded history of this period. There are no natural resources immediately to hand, no sea for fishing and no land suitable for farming, raising the question of why they needed to retire to such an impregnable fortress under such harsh conditions. But they did, and they built a city of some grandeur. It survived unconquered by all but the forces of nature. Perhaps the most famous attempt on it was made by Alexander the Great, who marched upon Termessos, but stopped at the gates when he realised the magnitude of the task. In the end it fell to a series of earthquakes which effectively destroyed the city.

This walk only takes you up to Termessos. Once at the site there is a good deal more walking to do, not only to see the various remains of the old city, but for the sheer pleasure of some splendid footpaths amongst scenery as fine as anywhere in this part of the Mediterranean.

Termessos is not like the usual historical site where you can stand at the entrance and survey the layout. Its unique location makes it impossible to see any of it on the approach. Since you should allow almost three hours to begin to do it justice (see notes and plan on pages 107-113) you are in for a very tough day. Ideally, treat this walk as an excursion in its own right, and explore the site at leisure another day.

Start the walk from the parking area in front of the **trout farm**: cross the access road to the restaurant and then go left at a fork, parallel with the water pipes. You pass through a barrier. Slender spikes of *Orchis anatolica* in the surrounding pine woods shyly offer their nectar to the passing butterflies in a peaceful setting, disturbed only by the intense gurgling of the river running its course. The track forks again (**10min**; a fenced building is ahead, hidden in the trees); go left again. Following the water pipes, ignore any turnings to the right as the track rises and falls beside the gurgling river on your left. Limestone mountains, stark and rugged, tower ahead — holding a promise of yet more fine scenery and some climbing in store. The plane trees along the stream splash light green against the dark of the pine, where the ripple of pink announces the presence of oleander. Impervious to this, the tall purple spikes of *Limodorum abortivum* seek only the oblivion of the darker recesses. Soon after a short excursion away from the riverside to negotiate a small stream, the route starts into a more noticeable climb until you are high above the river, before narrowing and dropping down to the river again. You can see the limestone gorge shaping up ahead: it looks formidable, but nonetheless inviting. It contrasts sharply with the soft greenness of the immediate surroundings. The route reduces to a path as you pass beneath the **leafy bower** (**45min**) shown opposite; green and shaded, in harmony with the gentle sounds of the river, it is a good place to take a short break before the walk becomes difficult — not far ahead.

At this point the **first waymarks** appear — **red spots** on rocks. For another 10 minutes or so you can continue along the riverside, enjoying shade one moment and open views the next, as the path leads you across a **boulder-strewn area**. About 150m further on, watch for **red spots** and a **large cairn marking your turn-off right, away from the river** (**55min**). You will know you are on the old trail within five minutes: old steps can still be seen, as well as **sections of retaining wall**. From here the way is all uphill, and you quickly rise high above the water. Proceed along the rocks arranged like steps as the trail narrows to a

The leafy bower by the riverside (45min) and the wonderful view to the mountains from the theatre at Termessos

ledge above a steep rockface. Just past here you should be able to see down to Antalya and appreciate that you are walking a more or less direct line from it to Termessos.

Then you're back once more in the bushes. As a relief from the uphill slog, there is a short section of **descent (1h20min)** which gets steeper as you cross a short but tricky patch of loose shale. Soon after, from the shade of overhanging trees, there are good views of a gorge ahead, but this is *not* the way that you are going. Your route soon swings around into a gorge on the right, leading up to Termessos.

The shrubs are left behind briefly, as you enter a **grassy clearing (1h40min)** brightened by the yellow flowers of Jerusalem sage, *Phlomis fruticosa*. Olive trees suggest that this might have been a cultivated area at some time in the past, but now it provides a somewhat different habitat for plants like the delicate, long-spurred *Linaria chalepensis*.

From the clearing keep to the right of the large trees (**red arrow**). The ongoing path is generally clear and easily seen, although overgrown in places. If you lose sight of it, turn back and pick up the **red waymarking**; sometimes there are also small cairns. *If you haven't seen any red waymarks for some time, you are not on the right path.* As the path zig-zags up to Termessos, soon you can again look back to Antalya, or over to the opposite face of the gorge, to see the remains of an ancient building in a seemingly inaccessible position. It may well have been a strategically placed watchtower in view of both Antalya and Termessos.

Just after passing beneath a rock overhang, you emerge on a rocky ledge where the remnants of the old trail are again evident and from where you can absorb the distant views. The short stretches of trail soon peter out into path as you push your way through shrubs like the bean trefoil, *Anagyris foetida,* which has yellow pea-like flowers, trefoil leaves, and bean-like seed pods.

There are some encouraging, if momentary, glimpses of the ruins of Termessos ahead now, but there is still a fair amount of walking and climbing ahead. The April visitor with an eye on the herbage might just spot the delightful monkey orchid, *Orchis simia*, along the way: its flower can be likened to a dancing monkey. Keep pushing your way through the foliage as you continue to zigzag ever upwards. When the path widens from time to time, there are spectacular views to be enjoyed. Further glimpses of Termessos are revealed when, looking ahead, you can just about make out a sarcophagus. But keep an eye on the path too, especially about six-seven minutes later, when it takes an unexpected sharp turn to the left (**red dots**; cairn).

More and more of the old trail is evident soon after this point, as you start the final approach. The outskirts are reached as you pass the **sarcophagus (3h50min)** spotted earlier — if you turn round here, you'll have magnificent views back down the gorge. From here you head into the narrowest section of the gorge, to reach **Termessos** at the **gymnasium (4h)**. Take note of where you came in, to locate your descent path easily. Then use the notes on pages 110-113 to explore the site, starting at N° 5 on the plan.

Allow about 3h for the descent back to the **trout farm (7h)**.

4 KEMER AND SURROUNDINGS

Orientation • Accommodation/camping • Food and drink/Nightlife
• Beaches and diving • Practicalities A-Z

Area code: (0242

Information: the official Tourist Office is located in the local administration building close to the marina, at Liman Cad. 159 (signposted); professional staff. Open daily from 08.30-17.30, in winter 08.00-17.00 and closed Sat./Sun.; (8141112.

Connections: every 20 minutes there is a *dolmuş* connecting Kemer with Antalya and the surrounding hotels (departures from the clock tower on Cumhuriyet Meydanı. The *dolmuş* from Antalya to Tekirova via Phaselis also starts there. Intercity **buses** leave the the bus station 2km outside town on the D400 (reached by Kuzdere *dolmuş* from the clock tower). There are regular connections to (among others) Fethiye (journey time 7h; £10.50), and Denizli/Pamukkale (journey time 6h; £12.50). The **taxi rank** is on Cumhuriyet Meydanı. Some prices: Phaselis return, including waiting time £42; Beldibi or Tekirova £17-21; Çamyuva £12.50; Tahtalı Dağı (lower cable car station) £25; Antalya airport £54.

I n Kemer you can have a *şiş kebap*, be served by Turks, buy a fez or a carpet. But otherwise Kemer has little to do with Turkey. The city could be on any sunny beach anywhere in the world. The same applies to the surrounding resorts, all of which are part of the Kemer region: there are gigantic, anonymous hotel complexes everywhere — at Kiriş, Çamyuva and Tekirova to the south and at Göynük and Beldibi to the north.

At the beginning of the 1990s development began on the 45km coastal strip between Beldibi and Tekirova, opening the area up for mass tourism. Kemer was at the centre and the project, called 'Kemer 2000', was paid for with thousands of millions in loans from the World Bank. The whole coastal region was transformed into a gigantic leisure facility with Bavarian beer gardens, go-cart tracks, large shopping centres and all-day markets. Nothing remained of the former fishing villages except their names. In their place are faceless resort cities, the beaches crowded with millions of holidaymakers — most of them attracted by inexpensive package tours. Russians and Germans are the most noticeable visitors in the area, where one week in a hotel, including flights, can be cheaper than the cost of the flight alone to some other holiday destinations. 'Kemer 2000' is an ongoing project.

If you decide to stay in the area around Kemer, be sure to get all the information you need about your hotel, its exact location, and your specific room! Because if you don't book a *hotel right on the seafront with a room overlooking the sea*, all you will see is dripping air-conditioners or the high security walls surrounding the enormous resorts on the beach. Some complexes have capacity for more than 2000 people, so you're guaranteed new faces. Inside these resorts you will find a kind of 'perfection' — a totally artificial idyll. On the outside, however, things may be different: in Beldibi, Çamyuva and Kiriş the make-over is still ongoing, and sometimes things look improvised or shabby, leaving a bad impression. At present, the 'most perfect' places are Tekirova, Göynük and Kemer itself.

Orientation

Kemer (20,100 inhabitants) is the only 'proper' small town in this area and has the corresponding infrastructure. The main shopping and pedestrian street in Kemer is Liman Caddesi, which leads to the well-maintained marina. Southeast of the marina is lovely Moonlight Park, with cosy open-air taverns behind Ayışığı Beach. North of Moonlight Park there's an open-air ethnographical museum on the Yörük Park promontory, where you can see the lifestyle of the Taurus nomads *(yörükler)*, who today have settled down.

In **Tekirova,** too, they try to offer visitors more than beaches and night life. There's the Ekopark, established by the zoologist Selami Tomruk; it protects about 1000 reptiles, both indigenous and foreign, as well as 360,000 rare plants. (To get there, take the Tekirova exit from the D400 and go left after 0.7km, then it's sign-posted. Open daily from 09.00-18.00, but quite expensive (£12.50 per person, concessions half; www.ekopark. com.tr).

The newest attraction in **Göynük** is the Göynük Kanyon Parkı (see page 124), opened in 2010 and the setting for Walks 8 and 9.

Accommodation/camping

(see plan opposite, but some places are outside the plan area)

No doubt 99% of people holidaying in the Kemer region book their resort through a brochure. They see how things look around the hotel pool — islands of palms, garden chess, creative studios, breakfast for late risers, midnight feasts, jacuzzis, games — maybe a free haircut if you book early. Individual travellers, who book their accommodation locally, are rare. So many resorts are not set up to accommodate this type of clientele — some receptionists would be helpless and speechless if you tried to check in without a voucher. Theoretically at least you have an agony of choice — there are more than 76,000 beds, and you can count on discounts of over 50% in low season. Below are some very pleasant places to stay for anyone stranded in the area — or keen to stretch their legs along the Lycian Way.

Berke Ranch, one of the loveliest places around Kemer, a small comfortable hotel near Çamyuva, away from the frantic coast. Several buildings idyllically located in greenery. Pool, horse riding (even for non-guests, £42 for 2 hours). 26 tasteful, slightly

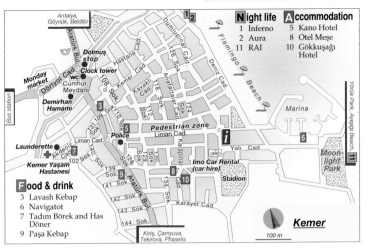

Kemer

rustic rooms and suites with views to the mountains, lovely restaurant. Children's activities. Per person with H/B from £38. (8180333, (8180560, www.hotel-berkeranch.com. Access: coming from Antalya, take the first turn-off for Çamyuva; it's signposted from there (another 1.8km).

Sundance Nature Village, a bungalow and camping area in the bay opposite Phaselis. Recommended by both German and English users, as well as the Lycian Way website. Beautiful open-air setting, spacious; the cabins are dotted about between old trees, with horses wandering around. Very simple facilities (some of the decorations in the bungalows have a socialist touch). The beach is large and not too crowded. Open all year; good restaurant in an idyllic garden. Tree houses with mosquito netting but no bath £29 for two people, two-person bungalows with private bath from £35, camping for 2 people £9.20.Horse-riding also offered (even for non-guests) for £17 an

hour. You can walk or swim to the Phaselis ruins from here. Access: take the Tekirova exit off the D400 and go left after 0.7km, then it's signposted. (8214165, www. sundanceweb.tr.

Kano Hotel (5), friendly family-run hotel in Kemer. Something different in the way of architecture and decoration (a lot of sculptures and paintings). Stone floors, many rooms with balconies. Small pool. Doubles £25. 110 Sok. 19, a quiet alley off Liman Cad., (/(8145217.

Otel Meşe (8), in Kemer, at Karapınar Cad. 10. Small 20-room hotel with a large pool. Clean but rather plain rooms without any personal touches. It has seen better days, but OK for the price. Doubles £25, singles £21. (8142119, (8144857, www. meseotel.com.

A similar place, with similar prices, is the **Gökkusağı Hotel (10)**, diagonally opposite the Meşe, (8147176.

Camping: The loveliest place in the area is the **Sundance Nature Village** (see above). Otherwise there's not much to choose in the Kemer area, most have closed in the last few years (replaced by resort hotels). But two alternatives in Beldibi are **Turkuaz** and **Orkinos**. They are side by side behind the cemetery (between the Ring Beach and Caretta hotels. Both are simple and rather forlorn, but OK and right on the beach. How long they will be around, with all the building going on, is anybody's guess.

Food and drink/Nightlife
(see plan on page 121)
Since the bulk of holidaymakers book all-inclusive, the number of good restaurants independent of hotels is quite small. But the choice is varied nonetheless. The best restaurants are around Kemer's marina and in Moonlight Park.
Navigatot (6), at Kemer's marina. Well-kept, cosy terrace restaurant facing the swanky yachts. Large choice of hot and cold *meze* (including seafood, £3.50-14), as well as grilled steaks and fish (£10-25). There's also lobster at £50 per kio. Liman Cad., (8141490.
Lavash Kebab (3), very popular with the locals. Large choice of kebabs, as well as pizza, *pide* and clay pot casseroles *(kiremit)*. Mains £4.20-14.50. *Lavaş* is also on offer — a paper-thin flatbread straight from the oven. Kemer Cad. 2, (8145520.
Paşa Kebap (9), an alternative to Lavash … so nothing for vegetarians. Nice place with wicker furniure. Kebabs, *pide* or *güveç* at £4.20-8.50. Atatürk Bul., (8142913.
Tadım Börek (7), Akdeniz Cad. 5, a simple *lokanta* with fair

prices. Soups, *börek*, kebabs und *döner*. The **Has Döner** *lokanta* next door is similar.
Yörük Park, local food but tourist prices at this open-air ethnographical museum: *saç kavurma, börek,* cheeses, etc.
Nightlife: The bars on **Ayışığı Beach** and in **Moonlight Park** are just right for evening drinks. You'll find the **RAI Club (11)**, a branch of the eponymous Moscow nightery, as well as **Inferno (1)** and **Aura (2)**. The hot spot in Beldibi is **Disco Jest** (in the north); in Tekirova **Disco X** (a lot of karaoke).

Beaches and diving
The most beautiful beach in Kemer is **Ayışığı** (= moonlight) next to Moonlight Park; it has fine sand and is well maintained, but is chock-a-bloc and has loudspeaker music. The same is true of **Flamingo Beach** north of the marina, behind which there's a new walkway.
The following rule applies to all beaches along the approximately 35km strip of coastline around Kemer: in the north there is more shingle, in the south more sand. Where the beaches are narrow and less attractive, the resorts provide pools. The beach at **Phaselis** is lovely (see page 140), as is **Paradise Bay** between Çamyuva and Phaselis (see Walk 11 on page 142). Further south, the **Çıralı/Olympos Beach** (see page 156), is definitely worth the trip. There are also several bathing bays **between Beldibi and Antalya** (admission is in the form of parking fees of up to £2). But with the widening of the new coastal highway these places have lost much of their charm.

Diving: There are numerous local bases; the larger hotels usually have their own schools. Courses for beginners start at about £250.
Water sports: everything from banana-riding to parasailing.

Practicalities A-Z
Boat trips and organised tours: Whether you're based in Kemer, Tekirova, Beldibi or anywhere in-between, the offers are basically alike and the prices almost identical. If any trips are offered substantially cheaper than with the bulk of the organisers, then they generally include several long shopping breaks. Boat trips to different bays for swimming cost on average £17; jeep safaris on predominantly dust- free roads £17; rafting in the Köprülü Canyon (including travel to the start) £17; daily tours to Pamukkale from £31; daily tours to Kekova and Myra £21.50.
Car and two-wheel rentals: There's a Rent-A-Car sign on nearly every corner. The big internationals nearly all have local branches, for example **Europcar** in the Hotel Amara Wing Resort, Atatürk Bul. 34, ℂ 8141140, www.europcar.com.tr. The cheapest model is about £54 per day. Local firms offer rather lower prices — a car starts on average (depending on the season) at £33 per day. For scooters allow £17 per day, 'department store quality' mountain bikes £8.50 per day (these are available from **Imo Car Rental**, diagonally opposite the Tourist Office, ℂ 8145275, www. imocarrental.com). Lykienbiker (see page 18) has high-quality bikes for rent.
Doctors and dentists, English-

Curious contrasts at 'Kemer 2000'

speaking: at the private hospital **Kemer Yaşam Hastanesi**, Akdeniz Cad. 26, ℂ 8145500 (see plan on page 121).
Events: The **Kemer Carneval** usually takes place in June, but some years it's cancelled.
Launderette: **Yeni Böwe Kuru Temizleme**, on Akdeniz Cad. er load £6.50.
Newspapers and magazines in English are available in many mini-markets.
Police: on Liman Cad; ℂ 155.
Post office: on Atatürk Bul.
Shopping: There is a large **market** in Kemer every Monday, on Dörtyol Cad. west of Cumhuriyet Meydanı. Friday is market day in Göynük.
Sport and leisure
Mountainbiking: see under Ovacık on pages 134-135.
Riding: see Berke Ranch and Sundance under 'Accommo-dation' on pages 120-121.
Walking: Walks 7-14 are easily reached from your doorstep or a short bus or taxi ride.
Türkisches Bad (Hamam): **Demirhan Hamamı**, a modern tourist bath on Cumhuriyet Meydanı by the clock tower. Separate times for men and women. £21 for 'the works'. Open daily 08.00-21.00.

Göynük Kanyon Parkı

The Göynük River runs into the sea between Beldibi snd Göynük. Parallel with the river there's a little road (*Kanyon Yolu*) running inland to the Göynük Canyon entrance. En route you pass **Ali's Garden Café** (see below). Several years ago, Ali took a paint brush and marked out some walks in the area, clearing paths and even building a bridge or two. Then he drew a reliable sketch map; despite the text being in German, the café and walks have been popular with English-speaking walkers for years.

In 2010 a lot changed, with the opening of the Göynük Kanyon Parkı for the general tourist, with the **Eco Fun Adventure Park** (www.ecofunadventurepark. com) opening at the same time. The quiet, fairly isolated Göynük Canyon changed into a noisy adventure park — at least in high season. Outside summer the place is still idyllic.

Between Ali's Garden Café and the park entrance you pass the **Yüksek Parkur**, a high-wire adventure forest (www.yuksek parkur.com) and a **quad bike** rental place. Not far past the park entrance you come to a tiny dam, where the Sarıçınar River meets the Göynük. You can see the confluence from the air — there's a 400m-long 'zip wire' (part of the Eco Fun Adventure Park), where you hang onto a high wire and skitter downhill (£8.50 per stage, £33 for the whole stretch). **The most popular walk** in the canyon starts by the dam: follow the signposting 'Canyon' from the restaurant. You cross the Göynük on a little bridge in a few minutes. Then there's a 30-minute gentle ascent along the good track, with fine views to the Taurus mountains and into the Göynük Valley. When the track ends, a steep path takes you down into the real Göynük Canyon, a narrow passage where the water can be cold and waist-high! Sometimes there's a 'ferryman' here, who will take you through in an inflatable boat (or you can rent helmet, wetsuit and shoes for £21). Otherwise, in summer and autumn (*but not after heavy rain, when the canyon is very dangerous*) you should be able to wade the final 500m to a waterfall (up to 6m high, depending on the season).

Getting there/opening times/prices: Drive up the road (Kanyon Yolu) beside the Göynük River (only accessible from the coast road or the west-bound side of the D400!). After 1.3km you pass Ali's Garden Café (see below), 500m further on the Naturhaus Otel. At the fork 100m past the hotel, go right. Eventually the road loses its hard surface and after 3.5km from the bridge you come to the park entrance. Dolmuşes from Kemer towards Antalya cross the Göynük River via the Göynük Bridge (Göynük Çayı Köprüsü). *Ask the driver to let you off there. From there it's 3.5km on foot to the park entrance (or about 4h to the waterfall and back). Open from sun-up to sunset; entry £2.25.*

Food and drink: Ali's Garden **Café**, on the river. A friendly open-air café/restaurant with good food (especially trout) and fair prices (mains £3.50-6). Lovely garden. Ali and his wife take a lot of trouble. Long recommended by Sunflower readers, since it's on the route of Walk 9.

Walk 7: Kemer • Çalıştepe • Çamyuva

Time: 2h40min
Grade: easy, all on track; ascent of 320m.
Equipment: see page 22.
Travel: 🚐 *dolmuş* from Antalya to Kemer (see page 64; Kemer service or Kemer/Çamyuva service), frequent departures, journey time 50min; return on the Çamyuva/Antalya service — to Kemer or Antalya. Or 🚗 to/from Kemer.

Alternative walks
1 Kemer — Çalıştepe — Kemer (2h40min; grade as main walk). Follow the main walk to the fire-watch station and return the same way.
2 Kemer — Çalıştepe — main road (2h20min; grade as main walk). Follow the main walk to the fire-watch station; on the return, follow the road towards Çamyuva, but take the right turn at the junction reached at the 2h20min-point. From here the main coastal road is only two minutes away, and you can wait for a *dolmuş* back to Antalya or Kemer.

If you look south from Kemer, there is a white 'house' to be seen perched high on a hill called Çalıştepe. So full of character is the hill, with its long sloping shoulder running seawards and an almost precipitous western flank, that it is a landmark for miles around, especially with the white building there as well. The converse is also true: from the top of this hill there is a panoramic view of all the surrounding forested hills, perfect for a fire-watch station — hence the white 'house'. Even before you reach the top, there are some fine views back over Kemer and to the coast beyond, bounded by the Beydağları mountains.

Forest fires are a hazard in such a hot, dry climate, and constant vigilance is required to prevent them. The Turkish people are justifiably proud of their forests, which cover over a quarter of the country and provide an industry for as many as 10 million people living in or on the fringes of the forest. Many of the forestry activities can be seen when you're out walking — including timber-felling and cleaning, resin-collecting from the pine trees, charcoal-burning, and the preparation of firewood. Perhaps a less obvious product of forestry is the handicraft work done by the village women, whose fingers are never idle. Crochet is universally popular and is done with meticulous care — even to the point of covering the work in progress to keep it clean. Likewise, hand-spinning is another activity you might notice among the goatherds.

Start the walk in **Kemer** (plan page 121), at the roundabout at the top of the road leading to the marina. Head south along the road, to pass the mosque with its white minaret almost immediately on your left. The old wooden houses of the scattered community that was once Kemer, the orange groves and farms, have all but disappeared under residential and tourist developments. As the wider road turns sharp left, keep straight ahead on Mehmet Egrutal Caddesi (**20min**) to begin your ascent. The way is wooded initially but, as you gain height, you start to get a view of Kemer and the marina above the pines, a view which gets ever better as you climb.
At a fork (**35min**), take the track to the left (the right-hand fork

125

leads to Çamyuva and is the return route). Continue your steady ascent. Virginia stock, *Malcomia maritima*, liberally sprinkles the rocks to the right with a dusting of pink and white flowers throughout early summer, while over to the left the views over Kemer are certain to get some cameras into action; on a clear day you can see the mountains following the coastline all the way back to Antalya.

Looking upwards from here you probably have the best view of the fire-watch station itself but, as the track leads you steadily upwards, the outlook changes as you start to look down on the south side of the hill. The plain of Çamyuva, divided by the stony river bed, comes into view. Beyond it, the coastline down to Phaselis (Walk 11) can be seen. Çamyuva itself is still partially a farming community, but new

concrete buildings stand out in the midst of orange groves and cultivated farmland.

The track continues to wind up the hill, revealing new view-points almost with every turn. One moment you're looking at the magnificent peak of Tahtalı Dağı (Walk 12) and the next you're facing northwards along the pine-clad mountain chain which hugs the coastline until it vanishes in the distant haze. Just before you reach the summit you enjoy a particularly fine view down to Kemer from a grassy area that makes a pleasant rest spot.

From the 312m-high summit of **Çalıştepe (1h25min)** the views are panoramic — especially if you ascend the few steps onto the balcony around the **fire-watch station**. There are also some remains of ancient buidings at the top — walls and a doorway. While not knowing their history, it seems most likely that they are from the Phaselis era, and one of the buildings may possibly have been a watch-tower.

When you are ready to return, retrace your steps along the track to the road junction and turn left, descending through pine woodland towards Çamyuva. Stay with the road when it swings around to the left at the next junction (**2h20min**), ignoring the track off right. (*Alternative walk 2 goes right here, to the main coast road.*) Very shortly, go straight over a junction. Then cross the **bridge (2h40min)** on the outskirts of **Çamyuva**. Not far past the bridge you can wait for a *dolmuş* bound for Antalya via Kemer.

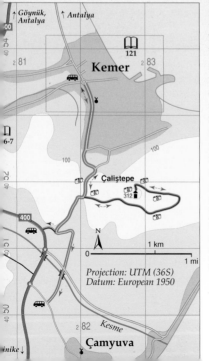

Projection: UTM (36S)
Datum: European 1950

Walk 8: Göynük's old trail

Time: 7h30min

Grade: moderate to strenuous; a fairly relentless uphill walk, with an ascent of just over 700m. Once you join the Lycian Way, the paths are mainly good underfoot and waymarked with red and white flashes.

Equipment: see page 22.

Travel: 🚐 *dolmuş* from Antalya to Göynük (Antalya/Kemer/Çamyuva service), frequent departures, journey time 35min from Antalya, 15min from Kemer. Or intercity bus; alight at the 'Göynük globe' roundabout on the D400 (saves 15min each way); return on the same service. Or 🚗 to Göynük, but see also Shorter walk 4 opposite).

Shorter walks

1 Tree-covered ridge (3h50min; moderate, with an ascent of 300m). Follow the main walk to the ridge at the 2h15min-point, from where you have views into wooded valleys on both sides and to the mountains beyond. There are rocks to sit on here and plenty of shade — a good picnic spot.

2 View to old fortifications (5h35min; fairly strenuous, with an ascent of 500m). Follow the main walk to the 3h05min-point, until you reach the turn-off to the rocky pinnacle with the ruins. Return the same way.

3 Göynük Canyon (3-4h; moderate, with an ascent/ descent of about 250m). After turning up onto the wooded slopes from the *kanalet*, ascend for 10-15 minutes, then take the right fork and descend the path to the river. You meet a wide track, which you can follow upstream for about 30 minutes. When the track ends, the going gets tougher, as a path descends to the river; see the notes on page 124 ('The most popular walk…').

4 Suggestion for motorists

🚗 Drive along the start of Walk 9 and park just before the canyon entrance barrier (or at Ali's Garden Café; see page 124); this saves about 50min walking time each way. Cross the nearest ford over the river (see map), to the path on the south side and turn right. Then follow the main walk, heading towards Ovacık on the Lycian Way.

This walk follows the line of an old trail which was possibly used as a route to Antalya or Termessos before the coastal road was built. It crosses the coastal range of mountains, before swinging north along the line of the valley beyond. It can never have been easy, even on horseback, and was probably used less than the route from Kemer through the Kesme Valley (Walk 10) with which it links

At the start of the old trail

View to Tahtalı Dağı from the Lycian Way trail towards Gedelme

up. Distances are far too great for day walkers to tackle more than just a short section of this route, to savour the marvellous mountain atmosphere and scenery. (At the point where this walk turns back, the Lycian Way continues west to Göynük Yaylası, then south towards Kuzdere or Gedelme.)

One of the botanical highlights of this walk is the lovely pink cyclamen found at the higher altitudes, Cyclamen trochopteranthum, *which has a distribution limited to southwest Turkey. It is easily distinguished by the arrangement of the petals which, half twisted, spread out almost horizontally — just like a propeller blade. Look too for the solid blotch of colour at the base of the petals and sample the primrose-like fragrance of the flowers. Plant lovers will be aware that now only is there a ban on collecting cyclamen in Turkey, but also a ban on their importation into the UK. But at least they can be photographed!*

Start the walk as you leave the

dolmuş on the coast road by the resort hotels (about 1.5km south of the Göynük River). Walk 1km inland along the dual carriageway road, to the roundabout with the **'Göynük globe'** on the main D400, and continue inland towards Göynük village. Straight away you can see your route into the mountains — the gorge ahead to the right, so you know where you are heading. Follow the dual carriageway as it bends right past the **school**, then turn left after about 130m, past the **mosque** (on the left). After another 130m turn right on a road running through the village farmlands in the general direction of the gorge; ignore two forks to the left and then one to the right (after which the road becomes a track).

When the track eventually forks (**55min**), go down right towards the river, but look for the small path off left in under a minute. The path is interrupted by an **irrigation system**, but keep ahead and you will rejoin the old route. For a time the way leads you through the oleander and pine alongside the river, until you walk up the bank to join the *kanalet* (irrigation system) and continue by following the watercourse.

Cross a **bridge over the *kanalet* (1h15min)** and head up into the woods, leaving the river behind. The gorge entrance is narrow, as you head along this beautiful woodland path, marked by the red and white flashes of the **Lycian Way** — and painted rocks advertising Ali's Garden Café. (Try not to be put off by all his advertising; for years users have been singing his praises and telling us what a superb job he is doing maintaining the paths and bridges in this area. You pass his restaurant on Walk 9.)

On the steep sections here you can see parts of the old trail still in evidence. The path climbs continuously, as you pass through the gorge to wind around to the left behind the mountains which form the backdrop to Göynük. Over to the right is a view down the steep-sided and wooded valley pursued in Walk 9. The purple limodore, *Limodorum abortivum*, can be seen around you now, as it is during many woodland walks. On the mossy banks you might notice the dense-flowered orchid, *Neotinea maculata*, if you are an early-season walker. Mountains rising steeply on the left somehow melt away as you wind upwards along the well-defined trail, skirting around a valley on the right.

After crossing the head of a valley, the path divides briefly only to rejoin ahead; the left path is slightly longer but a gentler ascent. Sections of old trail are still in evidence as you continue the steady ascent. Eventually you arrive at a **tree-covered ridge (2h15min)**, from where you have views into wooded valleys on both sides and to the mountains beyond. There are rocks to sit on here and plenty of shade — a good spot for a break.

Continue walking along the ridge towards a rocky outcrop and swing right between the rocks, before descending slightly alongside the valley on the right. Mossy rocks by the slightly sunken path suggests that this might also be a winter water course, and one surprise here was a garden of *Orchis anatolica* on the side of the bank flourishing under these damp conditions. Strawberry trees are ever present amongst the pines as you continue the ascent, now heading along the stony path towards some **huge rocks** on the right **(2h45min)**. Take a moment at this viewpoint to enjoy the view of a dense green forest trying in vain to cloak the rocky escarpment; then walk on around the top of the rocks.

In the midst of all this isolation you move suddenly into a **small glade** which looks as if it might have been under cultivation at some time in the past. If you can raise your eyes from the dark nodding heads of the fritillaries here, and look over to the towering **rock pinnacle** to the right, you should be able to discern signs of an **old fortification**. Neatly-constructed walls, serving perhaps as small terraces against the hillside, blend so naturally as to make them almost undetectable. You reach the closest approach to this pinnacle at a **fork (3h05min)**, where the main path goes off sharply to the left. If you want to explore this region a little more closely — since it is a vantage point with commanding views — then take the path off to the right. It leads around the back of the pinnacle. Then return to this sharp left turn to continue.

Climbing on from here, the terrain becomes more rocky and the vegetation less luxuriant, but you can still recognise bits of the old trail as the path zigzags up the mountainside. Soon open views of mountaintops, plunging valleys and gorges provide another excuse to stop for a breather — as do the wayside flowers, including cyclamen. Still clearly defined, the path continues its winding ascent until eventually **(3h35min)** you glimpse through the trees the ridge which is the destination of this walk. Some 15 minutes later, when the path divides, stay left and feast your eyes on the magnificent display of mountain scenery which opens up. From here it's just 10 minutes to the **top of the ridge (4h)** — where the views may be obscured. Continue over the ridge and descend a little on the far side, taking the path on the right a few minutes later. This leads you up onto a rocky outcrop with panoramic views, back to Göynük and across the valley ahead — where you can just discern a fertile meadow with houses (Göynük Yaylası, the next stage on the Lycian Way).

To return, retrace your steps to the **'Göynük globe'** or the *dolmus* stop by the coastal resorts in **Göynük (7h30min)**.

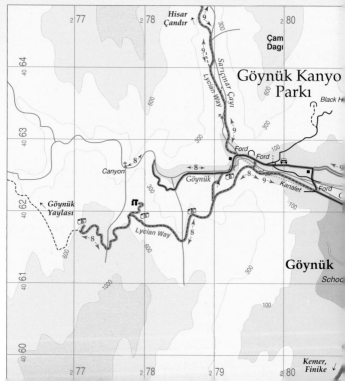

Time: 4h30min
Grade: easy-moderate. Although there is not much climbing (overall ascent of about 250m), the route along the river bed requires some agility.
Equipment: see page 22.
Travel: 🚐 *dolmuş* from Antalya or Kemer to the Göynük Çayı Köprüsü (Göynük River Bridge), (Antalya/Kemer/Çamyuva service), frequent departures, journey time 32min from Antalya, 18min from Kemer; return on the same service. If travelling by 🚗 see Short walks below.

Short walks

1 Göynük gorge (2h50min; easy). Go only as far as the bend in the river before the entrance to the gorge. Return the same way, but only as far as the ford over the river (the 50min-point in the outward walk). Cross the river here and follow the main walk from the 3h45min-point, to return via Göynük village. Travelling by 🚗, another possibility would be to shorten the main walk by using the car park at the entrance to the park.

2 Goynuk Canyon: (under 2h). 🚗 From the car park at the entrance to the park (see page 124) use the notes starting 'The most popular walk…'.

This walk explores the valley of the Sarıçınar Çayı (Yellow Plane Tree Stream) — only accessible when the waters have subsided after the winter rains and spring thaw. Once in the valley, the feelings of isolation and seclusion give the walk an added sense of adventure, as you penetrate deep into the region behind Çam Dağı, the 'Pine Mountain'.
The trees and shrubs along the way become more like familiar friends when recognition comes easily and their histories are known. The myrtle, for example, which you will see in plenty along the route, has been revered from ancient times for its powerful fragrance, which so conjures up images of innocence and purity that it became synonymous with love and virginity. The Greeks and Romans used it as a symbol of youth, beauty and marriage. All parts of the tree are aromatic, but it is the flowers which are used to make the perfumed water called eau d'ange. *Its botanical name is believed to have arisen from the comparison of its fragrance with that of myrrh. If you take one of the pointed evergreen leaves and hold it up towards the light, you can see the many oil glands, like translucent dots, which secrete oil onto the surface of the plant to minimise transpiration.*
This is just one of a number of strategies used by plants in the Mediterranean to survive the hot,

Antalaya ↑ Beldibi ↑

40 64

40 63

Otel 100
Garden Café

← 9

🚐 Göynük Çayı Köprüsü

40 62

40 61

N

globe'
ut

0   1 km
          1 mi

🚐 *Projection: UTM (36S)*
Datum: European 1950

40 60

/82   2 83

131

dry summers. Felting the leaf with hairs, as with Jerusalem sage, is another adaptation to achieve the same purpose, but most other techniques involve reducing the surface area of the leaf. The olive tree, for example, has a small leaf for the size of the tree, whereas plants like rosemary and heather have a rolled leaf. Others, like asparagus, have taken this method to the ultimate, by reducing their leaves to spines.

Start the walk from the **Göynük Çayı Köprüsü** by heading inland, crossing the main D400 and joining the narrow road signposted 'Kanyon Yolu' on the right-hand side of the **Göynük River**. As you contour round the base of **Çam Dağı**, layers of impregnable mountains dominate the skyline ahead. Down on your left, the wide flood-bed of the river, full of pebbles and boulders, might look inhospitable to plants, but the photograph opposite proves otherwise. The chaste tree, *Vitex agnus-castus*, another species which is happy on stony ground, dots the way as you follow the road up-river. The village of Göynük lies on the south side of the river, but villagers have spilt over to this side and made efforts to reclaim some of this stony ground. You can see the results around you with crops like sweetcorn and durum wheat which is used for pasta.

Keep right where a road goes left across a bridge to Göynük village (**25min**), almost immediately passing **Ali's Garden Café** (see 'Food and drink', page 124). Some 500m further on is the Naturhaus Otel, also on the right; 100m past the hotel, keep right at

a fork. When you pass a **café/shop** (**50min**) that looks like a mini-hacienda, the road reverts to track. A **ford** crosses the river here to Göynük village. Continue past a café selling çay from a steaming samovar, as well as fresh orange and pomegranate juice. You come to a **parking area** and then a track off right to the 'Schwarze Höhle' (Black Hole). Just past here there's a fence and a paybooth for the **Göynük Kanyon Parkı** (£2.25 per person at time of writing). Go down the track leading to the **Göynük River** (**1h10min**) and make your way up the river bed through the **gorge**, passing forests of oleander and tamarisk trees. Keep to the right-hand side of the river, to a Lycian Way signpost for 'Hisarçandır 19km', where the main river swings left. Head into the side-valley which runs off to the right on the bend in the river: this is now your direction.

The **entrance to the valley** (**1h35min**), with its small waterfall, is quite a beauty spot, where you may wish to rest before pressing on. Climb up to the left of the valley, to join a path which heads through pine, oleander and plane trees. The path soon levels out to follow the line of the small stream, the **Sarıçınar Çayı** (Yellow Plane Tree Stream), which you cross by stepping stones to reach the right bank. Plenty of shade is offered by the eastern strawberry and bay trees. Pipes on the right give the first clue as to the purpose of this path: it services a water installation.

Soon you cross the stream again and ascend the other side, to walk over a specially-built

The river bed at the start of the walk may look inhospitable to plants, but a number of colonisers have made inroads — like the pink oleander and the yellow-flowered aromatic shrub Dittrichia viscosa.

section retained by a wall. Hovering and darting in their silent flight, dragonflies inspect the waters of the stream, as it ripples and trips over small waterfalls on its way down to join the main river. Looking behind you, the mountains of this green, sun-filled valley seem to have moved in to enclose you in a mood of tranquillity. Only minutes later, the path leads you up and away from the side of the stream. Keep straight on following the Lycian Way marks (**2h05min**). Some sections of the path have been obstructed by uprooted trees from winter storms and landslides, and you will have to pick your way around obstacles to rejoin the path. Eventually the waymarking leads you into the centre of a shallow gully and you cross a man-made causeway at the foot of a rocky area *(take care here, as some of the concrete covers for the sunken stopcocks are missing)*. Duck under a large fig tree into a **boulder-strewn area**. Your day

walk ends here; there is plenty of shade, and you can rest or picnic before setting off again.

The Lycian Way path continues from here towards the **pass between Çam Dağı and Sarıçınar Dağı** (Yellow Plane Tree Mountain) — up on your left, with the TV mast. Along the route there are many more pleasant picnic spots and places to bathe in small rock pools — follow it for another half-hour or so if you have the time.

Return the way you came, but go only as far as **ford over the river** (**3h45min**), where you can cross on stepping-stones. Once over, follow the track (later road) away from the river and on to the village of **Göynük** (**4h15min**). Turn right on the main village dual carriageway road by the mosque, then follow it round to the left. Cross the main D400 by the **roundabout with the 'Göynük' globe** in the centre (intercity buses stop here) and continue straight along to the **coast road** (**4h30min**) for a *dolmuş*.

5 OLYMPOS NATIONAL PARK

Kesme Valley • Ovacık • Phaselis • Tahtalı Dağı • Beycik • Ulupınar • Çıralı • Olympos • Çavuşköy • Adrasan Bay • Karaöz • Kumluca

Area code: (0242
Walks: 10-14

Access/opening times/prices: see individual attractions

The Olympos National Park, encompassing some 700 hectares, stretches between Antalya and Kumluca. The Kemer coastal strip does *not* fall within the park's borders. The powerful Tahtalı Dağı massif (2366m) rises at the geographical centre of the national park, above pine forests hiding ancient ruins and coves opening out to a turquoise sea. Like some of its fellow peaks, in the past it had the rather unimaginative name 'Olympos'.

Apart from some lovely beaches, the park's main attractions are the ruined cities of Phaselis and Olympos and the eternal flames at Çıralı on the coast. In the hinterland there are charming remote alpine pastures, tinkling brooks and silent forests — a paradise for walkers. The summit of Tahtalı Dağı remains snow-capped well into spring. A cable car rises to the summit (see page 140). The concrete used to built the top lift station was flown in by helicopter, in order to protect the environment. But the regulations protecting the area around Tahtalı Dağı are considerably more relaxed than in those in Turkey's other national parks, so it's possible to rent a place to stay in the middle of nature — whether on the beach or up in the mountains.

Kesme Valley to Ovacık

Jeep safaris are the most popular way to see the wild, idyllic gorge Kesme Valley. The tours are so popular that several good walks routes were spoiled even before the road was asphalted — by jeeps throwing up dust. Only Walk 10 remains untouched. Following the little road to Ovacık, you'll pass the Roman bridge shown opposite and the inviting Kesme Boğazı Restaurant with divans just above the river bed; the trout is delicious, but ask about the prices in advance! Afterwards the bumpy little road goes through **Kuzdere Yaylası** (Kuzdere alpine pasture), where nomads once drove their

herds in the summer. Today there are a few places here catering for the jeep safaris, including a quite original cave restaurant. The last stop is usually **Ovacık**, where there are overwhelming mountain panoramas on clear days. Up here at 1250m there's a wonderful mountain freshness in the air, even in high summer.

Tip: Find yourself a mountain bike and a taxi in Kemer. Take the taxi to Ovacık and then cycle *down* the 20km-long road. (If you want to cycle uphill as well, you have to be in top condition.)

Access: Coming from Antalya on the D400, at Kemer take the right turn for the bus station (Otogar), then

keep ahead. It takes about 25min to Ovacık. Dolmuşes run from Kemer's clock tower to Kuzdere.
Accommodation: the **Gül Mountain Hotel**, on an isolated rise in Ovacık, with a 360° panorama. 28 unspectacular, but large rooms and apartments, sauna, *hamam,* indoor pool. Many groups. Doubles with H/B £66. (0533/3705324 (mobile), www. gulmountainhotel.com.

The Kuzdere Köprü (the Roman Kuzdere Bridge)

Walk 10: Sapandere from the Kesme Valley

Time: 8h35min
Grade: moderate-strenuous; all on road or good track, but long, with an ascent of about 650m.
Equipment: see page 22.
Travel: 🚌 *dolmuş* from Antalya or Kemer to the Kuzdere Yolu (Kuzdere Road) — Antalya/Çamyuva service, frequent departures, journey time 55min from Antalya, 5min from Kemer; return on the same service.
Shorter walk: Sapandere from

the Roman bridge (5h40min; moderate, with an ascent of about 525m, all on track). Although the main walk heads through a magnificent gorge, it follows a road frequented by jeep safaris. An option is to 🚗 drive or take a taxi from Kemer to the Roman bridge (Kuzdere Köprü) and begin and end the walk there. Park as near as possible (or arrange for the taxi to collect you on your return). Follow the main walk from the 1h35min-point.

If you want to experience the full sense of grandeur and vastness of the Beydağları, then this walk is a must. Penetration into these mountains is through the magnificent gorge of the Kesme Valley, where you share the way with a tumbling turquoise-green river (… and jeep safaris). It was an important old route to Antalya before the modern coastal road was built and is believed to be the route Alexander the Great's army used to travel towards Termessos. The gorge ends at the lovely arched Roman bridge shown on page 135 (Kuzdere Köprü), from where you head into the wooded valley of Sapandere along the Lycian Way.
The return route, at a higher level, reveals new glimpses of the surrounding mountains, dominated by the magnificent Tahtalı Dağı. This walk makes good use of orman yolu *(forestry tracks which are bulldozed largely to serve the*

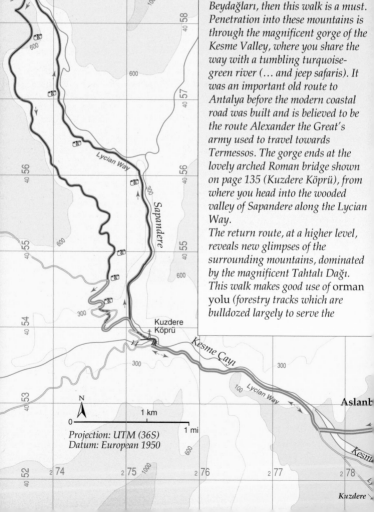

forestry workers). The Turks are rightly proud of the forests which cover around 26% of the country, and they are aware of the need for conservation. Most of the evergreen Mediterranean forest which cloaks the eastern shores of the Lycian Peninsula has been declared a national park (Olimpos-Beydağları Milli Parkı). Certain restrictions apply within these parks, including a ban on hunting, grazing goats and picking or collecting wild flowers. Unfortunately, the grazing of goats continues. It has been the practice in the past for the people living near these forests to use them as grazing grounds and, unfortunately for the flora, this still continues.

Start the walk at the 'Kuzdere Yolu' (Kuzdere road) bus stop on the D400 highway, and start walking along the road sign-posted to Kuzdere, but after only two-three minutes take the road off right. Keep right at a fork after 10 minutes or so and continue to a junction in **Aslan-bucak (25min)**, where the **school** *(okul)* is on your left. Turn left and follow the road across the **Kesme River (35min)**, then turn right inland along the road towards the narrow gorge ahead, joining the **Lycian Way**. As you can guess from all the stones around, the river might look lazy in the summer months, but it can be a torrent after winter storms. Soon you come to a sign indica-

ting the **boundary of the national park (50min)**. From this point onwards the gorge starts to look more spectacular as the steep-sided mountains close in. From here the road starts to rise, but it's unlikely that you will notice this, with the awe-inspiring scenery around. The river is fascinating to watch, as the white-crested turquoise water tumbles relentlessly over the now-smooth rocks.

The road opens out again as you pass through the narrowest part of the gorge, and a new pano-rama emerges towards the hills and valleys ahead. Eventually you come to the well-known **Kuzdere Köprü (1h35min)**, the Roman Kuzdere Bridge, where everyone takes a photographic break. In the season a café is usually open down by the river here.

Cross the bridge (which is wider than it looks on the approach), swing left on a track and, almost immediately, clamber up a very steep path on your right that cuts a bend off the road (keep the pylon on your right). Rejoining the road on a bend, turn right uphill. When you come to a fork a few minutes later, turn right down a track, to follow the line of another river below on the right, still on the Lycian Way. This *orman yolu* now heads along the side of a deeply-wooded valley known as **Sapandere**, plunging down a little at first, only to rise steadily and continuously later on. Cypress, pine and the eastern strawberry tree with its lovely orange bark seem to make up most of the forest here, but there are more open areas where you can hope

to find some interesting wild flowers like the naked-man orchid, *Orchis italica*. Another orchid which is totally at home in a woodland environment and which is fairly common in the region is the purple limodore, *Limodorum abortivum*.

There is little to do in the way of route-finding. Continue head for quite some time, relaxed and enjoying to the full the ever-changing sights and sounds of the woodlands, the mountains and the river below. One of the sounds that might perplex you for a time is the loud and inces-sant throaty chorus which dies only at the sound of your approaching footsteps. The small frogs around here do make an awful lot of noise! Somewhere along the route you may pass a forestry camp (they move from place to place), but it should be possible to see some evidence of their activities, including charcoal-making.

The track starts to wind more uphill, taking you further away from the river and into a region where the rock gives way to a fine shale. Although this area is perfectly stable in the dry season, in winter months there may be a series of **landslips** (beginning at about **3h**), although these can usually be negotiated with some careful scrambling without crossing the river. The valley broadens appreciably, and the changing perspective introduces

a more mellow landscape, with the higher mountains apparently receding behind the more softly cloaked lower slopes. The **track swings left uphill (3h35min)**, away from the main valley and into a smaller valley where some curious rocks protrude at peculiar angles. A series of small tight bends takes you still higher, until you can see all the way back to the gorge.

At a **junction (4h25min)**, be sure to turn sharply left uphill, *leaving the Lycian Way* (which continues to Gedelme or Göynük Yaylası). The track continues uphill through a region of old woodland for a time, then swings left to head back towards the bridge at the head of the gorge and,

more immediately, to the **highest point of the walk** (about 675m; **4h35min)**. At this higher level the views are quite different from those of the outward parallel track, particularly where the land falls away steeply to the left, opening up a vista across the valley. The track then starts a gentle descent through more open woodland (where you may find orchids like *Ophrys spliegodes ssp mammosa)* and continues to descend — sometimes more steeply — through patches of forest. Just occasionally, you may see some beautiful natural rock-gardens bringing together species like the lovely ivy-leaved toadflax, *Cymbalaria longipes*, the friar's cowl, *Arisarum vulgare*, and the musk hyacinth, *Muscari muscarimi*.

On reaching the **Kesme Valley road (6h05min)**, turn down left. The sea and of the plain of Çamyuva now come into view. You should be able to find some short cuts to avoid following all the loops of the road; two have been indicated on the map. Turn left as you rejoin the road for the last time, and continue downhill to the junction where you turned right into Sapandere earlier in the walk.

Continue on to the **Roman bridge (7h10min)**, cross it, then retrace your steps down the road, across the river and back through **Aslanbucak**, to the **Kuzdere Yolu bus stop (8h35min)**.

The Kuzdere road near Aslanbucak

Up to Tahtalı Dağı

A modern, Swiss-built 80-person cable car runs to the summit in just 10 minutes. Of course there are wonderful views to the Kemer region and the Bay of Olympos to the Kumluca plain and Finike — as well as to the Taurus mountains. At the summit there are terrace restaurants and cafés. The original plan was to create a ski area here, but that's no longer on the cards. Not because of the uproar from environmentalists (who already fought the cable car), but because of the lack of snow. And when it does snow, the snow is too wet because of the nearby sea.

Getting there/opening times: From the D400 take the turn-off sign-posted 'Teleferik Tahtalı Dağı' between Çamyuva and Phaselis; from there it's another 6km to the lower station. No public transport. Runs daily in summer from 09.00-18.00 half-hourly, in winter 10.00-16.00 hourly. Return tickets £21.

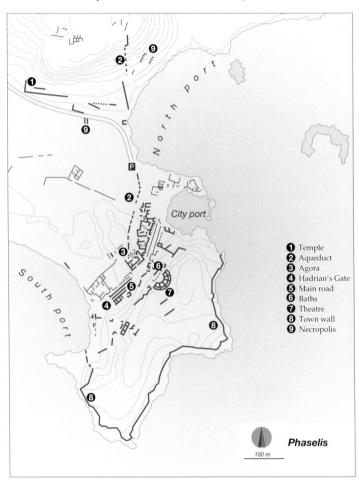

1 Temple
2 Aqueduct
3 Agora
4 Hadrian's Gate
5 Main road
6 Baths
7 Theatre
8 Town wall
9 Necropolis

North port

South port

City port

P

Phaselis

100 m

Phaselis

The ancient trading town of Phaselis is a lovely place to visit. You can wander among the wonderful ruins through fresh-scented pine woods and then have a swim in one of the old harbours. And the best way to approach the site is on foot — as described in Walk 11.

Phaselis was founded around 690 BC and within a short time grew into a city and became the main port on the Lycian east coast. The poet Theodektes was born here in around 400 BC. He wrote speeches for his famous contemporaries and also plays — the city honoured him with a statue in the agora. Alexander the Great spent the winter of 334/333 BC in Phaselis; it is said that he appreciated the local wine and took part in several drinking sessions. After his death Phaselis fell to the Ptolemy, then to Syria, and then to Rhodes. The philosopher Critolaus was born in Phaselis in the 2nd century BC; a Stoic, he condemned any pleasures of the flesh. With his belief that the virtues of the soul were paramount, he probably didn't make many friends. Whether that was the reason that Phaselis declined in the 1st century BC is open to question. Like Olympos, Phaselis became a target for pirates and was then destroyed during the Roman wars against the pirates. The Romans had the city rebuilt, but 400 years later it shared the same fate as the Empire: Phaselis fell with Rome. After this the people of Antalya plundered Phaselis for building materials for their own city.

It's not worth while wasting time on all the rubble at the site — far better to spend some time on the key remains.

Three **ports** are still clearly recognisable: the **north port**, near the aqueduct, the large **south port** and the central, heavily silted-up **city port**.

A 24m-wide **avenue**, flanked by what would have been some magnificent buildings, leads from the city to the south port; today only a few remains of walls serve as reminders of former grandeur.

The 2nd-century **theatre** had seating for up to 1500 visitors. At the **baths** you can still see some round arches — remains of the once-powerful barrel vaulting. The **aqueduct** it also interesting: it carried water from a spring rising in a cave past the north port and then south to a cistern in the city centre, from where it was distributed into the houses. It is supposed to have been one of the longest aqueducts in the Roman Empire.

Getting there/opening times/prices: The turn-off to Phaselis is about 10km south of Kemer, from there it's 2km to the site itself. You can also take a Tekirova dolmuş: see notes for Shorter walk 1 on page 142. Open in summer from 08.00-19.00, in winter from 08.30-19.00, in winter 08.00-17.00; entry fee £3.50.

Time: 3h15min, plus time to
explore the site.
Grade: easy, with very little
ascent; the tracks and paths are
mostly good underfoot.
Equipment: see page 22.
Travel: 🚐 *dolmuş* from Antalya
or Kemer to Çamyuva, frequent
service, journey time 1h from
Antalya, 10min from Kemer;
return with the same *dolmuş*
service. Or 🚗 to Çamyuva: drive
along the route of the main walk
and park at Paradise Bay.
Shorter walks
1 Phaselis by bus, return on foot
(2h10min; easy). 🚐 bus to
Phaselis, south of Çamyuva. The
Kemer/Çamyuva *dolmuş* also
provides a service to Tekirova,
passing close to Phaselis. If you
take this, there is a pitfall to
watch out for: if the *dolmuş* drops
you on the main road 1km from
the site entrance, then the normal
fare is charged (ask for 'normal');
this rate is very cheap. But if the
dolmuş diverts to the site *entrance*
for you, the private hire rate will
be charged (much more expensive). If you manage to leave the
bus or *dolmuş* at the main road,
just walk down the road signposted to Phaselis; you reach the
entrance in under 15 minutes.
From here continue along the
main track until you are
approaching the harbour. Take
note of the grassy track on the
right: this is the point where the
main walk joins this short
version and is your return route
back. Use the map to follow the
main walk back to Çamyuva.
2 Phaselis on foot, return by bus
(2h10min; easy). Follow the main
walk to Phaselis. To return, walk
along the main track from the
north harbour back to the

entrance and continue along the
road for 1km, to reach the main
road. If you are returning to
Antalya you can flag down any
coach or *dolmuş*, but for local
journeys be sure to take the
dolmuş.

*Nature conveniently sculpted a little
piece of the Lycian coastline to
produce three natural harbours. It
became Phaselis. If the historians are
not entirely sure who founded the
city, legend leaves no doubt: it was
Laicos of Rhodes. When he and his
men arrived at the site, they saw the
possibilities for a great city and
offered the shepherd Sylabras either
cereals or smoked fish in payment for
the land. He chose the fish and, thus,
smoked fish became a traditional
offering to the gods in this region.
Laicos's dream became reality as the
ancient ruins testify, and it does not
stretch the imagination too far to
visualise it at the height of its
greatness.*
*This walk, which takes you by the
shortest route from Çamyuva,
essentially follows the coastline to
enter the Phaselis site by an
unattended entrance. Those of you
with a conscience may later wander
up to the main entrance to pay your
entrance fees and perhaps take
advantage of the facilities there,
which include a café, museum,
bookshop and toilets.*

Start **the walk** as you leave the
dolmuş at **Çamyuva** by
continuing in the same direction,
to join the main coast road
(D400), where you turn left.
There is no choice now but to
walk along the main road for a
short while, at least until you are
through the cutting, but soon
afterwards you can look for the
wide track on the left (400m past

the sign denoting the end of Çamyuva; under **20min**). Turn left and follow the track down to the sea, arriving at secluded **Paradise Bay**, used as a fishermen's camp, where they mend their nets before putting them back out in the early evening. Cross the beach, heading south, to pick the footpath heading diagonally left up through the pines, with views back over Çamyuva Bay. The path continues over the headland and descends past a ruined building tucked away in the forest to a secluded **cove with a tiny pebbly beach (35min)** and the magnificent backdrop shown on page 148.

With the sea on your left, head along the bay and take the path up the headland. From the top of headland you look out to the Beş Adalar off the Chelidonian Cape, Musa Dağı (Mount Moses; Walk 14) and Porto Geneviz to the south. Do not let the good views distract you too much as you climb here, because the path stays close to the edge of the cliff in places, where care is needed. Very shortly the path reaches the edge of **Phaselis**, then heads

slightly away from the coast. Phaselis occupied an extensive area, and the area you are now heading towards was the necropolis, so you can enjoy a fine display of huge stone **burial tombs** along the way; the first comes up in six minutes or so.

Once over the hill, the path descends through the pines to a very small, secluded bay. Tread carefully on the slippery pine needles as you go down. Once by the bay, if you look northwards you can see the coastline at Çamyuva Bay and, above it, the white 'house' on Çalıştepe overlooking Kemer. This fire-watch station has commanding views which you can enjoy on Walk 7. Cross the beach and take one of the numerous tracks heading diagonally up the hillside. Aim slightly right until you reach the top.

The route now takes you over another headland, and you can see the sea through the trees ahead. Head towards the sea and, although the path is indistinct initially, once you have made your way through the trees

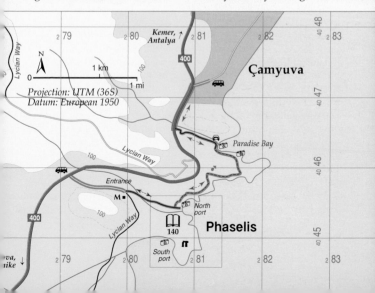

Coast near Phaselis

(again keeping slightly right), the path becomes more clearly defined. Soon the sea is again on your left and the path, which is now looking more like an old track, is leading slightly inland towards the main area of the **necropolis**. There are plenty of sarcophagi around, but don't lean on them because the limestone is flesh-eating (or so the ancients believed, hence their name). A few minutes later, *watch for a turning to the left* (which is by no means obvious): look out first for an unfenced, deep well on the right and, just beyond it, a sunken grave across the path. From here the turn is just 20m on the left, and it leads down (now on a clear path) into a gully. Cross the gully by going diagonally left up the far bank, to arrive at a **rocky outcrop on the ridge** (**1h15min**). There are plenty of jays around but, as you descend steeply through the woodlands down to the right, you may be lucky enough to spot a crested hoopoe. Also present is the unusual purple orchid,

Limodorum abortivum. As you descend into this next gully, with the sea on your left, notice the dense cluster of pines at the bottom. Once at the **bottom of the gully** (**1h20min**), skirt around these pines to the right, to continue more or less straight ahead. The path broadens out into a grassy track. Follow it as it wanders through the light pine woods, but leave it after a few minutes and head half-left downhill, steering just towards the right of some **old ruins** and a **well**. Then join the main track to the ancient site. Turn left to arrive at the **north port** (**1h40min**). (But turn *right* if you wish to head first for the facilities by the entrance, under 15 minutes away.)

From here you can wander around the remains of this once-beautiful city, using the notes and site map on pages 140-141. All the bays are lovely, but be sure to see the **south port** before deciding where to picnic and swim. Then retrace your steps to **Çamyuva** (**3h15min**).

144

Walk 12: Ascent of Tahtalı Dağı (Mount Olympos)

Time: about 9h

Grade: expert, only for very fit, very experienced walkers and only in fine, settled weather. The summit of Tahtalı Dağı, at 2366m, is over 1000m above the winter snow line. The snow recedes sufficiently from around mid-May to allow walkers access to the top. Snow patches remain well into summer, especially on the north face, but these can easily be avoided. This walk starts at 1000m, with an ascent of 1366m. Dean Livesley (see pages 8-9) prefers the walk in winter: 'on a clear sunny day the walking is spectacular', but warns that the snow starts at 1400m and if cloud blows in the temperature can plummet in seconds, turning the snow into sheet ice; take the right equipment! Up to the saddle, the walk is waymarked with red and white flashes (Lycian Way).

Equipment: see page 22; in winter/early spring you will need in addition: waterproof boots, gaiters, full waterproofs, crampons, ice axe, walking/snow poles, compass, warm clothing, sun protection, plenty of food and liquid (*2 litres minimum*). Remember to tell a responsible person that you are climbing the mountain; **mobiles** have good reception for nearly the whole of the walk.

Travel: 🚌 travelling by car, drive up through Beycik village (there is a small market where you can pick up supplies and a spring by the restaurant under the huge plane trees). Keep up through the top of the village, then fork right and continue uphill for another 1.5km (there are red/white flashes on lampposts). Park by the Lycian Way signpost and 'no hunting' signs. You could also arrange for a taxi or private *dolmuş* from Çıralı (21km), Olympos (25km) or Çamyuva (22km) to bring you to this point and collect you.

Shorter walks

1 Yesil Yayla (1h45min; moderate, with an ascent of some 275m). Follow the main walk to Yesil Yayla, enjoy the mountain atmosphere and some fine views, then return by the same route.

2 Descend from Tahtalı Dağı (3h30min; grade as main walk). Take the cable car to the summit (see page 140; *no* public transport). Follow the track down to the saddle and then the Lycian Way red/white flashes down to Beycik. You will also need private transport at the end of the walk (see 'Travel' above), so it's probably best to arrange for a taxi or private *dolmuş* for the day.

Tahtalı Dağı (Wooded Mountain) is the dominant peak in the Beydağları range of mountains and is easily seen from Antalya on a clear day. It stands proud and challenging, shrugging off centuries of history, disdainful of the influence of man. In ancient times, when the city of Olympos thrived down on the coast, this mountain was known as Mount Olympos. Stories of it are woven into legend. It was on this very mountain that Bellerophon earned the wrath of the gods when he endeavoured to ride his winged horse Pegasus to heaven. He was thrown from his horse and crippled.

You might wish that you had the advantage of a Pegasus at times, as you tackle the ascent of this mountain, although much of the walking at the lower level is mainly on a fairly well-defined path which is never short of scenic or botanical interest. There is a distinct change on reaching the saddle at 1800m: from here the going is very steep — which sorts out, in this case, the goats from the sheep. The mountain can be climbed in any season with the right equipment, Dean's favourites being a clear day in winter or a summer's night with a full moon (but remember a head-torch!). A very early start is strongly advised if the weather is hot, and be sure to allow some time in addition to the suggested walking time, for lunch and photography breaks.

Start the walk at the **Lycian Way signpost** (1000m): take the left track above the forestry road by the 'no hunting' sign, then go left immediately on a footpath heading up through the pine trees. The path is well way-marked with red and white flashes. Continue through the woodland, keeping an eye out for the tall purple spikes of the saprophytic *Limodorum abortivum* which revels in this kind of habitat. The path runs beside a small gully for a while, before crossing the gully then rising up the bank to reveal the dramatic cliff face speckled with snow in winter and the deep valley below. Here you may be lucky enough to spot a small colony of another woodland orchid, *Cephalanthera kurdica*.

The path continues along the bank before descending across two stream beds by deciduous planes (*Platanus orientalis*) and woolly-haired, yellow-flowering Jerusalem sage. The path ascends over stony ground through a clearing — to a flat green area with a spring and *kosk* (seating platform) at the top. This is **Yesil Yayla** (Green Pasture, 1275m; **55min**), where some of the villagers bring their animals for summer grazing. The high meadow also makes an ideal campsite, a perfect base from which to tackle the summit.

Continue up past the spring, and pause to enjoy the views back to the coast. Olympos Beach and Porto Geneviz can be seen, with Musa Dağı (Mount Moses) looking like a volcano with its cone-shaped summit. As you climb now, the pines, less comfortable at this altitude, give way to the prickly juniper (*Juniperus oxycedrus*), growing here as trees rather than shrubs, and to cedar. Interesting too, are the viviparous grasses whose strategy for survival, faced with a very short season at this elevation, is to produce a spike bearing young plantlets in the place of seed.

The route continues relentlessly upwards towards the saddle; in winter the snowline starts at around 1400m, and in between the patches of snow Persian sowbread (*Cyclamen persicum*) dots the ground with flashes of pink. In late spring, as you near the saddle, you start to encounter the mountain windflower, *Anenome blanda*, in shades of blue and, more unusually, white. The path zigzags up to the **saddle**, then veers right over the saddle, passing several fairly massive tree trunks — long since dead, but still standing — creating an eerie atmosphere with thin misty cloud swirling up through the pass. The path splits by a fallen tree trunk; the left fork carries the Lycian Way through Yayla Kuzdere and down the Kesme Valley (Walk 10). Fork right (east-northeast) through ancient cedars to the **edge of the treeline** (1840m; **3h**).

Facing the shoulder of the mountain, head east-northeast (70°) up the gully to the crest. At times the path merges with an old track to the summit, now mostly worn away. As the climb steepens, make long zigzags to lessen the angle of your ascent. You have stunning views over the Beydağları Mountains, with Kızlar Sivrisi (Maiden's Peak; 3070m) the highest. As the snow recedes there is a real chance of finding an exciting array of flowers off the track — including two different species of *Corydalis*, *C. solida* and *C. erdelii*, the dainty blue *Scilla bifolia*, crocus and a lovely small yellow fritillary, *Fritillaria carica ssp carica*. Reaching another **saddle** at the top of the rise (2200m; **4h**), you can see the cable car station at the summit for the first time — if the weather is clear. Now descend slightly, heading northeast, across to the main ridge. Then cut right, traversing below the main ridge line. For the most direct route stay below the ridge until you reach the last dip before the main peak. The precipitous cliffs drop down into the forest, and the whole of the western Lycian coast comes into view from the **summit of Tahtalı Dağı** (2366m; **5h30min**). The peak is disfigured by the cable car station and its infrastructure. In winter the buildings look like an Artic ice station, with freezing cloud swirling around, casting haunting shadows across the icy peaks.

Return the same way, taking care on the descent from the shoulder down the limestone scree to the treeline (in winter it's possible to slide down using an ice axe as a brake). Downward time will be about 3h30min to the **Lycian Way signpost** (about **9h**).

Beycik

Cows moo, dogs bark, sheep bleat and cocks crow — Beycik is a quiet, sleepy mountain village at a height of 800-1000m. The landscape is wonderful, and the climate extremely pleasant. It's a relaxing place to visit in summer, to escape the oppressive heat on the coast. Sitting on the terrace of the Panorama Restaurant, enjoying a glass of tea, you have fantastic views.

Beycik is also on the Lycian Way,

Tahtalı Dağı makes a dramatic backdrop on Walk 11; this is the view from the pebbly cove at the 35min-point.

and the ascent of Tahtalı Dağı (Walk 12) *can* start here, but it adds another 200m of ascent to an already long hike. It's a walk that should only be undertaken in perfect weather conditions; the mountain attracts clouds like light attracts moths.
Getting there: The turn-off to Beycik is signposted off the main D440 highway; from there it's 6km up to the village. No public transport.
Accommodation: Villa il Castello is a quiet little mountain hotel in a breathtaking setting at 1000m. 9 comfortable roomy suites (only non-smokers), all with TV, central heating and balconies with views to the pool and mountains. Pool. Per person with breakfast £24, H/B £42. (/(•0242-8161013, www.villacastello.de.
Food and drink: Riviera Park **Restaurant**, delightful 'tree house' restaurant; trout and dishes from the wood-burning oven. At the top of the village, signed. (0537-5070193 (mobile).

Ulupınar

This little village, on the route of Walk 13, lies about 1km below the main D400 highway south of Kemer. It consists of a few houses, a mosque and a dozen good restaurants with gardens, which are famous far beyond the borders of the national park. Trout — prepared in many different ways — is the speciality on all the menus. Make up your own mind as to which restaurant grills or fries the fish best. Two particularly recommended by readers are **Havuz Başı** (see page 155) and **Çağlayan**.

Çıralı

Area code: (0242
Connections: All **buses** plying the main D400 coastal highway between Antalya and Finike stop at the crossroads 7km above Çıralı. The way from there to Çıralı and the eternal flames (Yanartaş) is signposted and in the high season is also served by *dolmuş* (seven a day, between 09.00 and 19.00). *Dolmuşes* also run in the other direction, from Çıralı to the coastal highway seven times a day. Additional *dolmuş* services include: daily departures from Çıralı at 21.00 to the eternal flames; Monday mornings to Kemer; Friday mornings to the market in Kumluca. *There is no direct road connection between Çıralı and Olympos,* but you can walk to Olympos Beach from Çıralı in about 10 minutes.

For years Çıralı was just a small settlement at the eastern end of Olympos Bay. Today it attracts a large, colourful mix of visitors who like the outdoors life. One *pansiyon* after another has prospered in the midst of the sumptuous greenery — there are over 80 of them scattered about now (there is no village 'centre'). The wonderful beach on the doorstep is, like Patara and Dalyan further west, a breeding place for loggerhead turtles, and the World Wildlife Fund works with its Turkish partner, Doğal Hayatı Koruma Derneği, to support local eco-tourism. You may find you never want to leave!

Accommodation/camping/ food and drink

In winter most places are closed. **Arcadia** in an idyllic green garden behind the north side of the bay (signposted from the road to the beach) — five well-hidden, comfortable 60sqm wooden bungalows named for Greek gods; another 5 bungalows inland. £83-110 for 2 people. (8257340, www.arcadia holiday.com.

Myland Pension, well-tended grounds with 13 differently decorated bungalows, all with private terrace. On the north side of the bay, signposted from the beach road. Artists' workshops, yoga. Central bar. Doubles £79, singles £64. (8257044, www. mylandnature.com.

Azur Hotel, is relatively far from the beach. Eight comfortably furnished rooms in 'terraced' bungalow style and 20 new bungalows with modern baths. Pool. They also organise walks and jeep safaris. Signposted off the road to the eternal flames. Doubles £75. (8257072, www. azurhotelcirali.com.

Anatolia Resort, on the north side of the bay, signposted from the road to the eternal flames (Yanartaş). More hotel than pension. 7 rooms in the main building; 5 bungalows. Friendly. Evening meal if you wish. Good value for money: doubles £50 (H/B £71). (8257131075, www. anatoliaresort.com.

Olympos Yavuz Pension, on the southern half of the beach; two-storey house in a large, well-tended garden, somewhat back from the beach. Simple, tidy white-washed double rooms with air-conditioning/heating.

Doubles £38. (8257045, www. olymposyavuzhotel.com.

Blue Paradise Pension, On the first street off the north side of the bay, signposted from the beach road. 9 rooms, with lemons falling off the trees in front. Very relaxing garden with table tennis, hammocks and sunbeds. Good breakfasts. Doubles with air-conditioning £33. (8257013, (8257214, www.blueparadise cirali.com.

Sima Peace Pension, somewhat set back from the north side of the beach, signposted from the road to the eternal flames (Yanartaş). Very highly recommended by readers. Both rooms and little bungalows with air-conditioning. Lovely terrace for relaxation, where Coco the parrot is a source of amusement. The cheerful hostess, Aynur Kurt, is a wonderful cook, and the prices are fair. Children's play area. Doubles £29 (with H/B £50), singles £21 (H/B £29). (8257245, (8257181, www.simapeace.com. **Other places** recommended by readers are **Odile Hotel** (www. hotelodile.com.tr), **Rüya Pansiyon** (www.ruyapansion. com) and **Emek Pansiyon** (www. emekpansiyon.com.tr).

Camping: Spartan, but usually wonderfully idyllic camping places can be found in the gardens of guest houses behind the beach road.

Food and drink: Since most hotels and pensions have dining rooms with excellent home cooking, there are few restaurants. But the following are recommended. **Olympos Yavuz Snackbar**, on the road to the beach, a shady place within sound of the sea. Small choice of dishes, inexpensive and cosy. Two beach restaurants, on the south side of the beach, also come in for praise: **Yörükoğlu** (good *mantı*) and **Azur & Aida** (good choice of wines; meat, fish, *pide* and home-made bread). Another inexpensive place is the Çıralı Café, with a nice garden next to the 'boat park' — just behind the beach, by Sahil Pansiyon. *Tip:* For trout try the Ulupınar restaurants mentioned on page 155 or the Uluçınar Restaurant, 4km inland, on the road to the D400.

Sights

The Chimera and the eternal flames of Yanartaş:
This popular and easily reached sight lies on a ridge at 250m. There are many flames here; fed by natural gas, they flicker up through tiny cracks in the rock. They have been burning since ancient times, but have undoubtedly grown weaker in the last century or so. In earlier times they could be seen from far out to sea and were 'lighthouses' for sailors. The mythical Chimera lived here until slain by Bellerophon (see panel on page 109 and the introduction to Walk 13 overleaf). At the Chimera's fire-spitting hearth the Greeks worshiped the Olympic blacksmith and fire god Hephaistos, the Romans his successor Vulcanus. The Turks named this place Yanartaş — 'burning stone'. There are two fire fields, the first is above the ruins of a temple dedicated to Hephaistos, the other, smaller, is some 20-30 minutes on foot uphill. (The Chimera of course still lives on today — both as a synonym for fantasy and as biological terms both for an

The eternal flames are best seen at night (there are organised tours).

organism containing genetically different tissues or for any fish of the family *Chimaeridae*, with pointed fins and a long tail.)
To visit the flames, either follow Walk 13 or drive direct from Çıralı: follow the signposting 'Chimaera/ Yanartaş'. After about 5km you come to the car park with a kiosk where you pay the entry fee (£1.25). From there it's another 20-30 minutes on foot, and fairly steep.

Practicalities A-Z

Car and two-wheel hire: The cheapest cars locally cost £38/ day; scooters £21; bikes (available at many pensions) £4.20.
Money: *no ATMs or banks in Çıralı!*
Boat tours: Most pensions offer trips with friendly Captain Mikael. Adrasan is a good choice (£17 per person with food). (0535 5548772 (mobile).

Walk 13: Olympos • Çıralı • Yanartaş • Ulupınar • Olympos

Time: 5h15 min
Grade: moderate. On the section from Çıralı to Ulupınar there is a climb of some 300m, on a path which is stony in places, otherwise the tracks and paths are generally good. Tree trunk to be crossed (see photograph on page 154). Much of the walk is way-marked with the red and white flashes of the Lycian Way.
Equipment: see page 22; rather than picnic, you may want to have a trout lunch at Ulupınar (see below and page 149).
Travel: 🚌 from Antalya or Kemer to the Olympos bus stop on main highway (half-hourly, journey time 1h10min from Antalya, 35min from Kemer), then shuttle bus down to the Olympos Valley (11km), journey time 20min; return using the same transport (buses on the main highway run to Antalya every half hour until 20.00).

Alternative walks
1 Çıralı loop (5h15min. If you are staying in Çıralı, you can start from anywhere in the village and make a circuit.
2 Ulupınar — Yanartaş — Ulupınar (2h20min). Start from the main D400 highway, at the the *second* Ulupınar junction (if coming from Antalya). Follow the road downhill and turn right towards 'Havuz Başı Restaurant'. Use the map to do the walk in reverse from this point (all Lycian Way, with red and white waymarks), crossing the river and descending past the higher set of flames to the lower flames. Return the same way.

Apart from some very beautiful countryside, this walk takes you deep into the ancient past — into a world of myths and legends. There is no

chance now of meeting Chimera, a fire-breathing female monster looking like a lion in the forepart, a goat in the middle and a dragon at the back — because it was slain by Bellerophon on his winged horse Pegasus some while ago. But there still remains part of the legend for you to see: the eternal flames burning on the hillside next to the ruins of the temple dedicated to Hephaistos, the God of Fire and the lame and ugly husband of Venus. There is a very difficult decision for you to make at some stage: whether to include the ancient site of Olympos or leave it for another day. Like many of the other sites around the Lycian Peninsula, Olympos occupies a very beautiful position. It was built straddling a river in a lovely wooded valley, and although the remains are perhaps less significant than others in the region, you can spend happy hours just locating all major buildings up both sides of the valley. The valley opens up onto one of the most inviting beaches in the region — which only serves to make the choices even more difficult if you're short of time.

Start the walk from the **Olympos ticket office** (£1.50 entrance fee). Head through ruins and cross the stepping stones fording a fresh-water spring, then continue through the lush greenery opening out to **Olympos Beach** (**10min**). Turn left and walk 500m along the beach towards **Çıralı** village. Turn inland past the first restaurant, crossing the stream (dry in summer and autumn). Follow the dirt road 400m to the main bridge junction. Turn right here, following the yellow Lycian Way signs for 'Chimera, Yanartaş', walking past the shops and restaurants in **Çıralı**. You'll see that in this village farming and tourism have found a very good balance, with family-run *pansiyonlar* and small hotels hidden away in the middle of orange groves and exquisite gardens. Keep to the landward side of the village, on the road hugging the base of the hills. Just after you pass the **last house on the left (1h10min)**, fork left at the junction and continue to the **car park** at the foot of the hillside

(1h20min). There is a small café here selling refreshments, clean toilets, and a booth where you buy an entrance ticket (currently £1.50) to see the eternal flames. From here you ascend a track and then a stepped, well-maintained footpath through pine forest, following the red and white flashes of the Lycian Way. The path is clearly defined up the stony hillside, where lavender dots the way, interspersed with

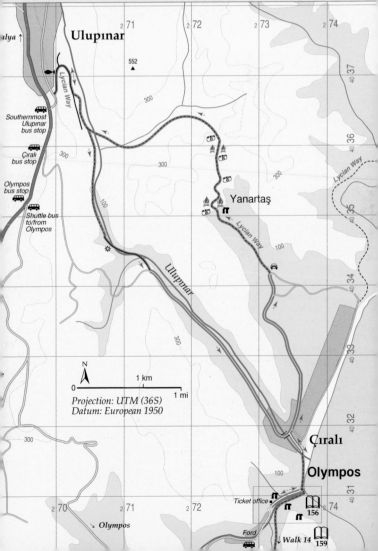

Crossing the fast-flowing Ulupınar River on the tree trunk. Users have written that some years there is a dicky makeshift bridge further upstream, but if you find it, you'll have to make your way back to the main Lycian Way route.

patches of quaking grass, *Briza maxima,* which nods gently to even the slightest breeze. Past the entrance to a rocky clearing with 'wishing trees' (where people have tied their plastic rubbish as 'ribbons', suffocating the smaller trees), you reach **Yanartaş** (the Burning Stone; **1h40min**). On your right, below the flames, are the remains of the ancient temple dedicated to Hephaistos, black-smith of the gods, surmounted by the ruins of a Byzantine church. Here the myth of Bellerophon slaying the Chimera comes to life, while the vents for Hephaistos's forge burn brightly as he tempers a new Excalibur for a mythical warrior.

When you are ready to leave, pick up the Lycian Way at the top of the flames and continue up the winding path. As the ascent steepens the terrain becomes harsher, with the stony ground less hospitable even to pine trees. Head over a low saddle where, if you pause for breath, there are good views to savour over the lower slopes in the direction of the sea and Olympos. The path

rises steadily, following the line of a small ridge for a while. With each step the views open up around you until, just as you start to move away from the ridge to continue alongside the valley on the right, you can look down over Yanartaş and the lower plain to the sea. Some five-six minutes later, unexpectedly, you find yourself at more **eternal flames.** This higher area is smaller and much less frequented than the lower site, but in some ways a more beautiful setting. If you continue along the path for just a minute, to breast the **saddle** (the **highest part of the walk; 2h15min**), you can enjoy breathtaking views of Tahtalı Dağı — ancient Mount Olympos, from where the city took its name. Looking down into the valley, you can make out a large pale green area of plane trees — your next destination. To leave the saddle, follow the red and white flashes way-marking the path down to your left. On this side of the hill you can enjoy greener surroundings, and, once through a boulder-strewn area, there is a greater abundance of flowers. The route continues in a steady diagonal descent down the lightly wooded hillside until you turn left, joining a footpath running parallel with the stream down on your right (**2h30min**). The path divides a short time later; go right here, using the stepping stones to cross the stream (look upstream to enjoy the sight of miniature cascading waterfalls). The path then contours around the hillside on your right until you drop sharply to the **Ulupınar River** (**2h40min**). Now your sense of balance is really put to the test, as you cross the river on a tree trunk. If you have any doubts about 'walking the log', then sit astride it and gradually haul your way across. The path climbs diagonally up the bank, to join the main path up to Ulupınar. After a right turn here, relax from route-finding and enjoy the sheer magnificence of the surroundings. Continue the gradual ascent, rising parallel with the ravine, with plane trees dotted along the banks of the river. Scents of sage, thyme, oregano and wild mint waft up as you brush past, continuing up to a **track** (**3h**).

Turn right on the track; around you is a beautiful green valley with rustic farms; Tahtalı Dağı stands towering above. Ignoring tracks both left and right, continue uphill until you pass a **trout farm**. Turn left at the junction and left again, to the two **Havuz Başı Restaurants** in **Ulupınar** (**3h10min**). The newer one, Havuz Başı 2, is on the right, with *kösks* under a canopy of green. The speciality is trout

baked in a clay dish with vegetables. They also serve *lavas* (pitta bread) hot from the oven and sprinkled with goats' cheese. Return by the same route to just above the river crossing, then continue on the path running parallel with the ravine (marked by *blue dots*). The path undulates through the pines before turning back sharp right, away from the river. From this bend you can cut down the bank towards the river, to a 'mini canyon', with amazing rock formations gouged out by immense water pressure over thousands of years. There is a perfect pool to swim in while listening to waterfalls and the wind whistling through pines. Continue along the path which open out into a tractor track winding down the valley. Set back from the river are the ruins of an old **mill**; the roof has collapsed, but the huge mill-stones are still in place inside. From here the track fords the main stream for a short stretch, before you recross the stream on stepping stones. Look out for frogs and fresh-water crabs scavenging along the bank. When the track emerges at a small green plain with some mandarin trees, cross the clearing and a side-stream to arrive at the **asphalt road** (**3h50min**). Turn left on the winding road, gradually descending. The road levels out along the valley floor; follow it 3km, back to the **main bridge in Çıralı**. Cross the bridge and turn right, back to the beach for a swim in the turquoise waters at **Olympos Beach**. Continue back along the beach and through the ruins, to the **Olympos entrance gate** (**5h15min**).

Olympos

For the majority of tourists the wonderful long sandy beach on the ancient city's doorstep is the best thing about Olympos. A river with crystal-clear water also flows into the sea, more refreshing than a shower — a hint of the South Seas!

Naturally you are not the first to be interested in Olympos. The tree house settlements on the approach road to the beach and site enjoy the same cult status on the international backpacking scene as Zipolite in Mexico or Hat Rin in Thailand. So while not a 'place' in its own right, Olympos has become a small centre for alternative mass tourism. Coachloads of young people arrive to party. At the improvised car park five minutes from the coast, rows of Suzuki jeeps disgorge day trippers, and in the bay elegant yachts moor alongside listing, overcrowded tour boats.

At the time of its founding in the 2nd century BC, Olympos was one of the six most important cities in Lycia, focus of the Hephaistos cult (see Chimera on page 151). At the beginning of the 1st century BC Olympos was under the control of Cilician pirates. Their leader was a man called Zenicetes (see Walk 14), who chose it as their main base. He introduced the cult of Mithras, which originated in Persia, a cult exclusively for men and which demanded the ritual sacrifice of bulls in order for the soul to gain redemption and immortality. In 78 BC the Roman wars against the pirates destroyed the city, and Olympos never recovered. But Roman soldiers continued the cult of Mithras, which spread across the entire Roman Empire. In many garrison cities Mithraea were developed, in which the bull-killing god was worshipped.

Sights: Alternative walk 13-3 on page 158 is the best tour of the ruins, which are hellishly busy in summer but wonderful out of season (start at the ticket office and cross to the south side of the

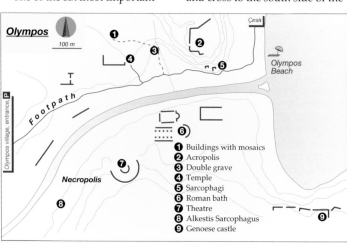

Olympos

100 m

Çıralı

Olympos Beach

Olympos village, entrance

Footpath

Necropolis

❶ Buildings with mosaics
❷ Acropolis
❸ Double grave
❹ Temple
❺ Sarcophagi
❻ Roman bath
❼ Theatre
❽ Alkestis Sarcophagus
❾ Genoese castle

river, to pick up the end of Walk 13). Highlights include the remains of a **Byzantine church**, a **bridge support** on the river (which hasn't changed its course since antiquity), a **theatre** hidden in the bushes, an interesting **temple gate** (5m high, in the Ionic style, with a beautiful lintel and an inscription dedicated to Emperor Marcus Aurelius). The somewhat difficult route up to the **acropolis** is worth it for the fabulous view over the bay of Olympos. Among the most worthwhile ruins are the burial areas: the **Alketis Sarcophagus** on the south side of the river, the large **double grave** in the jungle on the north side of the river, and the three **sarcophagi** in two rock niches on the way to the beach. *Getting there/opening times/prices: Olympos is most easily reached with private transport. Turn off the D400 about 30km south of Kemer (after Ulupınar and past the Cıralı turn-off) on a signposted road. All buses between Antalya and Finike will stop at the turn-off on request. In summer a shuttle bus runs down to Olympos and back every hour (in winter every 2h). From Cıralı you can walk along the beach to the site in about 10 minutes. The site is open daily from 09.00-19.00; entry fee £1.25. Out of hours free.*

Accommodation, food and drink:
On the way to the beach there are several **tree house** settlements with adjacent restaurants — most suited for the young, as there's nothing really comfortable. The following places are listed in order of their distance from the beach (Kadirs is furthest away). **Kadirs Yörük Top Tree House**, one of the oldest and best loved. Nearly a small wobbly city in itself. Only rented as half-board: for this you get a nice meal, eaten at a community table; in the evening there are large campfires and booming music. In season there are diving lessons; all year round kayaking and climbing. Per person in the dormitory from £9.20, in the huts with double bed/private bath from £15 and in the bungalows with air-con. from £21. (8921250, (8921110, www.kadirtreehouses.com.
Şaban, 10 tree houses (with H/B £11 per person) and 40 bungalows with bath/WC (H/B £17 per person). Good food; open to non-guests in the evening. Friendly. (89212655, (8921397, www.sabanpansion.com.
Bayrams, tree houses (£27 for 2) or bungalows with bath and air-conditioning (£37 for 2). Nice terrace, bar, laundry, book exchange. All H/B; buffet dinners. (8921243, (8921399, www.bayrams.com.

Practicalities A-Z
Bathing: Olympos Beach is only accessible from the places to stay via the site itself, so you must pay the official entrance fee (a weekly pass costs £2.25).
Boat trips and organised tours: Nearly all places to stay organise trips to the local sights. Four-day boat tours to Fethiye are also offered. A good company is **V-Go**, run by the eponymous guest house in Fethiye (office in Olympos near Bayrams). Cruises on yachts carrying from 16-20 with F/B (drinks are extra, a beer costs £2.25) £135 per person. (0252 6122113, www.bluecruise turkey.com.
Money: *No bank in Olympos, but a mobile cashpoint in summer.*

Walk 14: Olympos — Musa Dağı (lost city) loop

Time: 4h (add 2h to visit the site)
Grade: moderate-strenuous, with an ascent/descent of 700m. Most of the walk is through dense, humid forest.
Equipment: see page 22; plenty of fluid (the spring near the summit may be dry in summer).
Travel: 🚌 as Walk 13, page 152.
Alternative walks
1 Olympos to Adrasan Bay via the Lycian Way (8h; grade as main walk). This route is marked with red and white flashes. Use the map to begin at the southern necropolis (near the *end* of the main walk) and follow the Lycian Way up to the stone shepherd's hut near a spring. From here descend on the Lycian Way path into the Adrasan Valley and head left, circumnavigating the base of the mountains through farmland. When you meet a road, turn left and follow it down to Adrasan Bay, to finish with a swim at the beach. From here take a *dolmuş* back to Olympos (summer only), hitch-hike, or take a taxi (see page 163).
2 Olympos — shepherd's hut — Olympos road (10h; grade as main walk). Follow Alternative walk 1 above, but when descending to the first cottages, cut right, circumnavigating the base of the mountain on shepherds' paths. This will bring you out on the Çavuşköy road near Kilise Yakasi at the head of the Olympos Valley. Walk on to the Olympos road, from where you can take one of the shuttle buses down to Olympos or up to the Olympos bus stop on the main D400 highway.
3 Olympos ruins (about 2h; easy). Follow the end of the main walk from the avenue of vaulted tombs on the south side of the river, opposite the ticket office and car park (see last paragraph on page 162). When you get to Olympos Beach, cross to the north side of the river to re-enter the ruins on the main track. Turn right into the vegetation past a fine sarcophagus, by the fresh-water spring and stepping stones. The path ascends steeply to the Genoese battlements and small acropolis overlooking the beach. Return down to the main track over stepping stones. Ten metres further on, turn right, following the walled canal system past stone doorways and a mausoleum. Go through an arch and on to a sarcophagus. Turn back here, then go right, alongside the water channel, to a building with a geometrically-patterned mosaic floor and domed apse (probably the bishop's residence). Return along the channel and walk through a canopy of sweet laurel to the main track. From late spring the sound of frogs and summer cicadas is quite overwhelming, and dragonflies and damselflies hover around the marshy pools. A photo opportunity will draw you to a clearing by the main stream: arched windows sur-mount the polygonal stonework edging the river channel, and the bamboo lining the banks of the stream darts skywards like ruffled hair. Follow the signpost for 'temple', back into the lush greenery and to a 5m-high temple dooway; the temple was dedicated to the emperor Marcus Aurelius. Continue along the main track past ruined buildings and bulging walls — nature being the final conqueror of this city —and on to the ticket booth, toilets and car park.

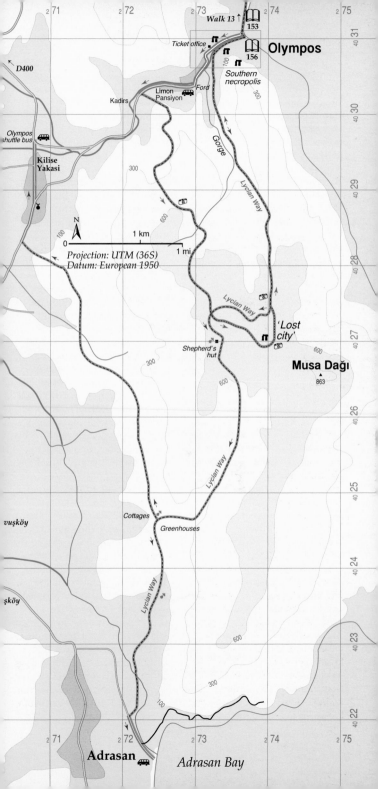

From the lush valley and stream of the Olympos ruins, this walk takes you up the forested slopes of Musa Dağı, to explore the 'lost city', a stronghold of the pirate leader Zenicetes (see page 156) before the pirates were crushed by the Romans in 78 BC. There are wonderful views from the walk's high points over to the Beydağları mountains, snow-clad through to early summer, with Kızlar Sivrisi (Maiden's Peak; 3070m) — the highest point in the whole of Lycia. Wild boar roam the mountainside and, although they are rarely seen, the scuffed areas along the route are evidence of their nocturnal foraging for food. On the higher slopes cukurs (rock partridge) fly out from their roosts at your approaching footsteps, and chameleons, changing colour to match the different shades of vegetation, stay motionless awaiting their prey. Abundant wild flowers make feeding grounds for the many species of insects amongst them, and you may spot yellow-and-black striped caterpillars forming a chain to ward off predators: from a bird's-eye view, they look like a snake. The walk ends by going through the Olympos ruins to the protected beach, where loggerhead turtles drag themselves cumbersomely up the beach to lay their eggs before disappearing back to their undersea world.

Start the walk from the **Olympos ticket office**: head up the valley on the dirt road, away from the ruins. Ford the (seasonal) stream and continue on asphalt. You pass *pansiyonlar*, bungalows and tree-houses. After passing the 'Limon Pansiyon' sign (**10min**), continue another 40m, to the end of the orange grove. Turn left and skirt round the edge of the trees for 30m, then take the footpath up the bank, to the back of a wood-clad house. Turn left, ascend through the terraced *tarla* (farmland), then fork right through a gully and pine trees, to more open ground and a huge carob tree (*Ceratonia siliqua*). Turn left here and head up the terraces, then follow the path into the vegetation. Continue on through pine forest and greenery into a rocky section: if you look up on your left here, you'll see a **'river' of boulders** coming down from the cliff face (**25min**). The path rises, then dips through a small clearing. From here the ascent steepens, as the path winds up the mountainside through thick vegetation, with a gully below on your right. Among the pines you can find different varieties of cyclamen with their intricately patterned leaves, sweet laurel (*Laurus noblis*) and three-leaved sage (*Salvia fruticosa*) which clears the nostrils as the pungent aroma wafts up from below. In Turkish it's called *ada çay* (sage tea), which is made from the dried leaves.

Occasionally the views open up across to the main Antalya highway above Yazir village and a forestry fire-watch perched precariously on the ridge line. The path continues upwards through twisted strawberry trees, where you will see evidence of wild boars scuffing the ground. Further on a large **fallen pine tree** (**1h10min**) obstructs the path. Pick your way round and rejoin the path, which is marked intermittently by **small stone cairns**. Later you cross a small gully and the path becomes more defined as you near a pass. The path swings right and follows a dry stream bed up to this **saddle and a small clearing (1h40min)**, where the stone foundations of an ancient building is set in the earth. Take a break after the hard ascent. If you scramble up the boulder on your left there are views of Musa Dağı (Mount Moses) and the surrounding ridges above the trees.

Turn right and follow the path, contouring round the mountain-side, perhaps over more fallen pines. Cross a gully; the path rises then levels out and crosses two more gullies. From here the path climbs the slope, switching back to follow the line of the gully. Look back now to get a view of Tahtalı Dağı through the trees. The path crosses the start of the gully and rises to another **saddle (2h15min)**. Continue over the crest and turn left; the path gradually descends through the forest in a southeasterly direction. Reflections of light bounce off the polytunnel greenhouses in the valley below, as you pass under the V of a fallen pine and emerge in an open meadow with several Valonian oaks (*Quercus infectoria*).

Keep to the left bank, by the pines, where you'll find the first remnants of an ancient settle-ment — faced stone blocks half buried in the earth. (If you are short on water, fork right down-hill towards a **stone shepherd's hut**; there is a good **spring** below it, which dries up from mid-September until the first seasonal rains. Retrace your steps up to the gully and the Lycian Way

path.) If you didn't go down to the spring, continue by dropping into the gully, crossing the Lycian Way path. As you cross the gully, an ancient wall is visible down to your right. From here there is no real path, so just zigzag up the slope; soon the defensive walls appear above you, through the pines. Head for the breach at the right-hand end of the walls and pass through, to come into the '**lost city**' below the summit of **Musa Dağı (2h50min)**.

Follow the path along its southern edge, threading your way among the ruined buildings, to a walled enclosure of cut block masonry. Cross the walled area, *being aware of the 8m-deep open cistern* (its stuccoed sides prevented water leakage). Leave the enclosure at the opposite end, then fork right and pick your way over the rocky ruins, where pottery shards are scattered among rubble and pine needles. Continue to an interesting double-apsed building the size of a small chapel. Pass more build-ings and walk out to a **rocky ledge (3h15min)** — a fine view-point. To the northwest is the mass of the Beydağları moun-tains, with Kızlar Sivrisi and Alaca Dağı further to the left; in between these two peaks is the Susuz (Waterless) range. Below is the fertile Adrasan Valley, with orange groves and greenhouses shimmering in the sun, leading the eye to Çavuşköy and the coastal mountains rising up from the Chelidonian Cape.

Climb up the bank, back to the shade of pines, and turn right, staying high along the southern flank. After five minutes you come to the best-preserved stone buildings, with a sculpted doorway. From here descend the bank into the start of the gully. There is no path, so pick your way down the wooded slope carefully. You cross a footpath by the city wall, then continue down the gully, which levels out, swings left, and after 15m joins the **Lycian Way footpath (3h35min)**.

Turn right, the path is now waymarked with red arrows and red and white flashes. Ascending slightly, there are more views through the trees to snow-capped Tahtalı Dağı. The trail now undulates through the forest, where cyclamen and sage carpet the ground, to the start of the **main descent (3h50min)**. The eastern strawberry tree (*Arbutus andrachne*) dominates the terrain here, its burgundy skin peeling like strips of wallpaper and its twisted muscular boughs forming a surreal forest-scape. Continue down under the canopy of green, twisting your way through vines entangled in bay and strawberry trees, with small ferns flourishing in the humid environment. The path runs alongside the start of a stream bed, and the gully becomes a gorge. Returning to pine forest, the path swings right, away from the gorge. Just after Christmas, wild iris will be dotted along the path and, lower down, patches of daffodils (*Narcissus tazetta*). Views open out to the Olympos Valley, with wooden bungalows set among the orange trees and dramatic cliff faces rising above the greenery. The path cuts across the bottom of a scree slope before continuing around the hillside. After five minutes the path descends sharply to some large vaulted tombs, part of Olympos's **southern necropolis**. Some of the inscriptions are curses threatening would-be grave robbers. Continue to the bottom, where you have a choice: you can either cross the stream on stepping stones (dry in summer and autumn) and finish the walk at the **ticket office (4h)** or continue, to visit the Olympos site and enjoy a swim.

To visit the site, turn right *before* the stream crossing, following the **avenue of vaulted tombs**. Continue on the path along the right bank of the stream, where the pink and white flowers of oleander (*Nerium oleander*) add a splash of colour to the greenery (all parts of this plant are highly poisonous). You pass a very decorative **sarcophagus** just above the path and walk on to a **Cyclopean masonry wall** — the blocks are cut and pieced together like a jigsaw. Take the right fork *before* the wall, to enter the **theatre** by the vaulted tunnel entrance, then continue past ruined buildings to the **harbour baths** and a **basilica** with the apse still complete and fallen columns filling the narthex of this early Christian church. Continue past the last harbour buildings to emerge from the vegetation on **Olympos Beach**. The battlements lining the cliffs were built by the Genoese to defend the port from a sea invasion. Cross the stream at the harbour mouth and use the notes for Short walk 3 on page 158 to walk through the ruins on the opposite bank, back to the **ticket office (2h)**.

Çavuşköy

Çavuşköy is a small place to the south of Olympos — a few farmhouses, a tea house, several shops, the fire brigade, a little hospital, a school, and a pharmacy. There's a single traffic light by the village square with its sleeping dogs, but it's hardly ever working. The inhabitants grow fruit, cotton and vegetables, the last mostly in greenhouses. So it's a pretty boring place, and tourists tend to give it a miss.

Adrasan Bay

Area code: (0242
Connections: In summer three *dolmuşes* a day to Antalya (in winter one). On Fridays a *dolmuş* goes to the market in Kumluca. Taxi drivers exploit the lack of choice and ask £17 for the 20km drive to the main road.

Adrasan Bay, 5km southeast of Çavuşköy, is appealing. It has an extensive beach, framed by rocks and backed by motels and *pansiyonlar*. Like Çıralı, Adrasan has the charm of simplicity and imperfection. But while Çıralı is harmonious overall, Adrasan looks a bit neglected.

Adrasan is a good spot for walkers: from the beach, footpaths lead into neighbouring bays and, to the south, a path runs towards the Chelidonian Cape (Yardımcı) and on to Karaöz (see page 165). Best of all, you can follow the Lycian Way to Olympos from here — or do a variation via the pirate leader Zenicetes's stronghold, the 'lost city' below Musa Dağı (see Walk 14).

Accommodation, food and drink

Adrasan has about 30 different places to stay, some of them in the fruit plantations which extend between the village and the bay; some are on the road to the beach, but most are right on the bay. Most of these places offer full board, but there is a selection of restaurants near the river bed on the north side of the bay, which make a pleasant alternative. Note that many of the *pansiyonlar* here are only open from mid-May to mid-October.

On or near the beach
Fordhotel is right on the beach — the last building on the south side. It's a kind of mini 'resort', beautifully landscaped with a pool and palms. Many reader recommendations; be sure to reserve a room with sea view. Air-conditioned, bright, friendly service. Doubles £83. (8831066, (8831026, www.fordhotel.net.
Hotel Atıcı II, small establishment in a meadow with a few trees behind the beach. Restaurant. 12 rooms with newly restored baths, plus simple, clean three-bed bungalows with small terraces. Nice atmosphere, popular with divers. Doubles with climate control £33, bungalows for 2-3 people £46. (8831097, www.atici2hotel.com.
Street Café is a small, jolly shack behind the beach with home-made cakes and probably the best cappuccinos in Adrasan.

The owners also rent out 5 well-furnished bungalows (large for families, smaller for up to 3 people). Friendly, laid-back atmosphere. Highly praised by readers. Bungalow for 1: £19, for 2: £29, for families with 2 children £35. ℭ/℣ 8831354, www.streetcafeadrasan.de (in English).

On the river

On the north side of the bay there is a collection of several idyllic guest houses and hotels — including the **River Hotel** 150m inland. Loungers and tables right on the water. Hammocks in the garden. Very cosy. The rooms are simple, but OK and clean. Friendly. Doubles £38. ℭ 8831325, www.riveradrasan.com.

Another good place beside the river is **Paradise Café**, just a few steps away from the River Hotel. Has an equally delightful terrace. Doubles £42. ℭ 8831267, ℣ 8831374, www.paradiseadrasan.com.

Between Cavuşköy and Adrasan

Papirus Hotel, small two-storey hotel with a well-kept pool area, about 350m back from the beach (where it has its own recliners). 22 comfortably furnished rooms with balconies, the most modern and loveliest on the upper floor. Discreet but very helpful service. Praised by users. Per person with H/B (very good food) £36. Çakmak Cad. 114 (signposted from the road to the beach), ℭ 8831046, ℣ 8831116, www.papirushotel.com.

Practicalities A-Z

Car and two-wheel hire: Various supermarkets and hotels rent cars and also a few bicycles. The prices for a car begin at about £33 per day.

Diving: **Adrasan Diving Centre** next to Hotel Atıcı II. Opened in 1998 by a German couple, Holger and Mediha Pollmann (who no doubt speak English). Beginner courses from £240, daily trips to beautiful cliffs and caves, 2 dives £42. ℭ 0532-3412943 (mobile),

The long beach collaring Olympos and Çıralı

www.diving-adrasan. com.
Money: *No cash machine or bank in Adrasan or Çavuşköy!*
Tours and day trips: Some boat owners at the beach offer trips. Many guest houses do as well, if they have enough clients — perhaps cruises (for instance to Olympos, Phaselis or various islands) or land-based trips to local sights. The prices depend on the number of participants.

Karaöz

This holiday village in the south of the Olympos National Park is not a place for tourists (unless you're doing the Lycian Way, which passes it): for walkers there are a couple of pensions, but otherwise it's full of summer homes. There is, however, a delightful road from Karaöz to Mavikent, where you can find wonderful, sometimes deserted (but not always easily accessible) bays — ideal for a swim. South of Karaöz is the Yardımcı Cape (Cape Chelidonia), which was feared by sailors in antiquity. Many ships went down here, and divers are constantly making spectacular finds.
Getting there: two dolmuşes a day run between Karaöz and Kumluca.

Kumluca

This town of 31,000 inhabitants, at the eastern end of a large flood plain full of greenhouses, is bordered in the west by Finike. In contrast to Finike, Kumluca is not on the sea, but a few kilometres inland. Oranges in particular are a major crop. The town itself is nothing special, but the large weekly Friday market is very colourful.
An ancient treasure was dis- covered by chance at the nearby site of **Corydalla** (the same thing happened at Elmalı; see page 173). In this case the find was made by an old woman who stumbled across it while taking her goats to pasture. It consisted of priceless silver and gold artefacts from a 6th-century Byzantine church. This treasure, like the one from Elmalı, was smuggled abroad, but later most of it was reclaimed from American collectors by the Turkish government and can be seen today in Antalya's Archaeo- logical Museum. Despite the amusing story of how this find came about by sheer chance, there is nothing to see today, so it is not worth a visit.

The remains of ancient **Rhodia- polis** doze on a hill high above Kumluca, 5km northwest as the crow flies. Opramoas, one of the richest men of the ancient world, lived here and made a name for himself in the 2nd century by commissioning many of Lycia's architectural monuments. He had a large tomb built for himself, the external walls of which were full of engraved inscriptions honour- ing him — modesty obviously not being his strong point. But Austrian archaeologists took this tomb out of the country 100 years ago. So you'll have to make do with a few Lycian rock tombs, a theatre with 16 rows of seats, remains of a stoa and a bath.
Getting there/opening times: Coming from Antalya on the D400 turn right at the first traffic lights in Kumluca, then keep straight on and watch for the obscure white signpost — not the obvious brown sign! From the D400 9km; the last 3.5km are horrendously bumpy. Free entry.

Accommodation • Food and drink • Beaches • Practicalities A-Z • Limyra • Arykanda • Elmalı

Area code: (0242
Information: Officially Finike has a Tourist Office, but at time of writing it had neither a location nor any employees.
Connections: There is a small **bus station** on the road to Elmalı. Buses stop here every hour on their way to Antalya (2h30; £4.20) or Fethiye (4h; £7). There is a minibus every hour to Elmalı (£3.50). The surrounding beaches and places like Turunçova (Limyra), Demre (Kale) and Kumluca can be all reached by *dolmuş* from the bus station. There are also **taxis** on several corners, notably near the marina; taxi fare to Limyra and back £15, Arykanda £29.

The small port town of Finike, called Phoinikos in ancient times, looks larger than it is. So far tourism is not the main source of income for the town's approximately 11,200 inhabitants — which is in Finike's favour! But with 30 kilometres of sandy beaches, large bays and small, nearby ancient cities, and the Lycian Way on its doorstep, Finike is ripe for more development. For the moment the town's prosperity is based, like Kumluca's, on rich yields from the fruitful flood plain — the reason for the founding of both towns. Orange groves extend far into the hinterland below the 3000m-high Taurus Mountains. Despite the unmissable growth of the last few years, the centre is still pushing itself towards the foothills.

Flair and style are not Finike's strong points; its trump card is efficiency, with everything that a small town needs. And in place of the annoying carpet dealer, one meets good-humoured barbers, who let the customer decide how much the shave is worth. The few international tourists who come here usually bring their boats into the modern marina. The area behind the marina was been completely rebuilt a few years ago (Finike's mayor gets suggestions for improving the town from Germany, since it is 'twinned' with Mosbach in Baden).

Turks often holiday in Finike, many of them within their own four walls. Innumerable apartment blocks, as well as a few *pansiyonlar* and hotels, have been built in the new Sahilkent district behind the four-lane D400. The kilometre-long beach isn't always spotless, but it *does* face out to a gleaming sea.

Accommodation

There is good choice of inexpensive and mid-range places to stay both in the centre and on the road to Kumluca. None has any personal touches, but all are good value for money. If you can spend a bit more, our tip would

Çağıllı Beach near Finike

be to stay outside town at **Villa Hôtel l'Orangeraie** (also called Villa Portakal). This place, under French management, is set inland among orange groves. A two-storey U-shaped building — Tuscan in style. Tasteful decorations, lovely pool area. Just 6 large rooms, a billard room and aliving room with an open fireplace. Doubles H/B £100 (and the food is super!). From the centre of Finike, drive past the bus station on the old road to Elmalı and turn right after 2.5km (signpost); then it's another 500m. (8554137, www. orangeraie-de-finike.com.

Hotel Grand Finike, on the (noisy) main through road near the port. Large and sterile standard hotel, built on the cheap. 56 rooms with climate control and TV. Pool. One plus point: almost all rooms have balconies, many with a beautiful view over the port. Doubles £38. (8555805, www.hotelgrandfinike.com.tr.

Finike 2000 is a friendly place west of the marina (from the centre take the road to Kaş, then it's signposted on the right). Only 20 rooms, almost all of them really large; looking a bit tired, but very clean. Only 4 of the rooms have no view over the bay. Helpful service; praised by readers and books up quickly. Good value for money. Doubles £25. (8554927, (' 8555076, www. hotelfinike2000.com.

Baba Motel, 2km from the centre on the road to Kumluca. 47 well-kept but rather narrow bungalows with tiled floors and small terrace. Pool, bar, restaurant. Bungalow for two with H/B £36. (8551568, (' 8552128, www. babamotel.com.

Engin Otel, inexpensive central hotel. Balcony rooms with climate control, TV, phone, badly laid carpeting and badly working wardrobes. But clean and OK for the price. On the main square behind the promenade (rather noisy), near the turn-off to Elmalı. Doubles £21. Şerbetçi Bul. (8553040, (' 8553041.

Food and drink

Deniz Restaurant, on Cumhu-

riyet Cad. (near the Hotel Sedir).
Quite good *meze* and grills in a
cantina ambience. Somewhat
more up-market is the affiliate
called **Deniz 2** on the main
through road near the turn-off to
the port. This has a huge choice
of starters from £1.70-£2, mains
from £3.20-6. Terrace. ℂ 8552282.
Petek Restaurant at the port has
a terrace and is the meeting point
for the yachting crowd. Fair
prices: *meze* £1.70, mains £3.20-8.
ℂ 8555029.
Öz Çoban is the locals' tip for the
best trout in the area. It's 26km
outside Finike on the road to
Elmalı, by the side of a rushing
stream in the little village of
Çatallar. Simple, but just right.

Beaches
As already mentioned, Finike's
beach is not the cleanest. **Gök-
liman Bay**, 4km west of Finike,
has a pleasant shingle beach with
a bar and sun- loungers for hire.
During high season, take the
shuttle tractor from Finike, otherwise take the Demre *dolmuş* and
get off at the beach. The only
disadvantage is that the coastal
highway is just behind the beach.
Another good beach (but also just
by the coastal highway) is **Çağıllı
Aile Plajı**, 3km further west
towards Demre.

Practicalities A-Z
Boat trips: You'll find some
offers at the port — maybe by
fishing boat to Kekova, per
person with meal £17. But many
people find this kind of trip
boring, since it takes so long to
get there and back.
Car hire: There are a few
companies at the port; cars start
from £38 per day.

Newspapers: English newspapers
are available from kiosks near the
port.
Police: on the edge of town,
signposted from the road to
Antalya. ℂ 155.
Post: in the centre (on the road to
the bus station next to the river).
Shopping: large Saturday market.
Turkish bath (hamam): There is a
very modern Turkish bath next
to the bus station. Different from
the traditional steam baths, the
Finike *hamam* also has a Finnish
sauna and a pool for cooling
down. Open daily from 08.00-
21.00; on Tue. from 10.00-17.00
women only. Entrance, including
massage, £6.50.

Inland from Finike
Limyra
The ruins of the ancient city
Limyra, called Zemuri by the
Lycians and founded around the
5th century BC, are 2km east of
the small town of Turunçova, by
the village of Zengerler. Ancient
inscriptions and coins found at
the site testify to the fact that the
Zemuri worshipped Zeus, whose
symbol was the thunderbolt, and
not Apollo or Artemis, the main
Lycian gods.
The small, tinkling watercourses
which gather in the Limyros
Valley and flow into the sea were
home to the well-known Spring
Oracle of Limyra: trout (!) fore-
cast the future. If they hurled
themselves at the bait, the omens
were good; if they circled it
skeptically…
As in all Lycian cities, Limyra
changed hands over and over.
One of the most stable rulers was
Pericles who, as the Persian
satrap, governed all of Lycia. He

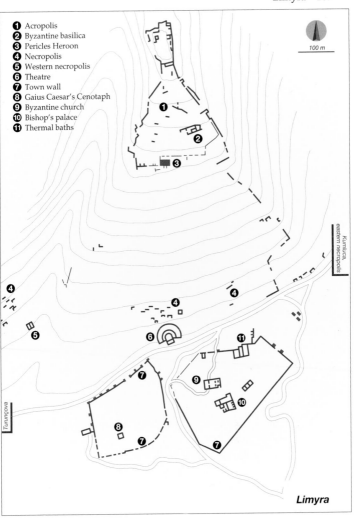

1 Acropolis
2 Byzantine basilica
3 Pericles Heroon
4 Necropolis
5 Western necropolis
6 Theatre
7 Town wall
8 Gaius Caesar's Cenotaph
9 Byzantine church
10 Bishop's palace
11 Thermal baths

Kumluca, eastern necropolis

Turunçova

100 m

Limyra

had so much self-confidence that he was the second person in the world to put his face on coins (up until 412 BC, only coins with the heads of gods were in circulation). In Hellenistic times, the city belonged to Egypt, until it was briefly conquered by the Syrians. Immediately after this Pergamon prevailed and finally Rome. The fact that Gaius Caesar, the very young grandchild of Augustus died here in the year 4 AD from a wound sustained during a Parthian campaign, was a stroke of luck for Limyra. Money flowed in from Rome to the resting place of the emperor's kin — whether to repair damage from earthquakes or to better

At Limyra's theatre

equip a temple. In Byzantine times, Limyra was a stable bishopric. Arab invasions and the silting-up of the Limyros River, encouraged the inhabitants to settle in Phoinikos (Finike), Limyra's port.

Sights: At the foot of the settlement hill are the scattered ruins of the Roman-Byzantine city, where cows and sheep now graze. If you approach from Turunçova, the first thing you notice are the remains of the once-proud **city wall**. Dating after the birth of Christ, there are still rows of seats in the **theatre** (141 AD), a **Byzantine church**, **thermal baths** and the **bishop's palace**. **Gaius Caesar's Cenotaph** is also of interest, even if only the solid interior tower remains; it was once 18 metres high.

But far more impressive are the traces of the pre-Roman past, above all the **necropolis** carved into the rock of the castle hill. The **western necropolis** in particular is superior to those in many Lycian cities for its location, condition and the number of tombs. Those that stand out are the relief-carved tombs of the Tebursseli (on the lower part of the slope) and the Teberenimi (further up), both from the 4th century BC.

Not far above the theatre is the monumental tomb of Xantabura (photograph page 57), who was probably related to Pericles.

The **eastern necropolis**, with many typical Lycian tombs, is more easily accessible — simply drive about 2km past the theatre towards Kumluca.

The ascent from the theatre to the 300m-high **acropolis** on the slopes of Mount Tokak takes about 45 minutes (without stops); today it's a desert of rubble, but the view is fantastic — taking in the whole of the site, the long beach culminating at Cape Chelidonia and Finike. In the lower part of the once-fortified compound, the remains of a **Byzantine basilica** catch the eye. At its feet, on a 330sqm terrace in an exposed position, is the 5th century BC **heroon** dedicated to the ruler Pericles. It consisted of a lower tomb surmounted by a temple. Instead of columns the architrave was supported by four caryatids. But none of this remains today. Antalya's museum has some surviving reliefs from the cella, which rank among masterpieces of Lycian sculpture.

*Getting there/opening times/prices:
From Finike drive 6km towards
Elmalı, then turn right in Turunçova (signposted), from where it's
another 3.5km. Or dolmuş from
Finike to Turunçova, from where it's
3.5km further on foot. At time of
writing, entrance was free, but this
could change.*

Arykanda

Even if you're not interested in
sites, make an exception for
Arykanda. Founded in the 6th
century BC, the city lies scattered
over the hillside, cradled by the
mightly Taurus Mountains. Its
backdrop is a sheer rock face —

the ideal protection. Praised in
antiquity for its beautiful location, Arykanda is as breathtaking
now as it was 2000 years ago.
But the ancients did not think so
highly of Arykanda's inhabitants;
they were reputedly wasteful
and pleasure-seeking. In 197 BC
they supported Antiochus III in
his fight against Ptolemy, not so
much as a power-political move,
but to get their creditors off their
backs. Otherwise, the basic
historical data hardly differs
from that of other Lycian cities.
Coins found testify to the fact
that Arykanda had embossing
rights by the 5th century BC.

❶ Bouleuterion (town hall)
❷ Bath
❸ Nymphaeum
❹ Stoa
❺ Agora
❻ Odeon
❼ Theatre
❽ Stadium
❾ Heroon
❿ House with inscriptions
⓫ Gymnasium
⓬ Thermal baths
⓭ Eastern necropolis

Arykanda

View to snow-capped peaks from Arykanda

From the 2nd century BC the city was a member of the Lycian League, and starting from the year 43 it belonged to the Roman province of Lycia and Pamphylia. Most of what remains today originates from that time. Christianity spread early to Arykanda, and in the Byzantine era the city even became a bishopric. It is also known that a settlement existed at Arykanda as late as the 11th century; why the city was given up remains a mystery.

Sights: Several excavations have taken place since the 1970s, allowing one to see the former layout of the site quite well. The foundations of the buildings lie one above the other on several terraces. The two-storey **thermal baths** near the **gymnasium** still look very impressive; behind them is the **eastern necropolis** with its remarkable temple tombs. The **agora** is still visible on its plateau. Mosaics were discovered during excavation of the **odeon** and the nearby colonnade — once 75m long. In the partially buried **stadium**, which is nestled perfectly into the slope, the spectators sat on the mountainside. The **theatre**, the city's most beautiful building, was completely excavated by archaeologists from Ankara: small and simple, it offered an intimate experience for the spectators, since the rows of seats begin just at the orchestra.

Getting there/opening times/prices: Take the Elmalı road from Finike to the village of Arif (about 32km), where a little road branches off right by the last houses (signposted); from here it's another 1km. The site is unfenced, but is 'officially open' from 09.00-19.30 daily (shorter hours in winter). Entry £1.25.

Food and drink: see Öz Çoban on page 168.

Elmalı

Backed by a powerful mountain massif, the minarets of the 600 year old main mosque, the **Ömerpaşa Camii**, rise skywards. When the muezzin calls, the men leave their tea untouched and stroll over to the mosque to pray. Elmalı is a small town of some 18,000 inhabitants. Set at the edge of a plateau at 1155m, it's a lovely place to visit — especially in summer, when you can escape the heat down on the coast (during the hot months the population rises to 30,000). By the way, *elma* means 'apple', and in the surrounding countryside fruit and grain are cultivated on a large scale.

The long, dead-straight main street leads up to the old centre (signposted 'Şehir Merkezi'), where small Ottoman houses in

---

Getting to and from Elmalı
The D635 road from Finike past Arykanda and the dried-out Avlan Lake is very well built and the countryside is beautiful. If you'd like to vary the return, you can take the road via Gömbe to Kaş or Kalkan. This also takes in wonderful countryside; it runs through poplar woods and past a large artificial lake. Be aware that the road is very winding, and the trip will take a good two hours.

---

half-timbered style cling to the slope. This is also where you find the market area, where you can buy some of the beautifully worked copper goods for which Elmalı is known. The old Turkish bath (**Bey Hamam**) by the main mosque is also worth a visit (open daily from 08.00-22.00; Saturdays between 10.00-18.00 women only; mixed bathing possible for groups of tourists). For £10.50 you'll be scrubbed and soaped for about two hours. A colourful weekly market is always held on Mondays close to the bus station. If you'd like to spend a night here, there are only a few simple hotels, because Elmalı is not geared for tourism. In the 1960s American archaeologists uncovered some sensational

finds from the early Bronze Age at **Karataş Semayük** about 5km southeast of Elmalı; they are on display in Antalya's Archaeological Museum — it's not worth visiting the site itself.

Equally sensational was a find north of Elmalı in 1984. Using a homemade metal detector, farmers discovered an amphora containing some 1900 Greek and Lycian coins from the 5th century BC — less than 20cm underground. The treasure was smuggled abroad and from there shifted to the international art trade. Individual coins were sold for up to US $300,000 at auction. Over 1600 coins (some are still missing) came back into Turkey from the USA in 1999 due to invention from Ankara and were shown in the Museum of Anatolian Civilisations in the Turkish capital. At the end of 2009 the treasure was transferred to Antalya's museum.

Several **tumulus graves** were also discovered around Elmalı, but they are not accessible to the public.

Getting there: Good bus connections from Elmalı to Antalya via Korkuteli, as well as to Finike or Kaş.

Accommodation: Otel Arzu, on the main road 100m above the Ömerpaşa Mosque. 24 small rooms with rather worn-out carpets; nothing special, but OK. Singles £15, doubles £25. Hanönü Cad. 27, (6186604, (6186605.

Food and drink: Sultan Sofrası, 500m below the Ömerpaşa Mosque on the main road. The best restaurant in Elmalı. Varied, very good food at reasonable prices. Also do breakfasts. Good kebabs und chicken specialities. Garden. (6186464.

7 DEMRE (KALE)

Accommodation • Food and drink • Beaches • Sights • Practicalities A-Z • Kekova and Simena

Area code: (0242
Information: The Tourist Office on the main square in Kaş (Cumhuriyet Meydanı 5) is responsible for Demre. Open year round, in season daily from 08.00-12.00 and 13.00-17.30, from Oct.-May open Mon.-Fri. from 08.00-12.00 and 13.00-17.00. (8361238, (8361695.
Connections: All **buses** on the D400 coastal road between Antalya and Fethiye stop in Demre. *Dolmuşes* run to (among others) Finike and Kaş.

Demre (less well known as Kale) is a fairly unappealing little town of about 15,600 inhabitants between Finike and Kaş. The ancient ruins of Myra, with particularly impressive Lycian rock tombs, lie on the northern outskirts of the town. Myra was also the domain of bushy-bearded Nicholas, who still makes his grand appearance on the 6th of December in many Christian countries. Andriake, to the west of Demre, was once Myra's port, from where St. Paul the Apostle boarded a ship to Rome. Today tour boats leave from here for trips to Kekova and Simena.

There are no longer any signs that Demre was once an important bishopric and that from the 5th century it was the capital of Lycia. Today the town is known primarily as a tomato-growing centre, its flood plain full of greenhouses yielding three harvests a year. Myra is a 'must' for all tourists, most of whom come by tour coach and rarely stay longer than a few hours, visiting the impressive rock tombs and the Byzantine church which for a long time was the last resting place of Bishop Nicholas of Myra.

Because Demre is so far only a day trip destination, there are few hotels and *pansiyonlar*. A kilometre-long shingle beach stretches out in front of the town, ending the Beymelek Lagoon. This wide, brackish lake, full of reeds, is also a nesting place for protected birds.

Accommodation

Rather than stay in Demre, we'd suggest Kaş or Üçağiz. But best of all would be **Hoyran Wedre**, 19km west of Demre. This idyllic place is covered in the *Kaş to Dalyan* guide, but you can see it, with prices, at www.hoyran.com. **Grand Hotel Kekova** is one of the best places to stay in Demre, though it needs a face-lift. 40 rooms with worn out carpeting, but balconies and acceptable plumbing; bar, restaurant. Singles £17, doubles £28. Lise Cad. PTT Karşısı 55 (diagonally opposite the post), signposted from the centre; (8714515, (8715366, www.demrehotel.com. **Kent Pansiyon**, simple family-run pension, popular with walkers. Plain rooms, not very clean baths, garden. Doubles £21. On the road from the centre to

A front-row seat at Demre

Myra, on the left. (8712042,
kentpansiyon@ hotmail.com.

Food and drink
There are several simple *lokantas*
in the centre. Another tip is the
Yüzer Köşk restaurant about
10km outside town on the Finike
road by the Beymelek Lagoon.
They serve really good fish
dishes, as well as freshly caught
crabs and prawns. The setting is
a plain but lovely terrace out
over the water.

Beaches
There's a lovely grey-sand (but
not very well kept) beach at the
ancient port of Andriake.

Sights
Church of St. Nicholas: The triple-
naved basilica signposted as
'**Noel Baba Müzesi**', in whose
forerunner the Bishop Nicholas
once worked, was a popular
place of pilgrimage in the Middle
Ages, attributed with several
miracles. The present building is
the result of repeated extensions
and renovations over the
centuries — the last full-scale
overhaul having been carried out

by Tsar Nicholas I of Russia. The
original church was not located
in a slight depression as it is now,
but at 'ground level', since the
high tides in the Demre Çayı
have fallen back, depositing less
sediment.
Inside there are some faded
frescoes as well as mosaics and
sarcophagi from early Christian
times. No sarcophagus has been
positively identified as that of
St. Nicholas. His sarcophagus is
thought to have been taken to
Bari in Italy, bones and all, in
1087. But some theorists believe
that the grave robbers stole the
wrong sarcophagus. Whatever
the case, it is clear that the mortal
remains of St. Nicholas are no
longer here. Whether the relics
displayed in Antalya's
Archaeological Museum
(including jawbones) actually are
those of St. Nicholas is certainly
open to doubt…
*Opening times/prices: May-Oct.
daily from 09.00-19:00, Nov.-Apr.
08.00-17.00; entry fee £4.20.*
Myra: Founded in the 5th century
BC, ancient Myra was one of the
prominent cities of the Lycian
League. The rock tombs of the so-

Santa Claus's family tree

During the lifetime of Bishop Nicholas (about 290-350) a very poor man is said to have lived in Myra. He had three daughters, but no dowry for them. The wealthy bishop wanted to help. One night he stole to their house, but found the doors and windows locked. So he climbed onto the roof and threw a pouch full of gold coins down the chimney. The girls happened to be drying their socks over the fire, so the gift landed softly in the wool…

Ever since then, on the evening before December 6th (the alleged day of the bishop's death) in many Christian countries socks or shoes are placed by the hearth (or if there is none, in front of the door), in the hope that they will be filled by the next morning. The good Bishop Nicholas from Myra is however not the only 'Father Christmas'. A research worker at the French CNRS took the time to trace the genealogical table of this strange old man with hooded suit, beard, boots and bag. He proved that Nicholas had up to 30 ancestors. The oldest was Gargan, son of a Celtic god, who also wore a red suit and excited children with his gifts — while at the same time frightening them with his appearance.

'Santa Claus' in his current form — particularly popular in America and Britain — is a product of the American writer Clement Clarck Moore (1779-1863), who also added the well-known sleigh. By the way, before Nicholas made a career as Santa Claus, he climbed through the ranks in the Eastern Church — first as the protector and patron of sailors and travellers (having once been involved in the rescue of shipwrecked sailors). Later, other professions lacking a patron saint — from bridge-builders to bakers and pharmacists — also chose him as their protector.

Wolfgang Koydl, a German journalist who was once a correspondent in Istanbul also investigated the history of St. Nicholas and found that he was the patron saint of prisoners as well. In Cologne prison there is a documented case of an inmate in 1933, on whose upper arm was the tattooed the words: 'Holy Nicholas, protect us from the police and the work-house.'

---

called '**Sea Necropolis**' dating from the 4th century BC are fascinating. Carved at eye-level into the side of a sheer cliff are dozens of caves with simple tombs, cells and houses — as well as temple tombs with elaborate façades and fake doors. Many of these tombs, which rise up out of the rock with their balconies and little gables, look like 'bijou mansions' with sea views. The most beautiful temple tombs are decorated with masterful coloured reliefs — warriors preparing for the fight or fighting, and motifs from the life of contemporary celebrities. Unfortunately the rock tombs are not accessible.

During the era of the Roman Caesars, Myra was extremely wealthy, as can be seen in parts of the stately **theatre** chiseled into the rock. The terraces were reached via a powerful barrel vault. The holes built into the terraces once held wooden posts to which canopies could be fastened, so that the spectators were shaded. In and around the theatre lie innumerable architectural fragments, including many of the mask reliefs from the theatre's friezes. Apart from the theatre, nothing else remains of Roman Myra — this was ensured at the beginning of the 9th century by the Arabs and later by mud and rubble from the Demre River. The remains of the **acropolis** above the theatre are meagre.

An excursion to the **eastern necropolis** is, however, worth while. From the car park in front of the theatre, either walk or drive back down the approach road and then turn left at the first opportunity (Lycian Way signpost: 'Baloren'). Turn left again some 400m further on (between greenhouses; again, this is the first tarred left turn, Güvercinlik Sokak). Entrance to the eastern necropolis is free and it is easily accessible. Stop at the millenia-old stairs hewn from the rock for the view. Then climb up to a tomb with life-size reliefs. *Getting there/opening times/prices: Myra lies on the northern edge of Demre, about 2km from the centre, near the village of Kocademre. The site is open daily May-Oct. from 09.00-19.00, between Nov. and Apr. from 08.00-17.00; entry fee £4.20. Warning: very pushy touts and self-proclaimed parking attendants!*

Andriake: Myra's (signposted) old port, Andriake, is 5km west of Demre and also known as **Çayağzı Bay**. In the year 59 St. Paul the Apostle changed ships here on his journey to Rome. At that time the bay could be closed by a strong chain. The meagre ruins of the port as a

Façades at Myra's Sea Necropolis

whole are unimpressive. The only exception is the still relatively well-preserved **granarium** with warehouses (on the left-hand side of the approach road, when coming from Demre). There is a silo consisting of eight sections, which could hold 6000 cubic metres of grain and was built in the year 129 to the order of Emperor Hadrian.

Today there are boat trips from Andriake to Kekova. There are no *dolmuş* connections to or from Demre.

Practicalities A-Z

Boat trips: leave from the port about 5km outside Demre, near the ruins of Andriake. There are both small and large tour boats, taking tourist groups to the

'Sunken City' and Kekova Island. Don't get into the first boat; give yourself time to bargain — you shouldn't pay more than £15.
Events: Every year there is a **Santa Claus Festival** from the 6th to the 8th of December, with Santa Clauses from all over the world, shows, competitions, etc.

Kekova and Simena

Area code: (0242
Walk: 15. This area is covered in more detail, with several walks, in the *Kaş to Dalyan* guide.

The sea between the island of Kekova and the mainland looks more like a lake and is dotted with innumerable islets. On the mainland, facing out to these islets, is Simena, an idyllic village without roads and only accessible by boat or on foot. In the straits in front of it lies the fairy-tale 'Sunken City'. Kekova, once an idyllic island, is today uninhabited (and you cannot disembark there), but the sea around it is swamped by boat-trippers.

The island world of **Kekova** is famous for its underwater ruins, widely extolled as the 'Sunken City' (**Sualtı Şehir**). By boat you chug in comfort over the foundation walls of buildings which are easily visible in the crystal-clear water. Here and there a sarcophagus rises up out of the water. You'll also see the ruin of a **Byzantine church** in the cove of Tersane — only the apse rises

Necropolis rising from the seabed in front of Simena

above the beach. The Sunken City, once on Kekova itself, lies under water now because the whole coast is slowly sinking (at the rate of about 15cm every 100 years).

Directly opposite Kekova is the picture-book village of Kaleköy ('Castle Village'), commonly known as **Simena**. Like a few other places on the Turkish coast, it is reminiscent of an old Greek fishing village in the Aegean. The houses tumble picturesquely down a slope crowned by a Byzantine fortress. The hill itself was settled back in antiquity. Inside the castle walls (*entrance £3.20*) you can still see the remains of a small **theatre** (without stage) chiselled from the rock, which once seated 300 people. A **stone sarcophagus** typical of this area stands at the foot of the castle. Since no public road has ever been built to Simena, the village of just 200 souls has a very special charm — one of the last truly idyllic spots on the Turkish south coast (at least outside the hours of 13.00-

15.00, when the boat-trippers come in for lunch).

Most tourists come on organised day trips from Andriake (40min) or Kaş (even longer). On the way they enjoy a unique view over the bizarre coastal landscape. But you can also approach via **Üçağız** (500 inhabitants), the nearest village accessible by car, and take a boat from there (just 15min). Üçağız (Teimiussa in antiquity) is today a grouping of restaurants and small *pansiyonlar* with a mosque beside the quay. As in Simena, the boat- and bus-trips determine the rhythm.

Getting there/prices/beaches: Once a day at 14.15 a dolmuş leaves from Antalya (bus station) via Demre to Üçağız. It returns the next day at 08.00. Most pensions offer guests staying four days a free pick-up service from and to Demre. A taxi from Kaş costs £21, from Demre £17. The boat fare from Üçağız to Simena is £8.50; two-hour private boat trips £25 (minimum 4 people).

Beaches: There are no local beaches, only simple stony bays. Swimming over the sunken ruins is forbidden.

Accommodation in Üçağız: There are serveral good guest houses.

Onur Pension, on the sea, with a jetty. Simple, friendly. Rooms with bath/WC. Lovely terrace just for guests, with restaurant. Doubles £38. (8742266, www. onurpension.com.

Kekova Pansiyon, right on the sea; 8 large rooms with air-conditioning, wooden floors. Common first-floor balcony with good sea view. Doubles £29-38. (8742259, (8742259, www. kekovapansiyon.com.

Ekin Hotel, 13 rooms, 5 with own terrace and bay view. Roof terrace above the restaurant. On the way to Kekova Pension. Open all year. Doubles £32. (8742064, www.elkinpension.com.

Camping: possible at **Kabay Treehouses** at the village entrance (£3 per person). The treehouses themselves (£12.50 for 2 people) are neither comfortable nor clean. (0535 4454996 (mobile), www. kabaytreehouses.com.

Accommodation in Simena is more expensive than at Üçağız.

Kale Pension, on the sea with a lovely terrace, jetty, hammocks. 10 cosy doubles with air-cond. and sea view, £63. Very friendly. (8742111, (8742110, www. kalepansiyon.com.

Ankh Pansiyon, near Kale, 8 nice rooms with stone floors, folkloric carpets, balcony views. Doubles £63. (8742171, (8742147, www. ankhpansion.com.tr.

Mehtap Pension lies further up. 10 rooms with air-conditioning, four with sea view. Super terrace. Hammocks. Doubles £54. (8742146, (8742261, www. mehtappansiyon.com.

Food and drink: There are several restaurants with seaside terraces in both Üçağız and Simena, all profiting from the boat trips. It's hard to say which is the best. The best-known of these for years was 'Hassan', mentioned in all the guides. Naturally others took note, so now there are other 'Hassan's in the bay. The 'real' one is in Üçağız and has a board with the German slogan 'Bester Koch vom Mittelmeer'. Hassan is very helpful and will advise on everything from finding accommodation to boat trips. Fair prices, fantastic fish dishes. (0532 5130208 (mobile).

Time: 2h15min
Grade: easy, but with a fair number of steps to climb.
Equipment: see page 22; refreshments are available in Simena.
Travel: If you are not staying in the Kekova area, you will need private transport, as bus times are inconvenient (see 'Getting there' on page 179.
Longer walk: Üçağız — Smugglers' Inn — Simena (about 6h30min; moderate and over rocky terrain, undulating throughout). Extend the walk to Burç Castle or even the Smugglers' Inn, then retrace your steps. Follow the main walk to the Lycian Way fingerpost near the walled cemetery. Then head towards 'Kapaklı 7km', skirting the cemetery wall. Continue along the walled route, lined by eucalyptus and carob trees, with purple anemones dotting the ground. The route goes past the open cisterns and village football pitch, then across the centre of a plain. The path continues through olives trees, rises, and carries on across another open plain with an ancient ruin on the right.
From the edge of the plain the path heads through rocky vegetation to the next open plain, with a fortification atop the hillside to your right. Head across the plain towards this small fortress, past some open keyhole cisterns (the ramps allow animals to walk down into the cisterns as the water table lowers). At the edge of the plain take the path marked with red paint up through the saddle, and fork right to clamber up to Burç Castle. There is evidence of an ancient settlement down below

on the right, with heavy ashlar walls. The path passes through the doorway and runs up to a flat terrace inside the battlements, where a rusted medieval cannon points out to sea. The view is spectacular: you look out over the eastern end of Kekova across the sea to the Chelidonian Cape on the horizon. Alaca Dağ (2328m) rises inland above the tree line of cedar forest, clad with snow until late spring. Return through the doorway and take the path winding down to the small cove, sometimes on worn steps hewn from the rock. The cove (2h) is an ideal swimming and picnicking spot in summer, popular with day-trippers anchored in the inlet.
Return over the saddle to the right of the castle and drop back into the plain. Head to the far right-hand corner and pick up the Lycian Way again. The path continues through maquis to a narrow inlet in a corner of Gökkaya Bay. It then follows the shoreline, past an abandoned metal-framed shack (possibly used by charcoal burners). Continue along the coastline to the opening to the bay, from where the path cuts left over a rise by a terraced olive grove. Soon you arrive at the Smugglers Inn (3h20min). This bar/restaurant is popular with the *gulet* crowd. From here retrace your steps to the signpost and cemetery, and pick up the main walk.

Kekova is the jewel of Turkey's southern coastline, steeped in history and with many islands and secluded bays. Most people enjoy this paradise by boat or gulet — the traditional sailing vessel built locally in the

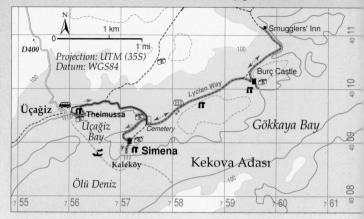

boatyards of Üçağız and Demre.
Since the villages of Üçağız and
Simena are protected sites, there are
no badly-designed concrete apartments to spoil the idyllic setting. To
really appreciate the area, stay a
night or two in a friendly pansiyon
overlooking the bay. Another
excellent way to see the area is by sea
kayak — either on a day tour set up
for all comers or a camping trip,
staying out under the stars (see
'Exploring the Kekova area' on page
179). This short walk takes in the
villages and ancient sites of Üçağız
(Teimiussa) and Kaleköy (Simena).

Start out from the main **car park**
in **Üçağız** village. Turn right by
the public toilets, through the
alley, to walk along the shore by
the ruins of **Teimiussa**. Continue
past the Kale Alti Pension, then
take steps up the side of this
guest house, into the ruins. The
right fork heads down to the
necropolis by the shore, full of
sarcophagi. The next right fork
heads up to the **acropolis**, for a
fine view looking down on
picturesque Üçağız with its
many jetties stretching like
fingers out into the bay.

Return through the fortified
ruins and descend north to a
wide track by the last of the
village houses. Turn right and
follow the mains water pipe
running along this track. The
way gradually rises through
rocky terrain, then drops towards
the shore and a corner of Üçağız
Bay, from where you look across
to the battlements of Simena
Castle (with the Turkish flag).
The track runs past an unkempt,
walled **cemetery** near a **Lycian
Way fingerpost** pointing
towards 'Kapakli 7km'.
Ignore this (unless you are doing
the Longer walk), and continue
round the coast by the marsh
area (full of egrets and grey
herons in spring). Follow the
path up the worn limestone steps
to the **eastern necropolis** below
the castle walls. Some of the
sarcophagi have sculpted lion's-
head bosses protruding from the

Kekova area for walkers
The companion book, 'Turkish
Coast: Kaş to Dalyan' describes a
host of walks in this area — along
the coast and in the hinterland.

Simena's houses shelter below the castle hill.

Gothic-style lids. Continue round the hillside past the tombs and ancient olive trees (possibly planted with the tombs over 2000 years ago). The path runs past the village **schoolhouse** — rebuilt and financed by the richest businessman in Turkey, Rahmi Koc.

Opposite the school is the ticket office for **Simena Castle** (entry fee £0.90). Climb the steps to the fortress: to the left is the rock-cut **theatre**, carved out of the hillside. The route winds up the side of the theatre on worn steps cut into the rock, to the flagpole at the top. From here there are fantastic views over the battlements to Kekova, Üçağız and the water-front jetties. The house to the right, built above the Lycian tomb, belongs to Rahmi Koc who sometimes arrives by helicopter and lands at his crazy-paving helipad in the garden. Head to the east side of the battlements and go through the break in the wall, from where the path twists down the hill back to the eastern necropolis.

To explore **Simena**, take the upper path by the ticket booth; this runs below the castle walls and descends past small stone houses dressed in bougainvillea, with lush gardens full of exotic plants. Continue down past Mehtap Pension (a lovely, peaceful place to stay, with wooden terraces looking out across the bay). Down at the water's edge is the partially submerged sarcophagus shown on page 178 — and all the postcards.

From here return through the village on the lower paths. Simena is a collection of old stone houses built on top of and in between the ancient structures. There are plenty of waterfront restaurants, and it's possible to take a taxi boat back to **Üçağız** or organise a short boat trip over to the sunken city at Kekova Island.

● Index

Only geographical names are included here; for all other entries, see Contents, page 3. **Bold type** indicates a photograph; *italic type* indicates a map or plan; both may be in addition to a text reference on the same page.